unstartup

How **Unacademy** Ignored Conventional
Advice to Become a 3x Unicorn

Nistha Tripathi

RUPA

First published by
Rupa Publications India Pvt. Ltd 2022
7/16, Ansari Road, Daryaganj
New Delhi 110002

Sales Centres:

Allahabad Bengaluru Chennai
Hyderabad Jaipur Kathmandu
Kolkata Mumbai

ISBN: 978-93-5520-158-4

First impression 2022

10 9 8 7 6 5 4 3 2 1

The moral right of the author has been asserted.

Printed in India

To my father,
Ramesh Ranjan Tripathi

Khan Market Delhi
Faqir Chand Store
28/9/23

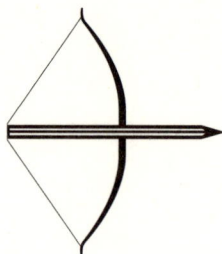

CONTENTS

FOREWORD

Today's India is dynamic and ready to lead in building the technology and talent of tomorrow. World over, trailblazers of Indian origin are changing the way we operate, think, order, shop and travel, amidst other things. This book comes at such an opportune moment to help unleash the entrepreneurial firepower that India is carrying within its human capital.

Unstartup is an apt name for a book that documents the making of a start-up as unconventional as Unacademy. As I look at Unacademy, I see the future of the internet ecosystem and education in India. As a board member, I not only believe in its vision but also endorse its unparalleled leadership in the edtech space.

Even in our initial meetings in 2016, Unacademy founders made me think deeply. We, a 138 crore population (and growing), were still milestones away from quality education and access to all. Today, in a post-pandemic world, access to education comes at an even bigger price with schools shutting down and internet availability still sporadic in remote corners. Unfortunately, the loss of school time will only show its fault lines and fractures in the years to come. This is why I believe in Unacademy's game-changing innovation that can help us cross such learning chasms.

Who would have thought that a YouTube video tutorial on computer graphics in 2010 would give birth to an education revolution? The unicorn start-up is witnessing a tremendous

growth with 3 billion monthly watch minutes, 1.5 lakh monthly live classes and 2 million monthly sign-ups on the app. Already, more than 14 lakh paid subscribers have trusted Unacademy for their academic goals. It proved back then (and continues to do so) that technology and entrepreneurship is the way to level the field of excellent education experience.

Unacademy is one of the best product companies being made in India, and I have witnessed its tremendous growth from close quarters. To come up with an idea is one thing, to build a multibillion-dollar growth business is another. Gaurav Munjal, Hemesh Singh and Roman Saini continue to defy the traditional practices and prove that it is possible to innovate even in the most competitive spaces.

When I was asked to lend my words and time to pen this foreword, I was humbled to share my observations and learnings from building one of the largest, hyperlocal food ordering and delivery companies in India. But I also started thinking about what has made Unacademy so successful.

My first thoughts went to the founders. All our school lives—and I am sure I speak for many generations before and after me—we were taught to answer questions but not to *question the answers*! I think it was a wave of agitation and discontent that gave birth to founders like Gaurav and me—we just had so many questions and had to find or build the answers on our own. We both were two mad hatters who saw a problem and error in the system and were hell-bent to correct it, or rather rejig the entire system. The founders have assembled a formidable leadership team who are not afraid to solve the harder problems.

I, then, think of the many moats that Unacademy has built over its lifetime. As the book points out, blistering speed of execution, ability to make tough pivots, finding new traction channels and building a capable leadership team are a few of

them. There is so much going on when you build a company that it is hard to put a finger on what is working and what is not. I am glad Nistha chose to write *Unstartup* because it gives us exactly this peek into the making of Unacademy. We need more such behind-the-scenes books that talk about the strategies, tough decisions, dilemmas and the visceral making of a breakout start-up.

I will end my note with this thought: whenever you feel uncomfortable, change the situation and whenever you feel restless, change the game. I strongly believe that *Unstartup* needs to be read by every founder—it can transform entrepreneurship in the manner Unacademy has transformed education.

My only advice to you: chase impact and opportunity together! The two are conjoined at the hip and are the secret recipe to changing the game. To date, I have never gotten bored!

To Unacademy, cheers to another disruptor! I will continue to serve as an advisor and board member and am thrilled to be part of this revolution in every way possible.

Deepinder Goyal
Founder and Chief Executive Officer, Zomato

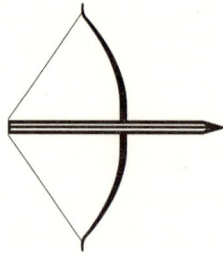

PREFACE

Most start-ups neither succeed nor know why they are not succeeding. A few start-ups succeed but do not know why they are succeeding. A rare few succeed and know why. Note that this knowledge does not make them immune to failures, but it makes them a wonderful subject to learn from.

I wrote a chapter on Unacademy in my previous book *No Shortcuts* that covered its journey up till the summer of 2017. The infantile company that was not even two years old at that time had grabbed headlines because of its founders. Roman Saini, the young doctor from AIIMS who had cracked the IAS in his first attempt, was quitting the IAS to democratize learning. He was joining his friends Gaurav Munjal and Hemesh Singh, two young engineers who had previously built and sold their small real estate start-up. It was an interesting team but nothing could have predicted their stellar rise to becoming India's second-biggest edtech company one day. Their fame was not short-lived though. The way their YouTube audience was growing, and their ability to attract young people to teach on their platform could not be attributed to luck alone. They were garnering more than 5 million monthly views on their content and had convinced an enviable team of angels and a few bigger investors. More interestingly, they were not rushing to monetize. They kept saying they are playing the long-term game. This is the story that I captured in *No Shortcuts*.

The chapter ended with 'On the whole, the team is looking ahead at the mountain of challenges with cautious optimism.' The challenges included figuring the right revenue model, keeping educators incentivized to add quality lessons and, lastly, building an intelligent discovery mechanism in the product to help users find the right courses for themselves. 'And if their past drive is anything to go by, this would be a fun ride to watch.' In this book, I have covered that ride.

I, and for that matter the founders themselves, did not know how high that ride would go. By the time I met them again, they were a twonicorn. They had already tackled the first challenge and hit it out of the park—finding the right business model. I became curious. By the time I finished writing this book, they were worth $3.4 billion.

In the writing of *No Shortcuts*, I had provided a bird's-eye view of the early years of 15 start-ups. As I realized from the appreciation shown by the readers later on, the stories gave them real motivation for entrepreneurship. However, motivation alone does not suffice. Even when one is brave enough to undertake the tortuous road of starting up, more daunting challenges lie in wait. This time, I wanted to zoom in on those challenges, and Unacademy appeared to be a compelling subject for study, mainly for three reasons.

One, the company had not just climbed up the rungs of the valuation ladder but had also created a $218 million ARR (annual recurring revenue) business. Notably, the revenues and number of subscribers had grown five times since March 2020. Numbers do not lie. Two, the growth was not sales-driven but product-driven. Three, the founders were approachable and willing to talk about their strategies. Having talked to numerous start-up founders, both in the United States (US) and in India, I knew how important this

consideration was. A researcher has a nose to smell the self-aggrandizements and fluff jargon. I have had my share of successful founders who talk a lot but say nothing.

There is another reason I felt inclined to dig deeper into the company. As a certified career coach and practising counsellor, I deal with young students and professionals all the time. When a girl from a lower-income family mentioned to me that she was studying for banking exams using Unacademy those days and was very happy with the content, my ears perked up. Unacademy had truly penetrated beyond physical and economic boundaries. They must be doing something right, was my thought.

The deeper I went, more questions I had—

How had they zeroed in on the right revenue model?

How had they managed to find investors even when they had no clue how they would make money?

How much had they spent on marketing?

How had they convinced teachers who were earning crores in Kota to start teaching on Unacademy?

How had they competed with offline coaching classes?

How would they compete with BYJU'S?

How have they hired 5,000 people in two years?

I am sure many other people would also like to know the answers to these. However, Unacademy was barely five years old at the time. Writing a whole book on a five-year-old company seemed presumptuous. So, I started digging to see if the unicorn is built on hype or substance. I found a few promising specimens when I sifted through my notes. Most importantly, I felt personally inspired. I started seeing how I could grow personally and professionally by practising some of Unacademy's strategies. This, to me, was the ultimate litmus test. I became convinced that if I can learn something from Unacademy's model, there must be more people who

can benefit from it, too. So, I decided to continue with my excavations.

The treasure was discovered in the events that unfolded somewhere between early 2018 and mid-2020, where Unacademy saw more action than many start-ups do in their entire lifetime. This was also the period when Unacademy reinvented its monetization model and rapidly scaled from 500 to 5,000 employees. This forms a major portion of the book.

Most of my research was conducted by talking directly to 50 plus people associated with the company including the founders, employees, ex-employees, board members, investors, mentors and friends. After the research had culminated, writing the book itself was an immersion in interpretation and connecting the dots. I picked up a few quotes and episodes from news reports and media interviews, too. Piecing them together, I was able to reconstruct the pivotal moments of Unacademy's hyper-growth journey.

In the process, some common principles started surfacing. One could call them principles or values or cultural touchstones. I have called them superpowers as a homage to my admiration for Batman—the only superhero with no divine superpowers. I believe real superpowers are *human* and *cultivable*. There is ample reason to suggest that any company, irrespective of size, can take elements of these superpowers and adapt to their own individual circumstances. For example, a lot of traction strategies that worked for Unacademy were taken from the book *Traction* by Gabriel Weinberg and Justin Mares but the founders went on to discover their own organic strategies on the way, such as using acquisitions or government collaboration as a traction channel.

Some of these superpowers were not even apparent when the company started inadvertently practising them. It is only in hindsight that one can correlate those with the results that

were achieved. For instance, setting aggressive deadlines and willing the team to execute in seemingly impossible time frames was the way founders worked and its unintentional benefits became apparent later on. It is a lesson in leadership how such successful strategies were imbibed in the day-to-day working and broader conduct of its employees.

Unacademy is not alone in embracing some of these principles. However, the combination of these superpowers correlates well with its hyper-growth journey.

Did they cause the hyper-growth?

Would an absence of these strip Unacademy of its success?

Would any company adopting these experience similar growth?

I have no intention of falling into the traps of narrative fallacy that many business books are prone to. As Nassim Nicholas Taleb would tell you, nobody can answer those questions definitively. However, we can say with greater confidence that in the non-random environment such as that of entrepreneurship, practising these traits can make success less dependent on luck. And that, is the best one can hope to learn from any business book.

We are not creating a blueprint of success. Rather, we are reverse-engineering Unacademy's walk of success. What you can do is to examine these superpowers, understand how Unacademy used them successfully and adopt the ones applicable in your situation.

I have gone to the depth that seemed exhaustive yet practical so that the reader does not get bogged down in the details. Data is used generously because numbers have a concrete feel to them. Saying that Unacademy has 6 lakh paid subscribers and $218 million in revenues makes it more real than saying Unacademy is successful, because success is subjective. Further, I use dates and timelines to make the

reader feel that you are taking a ride with me in the time machine and witnessing the becoming of Unacademy as it happened.

To say that Unacademy has not slipped on the way would be spurious. It came under attack for some of its content, which goes on to show the nature of responsibility expected, especially from companies in the education domain. While these issues are important and would test the resilience of Unacademy, they are outside the purview of what I have covered in this book.

I have made an attempt to decode the factors behind Unacademy's blitzscaling growth. The objective behind writing this book is to present my study and help start-ups make fewer mistakes and course-correct before it is too late. And, if the book can help you save a few months or years of rework, I would consider it a success.

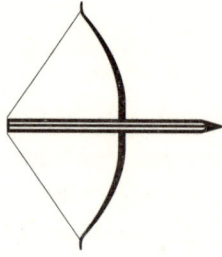

A PRIMER ON UNACADEMY

The book refers to the Unacademy business and app at multiple places. If you are not familiar with Unacademy, here is a primer:

Unacademy has two Apps:

1. Learner app for learners (students)
2. Educator app for educators (teachers)

When you log in as a learner, you can see the examination categories offered on Unacademy such as UPSC, IIT-JEE, NEET, SSC, etc. These different kinds of examinations are referred to as 'categories' in the book. So, UPSC is a category, IIT-JEE is a category and so on.

You can then subscribe to the examination category you are trying to crack. The subscription plans vary: you can see 1-month, 3-month, 6-month or annual subscription plans. The pricing varies from examination to examination depending on the complexity of the curriculum and number of subjects involved. Once you subscribe to an examination, you can access all the course videos (live and recorded) in that particular category for the duration of your subscription.

Category leader refers to the business leader who is in-charge of the respective examination category. Their job involves hiring the educators who can create live courses in that category, making sure more learners subscribe to their courses, managing the P&L, etc.

When you are signed up by Unacademy as an educator on the platform, you use the educator app. When you log in on this app, you can see creator tools which allow you to conduct live classes, doubt-clearing sessions, mock tests, etc.

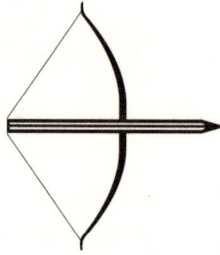

THE TIMELINE

The narrative features a lot of dates. Many readers will find it helpful to have a timeline handy for their reference. So, I have summarized the pivotal moments in Unacademy's history here:

2010—Gaurav Munjal creates Unacademy YouTube channel and uploads first video

2014—Roman Saini joins IAS and uploads UPSC related videos on Unacademy YouTube channel which helps grow the number of subscribers to 24,000

2015

- Unacademy YouTube channel crosses 100,000 subscribers
- Gaurav and Hemesh quit CommonFloor to formally start Unacademy as a YouTube(esque) platform where anybody can teach anything. No monetization model decided yet
- Roman quits IAS to join them
- Raise a seed round of $500,000
- 10 December 2015—Unacademy.in is launched

2016

- Cross one million monthly views on YouTube channel
- Encouraging more educators to start teaching on the website. Get influencers like Kiran Bedi and Shashi Tharoor to post videos

- Raise a Pre-Series A investment round of $1 million

2017

- Raise a Series A investment round of $4.5 million
- Cross 1,000 educators and 40,000 lessons on Unacademy platform
- Android learner app launched
- Educator app launched publicly; anybody can download and start teaching
- Founders start thinking seriously about monetization and conduct many experiments
- Raise a Series B investment round of $11.5 million
- Cross six million monthly views across YouTube channel and the app but the growth is stalled
- Launched first live class as another monetization experiment, results seem promising
- Launched courses for non-government exams such as IIT-JEE and NEET

2018

- Ramp up the number of paid live courses for monetization
- Raise a Series C investment round of $21 million
- Acquire WiFiStudy and add courses for more exams
- Onboard star educators like Mrunal Patel
- Overall 30 plus educators teaching paid classes
- Paid live courses generate monthly revenue of ₹3 crore in December

2019

- Surprise everyone by shutting paid live classes and launch Unacademy Plus subscription product instead
- TVF's *Kota Factory* premiers with positive reviews
- Raise a Series D investment round of $50 million

- Cross 62,000 paid subscribers, 2,000 plus daily live classes, 500 plus Plus educators, 150 million plus monthly views across YouTube channel and the app
- Plus subscriptions generate monthly revenue of $1 million in July. All doubts are laid to rest and Unacademy finds its business model for good
- More courses launched on GATE and other exams
- Karan Shroff joins and helps create Unacademy's first TV campaign
- Tina Balachandran joins to scale the hiring

2020

- Raise a Series E investment round of $110 million
- Touch $30 million in ARR in February
- Cross three lakh paid subscribers across 40 examination categories
- Becomes a unicorn after raising a Series F investment round of $150 million in September
- Touch $140 million in ARR in September
- Win IPL sponsorship and lauded for innovative IPL campaigns
- Crosses a valuation of $2 billion after raising an undisclosed Series G investment round in December

2021

- Cross six lakh paid subscribers across 70 examination categories
- Touch $218 million in ARR in August
- Crosses a valuation of $3.4 billion after raising a Series H investment round of $440 million in August

◆

ONE

FROM YOUTUBE CHANNEL TO AN EDTECH GIANT

History of Unacademy

JAIPUR JOURNALS

They both hailed from Mansarovar Colony in Jaipur and would share the ride to their Chemistry tuition classes every day. But, it was playing the video game *Age of Empires* that really sparked their chemistry. Gaurav Munjal looked up to Roman Saini's academic brilliance and wisdom, and Roman found Gaurav to be the most genuine person he could talk to.

Coming from a family of doctors, where medical jargon was a part of everyday conversations, Roman naturally drifted towards medicine. He was the kind of kid who excelled in Olympiads and essentially any examination that he chose to write. His inclination towards biology and chemistry served him well, as he passed the All India Pre-Medical Test (AIPMT) with flying colours. At the age of 16, he got into the crème de la crème of medical colleges in India—All India Institute of Medical Sciences (AIIMS).

Gaurav was nothing like his friend. Always up to some mischief, he spent a lot of his teenage years in cybercafes,

learning how to create his own websites. 'When I was in the sixth standard, I told my parents that if Bill Gates could start Windows, I would start "Doors".'

When Gaurav was attending St Xavier's Senior Secondary School, Jaipur, he applied to be a part of the editorial board of his school magazine *eXrays*. When he did not get that, he walked up to the principal and proposed that he be allowed to start an online version of the magazine. He agreed and permitted Gaurav to bring a digital camera and create vox pop videos (short videos made up of clips taken from interviews with members of the public) on campus. Gaurav interviewed students, asking them about their favourite teachers, what they would like to do when they grow up, etc., and uploaded the videos on the magazine website. Eventually, *eXrays* (http://exrays.net) became the official website of the school. It was then that he realized that he enjoys bringing together people who are as motivated as him and achieving something that has never been done before.

This theme of turning rejections into bigger successes would play constantly throughout his life. It is almost his way of making people regret that they ever said no to him. His confidence would blossom further with every initiative he took on, and form the foundation of a leader who can not only charm people, but also get them charged up.

In 2006, Gaurav did what any teenager studying mathematics does in India. He started preparing for the Indian Institute of Technology-Joint Entrance Exam (IIT-JEE) and the first step was to get into a good coaching institute. Gaurav's heart was set on studying with Ashish Arora, a well-known physics teacher teaching at a popular coaching centre. 'To enrol there, you needed to take a test and I failed that. So, forget IIT, I had even failed to clear a coaching centre's admission test. I could not get to study under the teacher I

wanted to because the coaching class would only admit the top 200 students, and I was not one of them.'

In 2008, their paths drifted apart when Roman headed to AIIMS and Gaurav headed to the Narsee Monjee Institute of Management Studies (NMIMS).

FORMATIVE YEARS

Roman enjoyed studying medicine for some time. After two or three years, though, he started preparing for the Union Public Service Commission-Civil Services Exams (UPSC-CSE). This was partly motivated by his senior Shena Aggarwal who had topped the exam in 2011 and secured first rank in the Indian Administrative Services (IAS). '*Doosri cheez ye thi ki neurosurgeon banne ke liye* (the other thing about becoming a neurosurgeon is that), you need another 10–12 years of practice. After my MBBS [Bachelor of Medicine, Bachelor of Surgery], I started working as a junior resident at the National Drug Dependence Treatment Centre, AIIMS, where I treated people with substance dependence issues,' he told me. Somewhere, his desire to crack the most prestigious examination in the country, the UPSC exam, overtook his drive to be a neurosurgeon.

Meanwhile, Gaurav's life had taken him to the city he would come to love more than any other place in the world— Mumbai. He resonates with the professionalism and quick pace of the city that author Kiran Karnik beautifully described in his book *Crooked Minds: Creating an Innovative Society*[1]:

Mumbai's long commercial history has shaped and defined its business-like, efficient culture, exemplified by

---

[1]Karnik, Kiran. *Crooked Minds: Creating an Innovative Society*, Rupa Publications, 2017.

the '8.48 super-fast to Churchgate'. Even outsiders quickly absorb the '8.48 syndrome'. They learn that missing a super-fast may mean riding aboard a slow local, which, even though it may depart only two minutes later, will get them to their destination fifteen minutes (or more) later. The local trains thus help create a culture where punctuality is important and time is valued, thereby contributing to the business-like efficiency of the city.

NMIMS was located in Juhu, and accessed the entrepreneurial energy that was unleashing in nearby areas. 'Entrepreneurs like Kunal Shah would come and judge our college events. I met Ankur Agarwal of PriceBaba and started writing blog posts for him as an intern. I would study just enough to pass examinations and instead, spend most of my time coding and participating in competitive coding websites like TopCoder and CodeChef.'

It wasn't as much the love for coding as it was to start new things that kept Gaurav hooked on computers. He had started a fashion blog called 'Fashionama' that was earning ₹1 lakh every month because he had figured out how to use AdSense. 'My friends will vouch for the fact that I do not know the f of fashion. I would pay a stipend to my friends for writing posts for it.' Similarly, in 2010, he created a YouTube channel called Unacademy to explore video creation. In December 2010, he uploaded a video of himself explaining a computer concept on a whiteboard. Blogging and creating videos showed him the power of the Internet. He was reaching thousands of people he did not even know. Such exposure to technology and the Internet would leave an indelible mark on his mind in those impressionable years.

In the second year of college, Gaurav was raising sponsorships for a college event and decided to approach

CodeChef (a business unit of Directi). He went to Directiplex, which is their office building in Andheri East, and what he saw would change him forever. 'The moment I entered, I was in awe. People were wearing shorts and playing table tennis. The vibe was like Google's office in San Francisco but this was Andheri. It was so far ahead of its time. I knew that this is the kind of place I wanted to work at.'

His dream came true when he bagged an internship at Directi in 2011. During this time, he also helped a friend find a flat through a broker. In return, the broker gave him a 10 per cent commission. He could see that students needed good brokers because it was hard to find flats in Mumbai and even brokers needed leads. 'If I can earn ₹4,000–5,000 by referring one friend, what would it be like if all the college students rented their flats through me? This is why I started Flat.to.' To code a prototype for his idea, he joined hands with Pratik Tandel, an engineer from D.J. Sanghvi College of Engineering, whom he had met at Directi. They created a website with Google Maps integration but could not figure out how to acquire users quickly enough. It looked as if they had reached a dead end.

THE HOUSING WARS

Gaurav graduated in 2012 and joined the media.net department at Directi as a full-time engineer. On 7 June 2012, he read the news that 12 engineers from IIT Mumbai had launched housing.co.in, which allowed users to search for flats based on geography, number of rooms and various other filters. He immediately realized he had made a mistake.

Back at Directi, things were happening at as fast a pace as they had when he had been an intern there. The media.net project was a contextual advertising network that would be

acquired by a Chinese consortium, Miteno Communication Technology (also known as Shuzhi.AI), in 2016, for a whopping sum of $900 million. But Gaurav's heart was no longer in working for anyone any more. The housing.co.in news had shaken him hard. He could not brush away the feeling that had he stuck out longer and put more efforts into his Flat.to idea, things could have been different. The silver lining was that his faith was reinstated in his entrepreneurial thinking and the promise of real estate as a market.

Previously, in the final year of his college, Gaurav had attended an event in which Aakrit Vaish had been invited to present a guest lecture. Aakrit, a graduate from University of Illinois Urbana Champaign had started his career in technology as employee number 12 with a San Francisco-based start-up called Flurry. After helping grow Flurry from nothing to $100 million in revenue, he moved to Mumbai to start Flurry's operations in India. At the end of his lecture, Aakrit had mentioned that he also invested in start-ups. As the crowd dispersed after the session, Gaurav lost no time. '*Wo jaise hi bahar nikla, maine use pakad liya* (I caught hold of him as soon as he came out). I introduced myself and told him the idea behind Flat.to.' Aakrit found it interesting and agreed to meet for coffee to discuss it further. The next day, Gaurav came to meet Aakrit at Costa Coffee with a friend who was also helping him with Flat.to. Interestingly, Gaurav pitched two ideas to Aakrit. One was Flat.to and another was this YouTube channel for students that Gaurav was creating some videos on. He asked Aakrit which idea looked more appealing to him. Aakrit did not think for long and told him that he had no interest in the YouTube idea and that he would be interested in investing only if Gaurav wanted to pursue the real estate idea. All Gaurav had said was, 'Cool, let's do the real estate idea then.'

'I wonder how different things would be if I had said yes to his YouTube idea back then,' Aakrit shares with a smile. Gaurav went on to show him the Flat.to website, and Aakrit offered to invest. They kept discussing it on and off but they lost steam. Gaurav was joining Directi, Pratik was taking another job, and the future was not clear.

Now that he had read the housing.co.in news, bitten by remorse, Gaurav reached out to Aakrit once again and asked if his offer was still open. Aakrit told him to put in more work on the product first and if it looked good, he would join Gaurav as a co-founder. Also, Aakrit agreed to make the investment only if Gaurav would work on it full-time. Gaurav did not want to make any more regrettable decisions, so, he got a no-objection certificate from Directi and started building the Flat.to product. After one year, he quit and started Flat.to full-time with Aakrit, who, apart from investing ₹20 lakh, also gave them space in his office to work from. Aakrit was a co-founder but also an investor and juggled his roles of being a mentor, a partner, a devil's advocate or whatever it was that the company needed. 'We were both young and figuring it out.'

One day, Gaurav informed Aakrit that he had hired another engineer who was coming to work with them.

'Coming from where?' Aakrit asked.

'Allahabad.'

The employee Gaurav had hired was Hemesh Singh. Aakrit recalls meeting Hemesh for the first time in June 2013, 'He is still lean but back then, he looked barely more than a kid.'

PAWN OR A VAZIR

September 2013

A salary of ₹14 lakh is no laughing matter, especially when you are all of 21 years in age. It was almost double of what

Hemesh was getting paid at the time. Plus, the brand value of the company that was extending this job offer could dwarf any start-up in Bengaluru back in the day. Nevertheless, he had his doubts.

'I visited Flipkart's office in Bengaluru and it was impressive. It was huge,' Hemesh Singh shares in his quiet monotone. In fact, it was so big that it made him feel small. Flipkart had offered him a front-end engineering role and a good salary. His parents were already convinced that he should go for it.

Barely three months ago, he had been finishing his bachelor's in electrical and computer engineering from Motilal Nehru National Institute of Technology, Allahabad. He was never into chip designing or control systems or any of the electronics subjects. He had spent most of his high school and college days coding and building software. 'I was surprised when I was able to finish my engineering course in four years to be honest,' Hemesh recalls. He had also managed to get a campus placement at Snapdeal but for some reason, Snapdeal had delayed the joining date for all its campus recruits. Hailing from a middle-class family in Agra, Hemesh did not want to sit out for another five to six months. So, he started scouting for other jobs and asked his seniors for any leads they might have.

One of his seniors had previously worked with Gaurav at Directi. Gaurav had recently quit to start Flat.to and was looking for engineers. He talked to Hemesh and extended him an offer to join the company right away. Within a week of graduating in June 2013, Hemesh had moved to Mumbai and had started working with Gaurav. It had been three months since they had been working together when the offer from Flipkart arrived. Although not many people had heard of their app, Hemesh had identified a familiar drive in Gaurav.

'Nothing is enough, there is always more that you can do—that is what I had seen in Gaurav. I was also like that. We were both product people, he appreciated the work I was doing. At Flipkart, I would be constrained to working on one small area within product building. With Gaurav, I was doing everything.'

When Hemesh told Gaurav about his new offer, it did not take long for Gaurav to read the situation astutely.

'I knew he was considering this new job offer. Anyone would. I was paying him ₹40,000 per month and Flipkart was offering him so much more. We had barely raised ₹20 lakh until that point but I couldn't let him go. I increased his salary to ₹8 lakh right away and told him that I would increase it further as soon as we raised more funding. I spent two days talking to him and trying to convince him.'

Ultimately, Hemesh had to decide what game he wanted to play. Did he want to be a pawn in the army of the Flipkart engineering team or a vazir (queen in chess) in a small start-up's tech future? The pawn moves one place at a time. For the vazir, the whole board is open and with the support of the right pieces, a checkmate is never too far.

'Having worked with Gaurav for close to four months, it was clear that he got things done and was aggressive with his goals. Whenever he said something, he would start working on it from the next day itself. Whenever we had to launch our app in a new city, he would get it done within a week. When we decided to build a video for marketing, it took literally 15 days from the basic idea to the video getting released. Taking ideas and making them real was Gaurav's thing.'

Hemesh thought about the ₹14 lakh offer once again. His needs were limited but ambition not so much. The fact that Gaurav was willing to do whatever it took to make him stay, that he could work on broader and more exciting things in

his more powerful role and above all, that he could work with a guy as decisive, ambitious and aggressive as Gaurav was enough to have him pass on Flipkart's offer.

'Somehow, he stayed. My history, his history, our history— it would have been very different if he had taken that other offer,' Gaurav told me. Hemesh would not regret his decision because Gaurav made sure he made some money when Commonfloor acquired Flat.to six months later.

One thing was clear—they both wanted to play the same game and create something big. Gaurav had found his tech co-founder and Hemesh had found a partner worth trusting. The entrepreneurial bond had been forged. Hemesh would serve as the chief technical officer (CTO) at Flatchat, the revamped version of Flat.to, and at Gaurav's next company— Unacademy.

THE COMMONFLOOR EXIT

In September 2013, housing.co.in purchased the housing.com domain for $1 million. '*Housing.com ki wajah se hamara blood pressure high rehta tha* (Housing.com was the reason for our high blood pressure). Here is a company that was buying a domain for a million dollars and we had a total of ₹20 lakh in our accounts. Just imagine!'

Gaurav wanted to raise more funds, so, he started connecting with other founders and start-up networks. One such group was Morpheus, which was run by Sameer Guglani and Nandini Hirianniah. Sameer had sold his company Madhouse (India's version of a Netflix-like DVD movie rental business) to 70mm and created one of India's first start-up accelerator programmes, Morpheus, with the sale proceeds. In 2007, Morpheus had invested in a start-up called Commonfloor, founded by Sumit Jain. Commonfloor was a

real estate listing app based in Bengaluru that was growing 100 per cent quarter on quarter and had raised $10 million from Tiger Global and Accel in its latest funding round in 2014. Gaurav used to attend Morpheus meetups in Mumbai and got close to Sameer. Sameer noticed Gaurav's energy and his itch to do something about the student accommodation space and introduced him to Sumit.

Sumit had initially been wary because Gaurav was trying something in the real estate space, and that could create conflict. But after Sumit talked to him a few times, he found Gaurav to be 'energetic and innovative'. 'His interface in Flat.to was very sophisticated. Back then, products were not very refined. Gaurav followed this minimalistic and modern approach to product design that I liked a lot. He was good at simplifying things and applying first principles thinking,' Sumit told me. Gaurav persistently followed up with him after they talked and requested to meet in person. Multiple calls later, Sumit told him that they could meet at 8 a.m. for breakfast in his office in Bengaluru. He further added, 'This is it. We either meet tomorrow or we will never meet.'

This conversation took place at 9 p.m., which meant Gaurav had to book flight tickets and make it to Bengaluru in time to meet Sumit first thing in the morning. Sumit had wanted to see if Gaurav was resourceful and committed enough. Later, Gaurav would use this tactic for hiring his own people at Unacademy.

Not only did Gaurav make it to that meeting but their meeting further convinced Sumit that Gaurav was indeed someone who could help him innovate at Commonfloor. Gaurav was interested in the student rental space which was a very niche market, whereas Commonfloor had two lakh active listings on its platform.

Sumit wanted Gaurav to work with him. The deal they

eventually agreed upon was that Commonfloor would acquire
Flat.to and Gaurav would keep running Flat.to independently
within Commonfloor. Sumit flew down to meet Aakrit and
close the deal. Aakrit wanted stock options in Commonfloor
but Sumit was adamant on doing a cash-only deal with him.
'I was acquiring Gaurav, not Flat.to,' Sumit candidly shares.

In this deal, Gaurav made ₹50 lakh in addition to
Commonfloor stock options. The deal also gave a 2.5x exit
to Aakrit Vaish. The only downside for Gaurav was that he had
to now leave his beloved city Mumbai and move to Bengaluru.
But he did not go down without a fight. He did his best to
convince Sumit to open an office in Mumbai and let him run
it but that idea did not materialize. Gaurav and Hemesh ended
up moving to Bengaluru.

Within Commonfloor, Gaurav was unstoppable. He would
flout rules and processes openly because he was too impatient
to wait for approvals. Human Resources (HR) would complain
to Sumit whenever Gaurav would hire someone without
following HR processes. The admin would complain when
Gaurav would spend ₹50,000 on Google AdWords without
submitting proper bills. People could not understand why
Sumit had brought in such a young guy, who kept running
around the office telling people what to do.

Gaurav had unconventional ideas for marketing as well.
With a big fundraise from Tiger Global, Commonfloor had
released its first TV commercial. Gaurav proposed doing a
sponsored web series with The Viral Fever (TVF). Sumit recalls
that the Marketing team at Commonfloor was not too keen
on this idea, partly because they did not understand it. They
were traditional marketing people and could not imagine why
someone would pay to do a web series. Gaurav's ideas had
always been ahead of their times. While the Marketing team
was dilly-dallying on his requests, Gaurav went ahead and got

in touch with the TVF team online. Finally, one of the TVF founders replied to him and one conversation led to another. TVF's *Permanent Roommates* was born and seamlessly integrated the Commonfloor brand in its storytelling. The first episode, which premiered on 31 October 2014, accumulated more than 4.5 million views before it was moved to other channels. The series ran successfully for two seasons and took the concept of web series to new heights. Later, Gaurav would repeatedly mastermind such integrated brand content successfully with TVF's *Kota Factory* and *Aspirants* and Dice Media's *Operation MBBS*.

Sumit could see the potential in his innovative ideas and gave him the freedom to do whatever he wanted within the company. Sumit would only intervene when Gaurav's disregard for authority would escalate. He recalls, 'I would call him to my office and tell him, "Boss, don't put me in these situations".' Gaurav would happily apologize when he realized this. Sumit could see that Gaurav was not doing it to offend other people; all he wanted was to get things done quickly. He was young and eager to accomplish bigger things.

Over the course of the next eight to 10 years, this impatience would mature into a tendency to do things at lightning speed. Once he built his own company, the whole organization would have to step up to match his pace. He made sure it did, as we will find out in chapter 'Velocity as moat'.

Next, Gaurav came up with a concept that would revamp Flat.to into a chat-based app called Flatchat. In 2014, he had grasped that apps were moving to instant chat-based communication. He felt that the market was ready for an app that would facilitate instant message exchanges between property owner and renters. Sumit backed this idea with funding from Commonfloor. Instead of continuing the new idea within Flat.to, Gaurav rebranded the whole app and

floated a new organization with Hemesh as the CTO. Thus, Flat.to was shut down and Flatchat was launched in October 2014. Flatchat not only showed flat listings but also allowed users to chat instantaneously.

While Gaurav and Hemesh had put their heart and soul into it and had built a good app, the real estate world was full of regulatory headaches and operations overheads. Most brokers would put fake listings on the websites. Unless one spent resources validating the listings, the platform would be filled with dubious listings, making the whole search process exhausting for the end user. Sumit had made some wise strategic decisions at Commonfloor. It had started as a social network for a residential community and had organically evolved into a real estate listing platform. Sixty to 70 per cent of the properties on Commonfloor used to be listed by owners, which led to more authentic and verifiable listings than any other platform. Housing.com and Flatchat were focused on the rental category, which was a messier and a smaller space to work in, and could not figure out a way to effectively handle the broker problem. Sumit adds that while new apps had better user interface and user experience (UI/UX), they would take two days to verify a property, by which time, a property on a platform like Commonfloor would be sold out. 'People did not care as much about photos and UI as they did about the quality of the listing itself,' Sumit noted.

However, Gaurav was running out of steam with Flatchat at this point. He knew that his and Hemesh's strengths were in product thinking. Unfortunately, no amount of effort in tech or product could solve some of the problems they were facing. In the end, he was a storyteller who was good at product and design thinking. 'I sometimes wonder why Gaurav was in real estate, it was clear that it did not excite him,' Sumit adds. Gaurav was feeling drained with all the operations and

procedural headaches of the business. It was growing too slowly for his liking.

'This was both Gaurav's strength as well as weakness. He was so uninterested in processes that he would solve some of the process-oriented requirements within the product itself. This made him a very good product person,' Sumit told me. However, there was no getting away from operations in Flatchat. By the middle of 2015, Gaurav's attention started to wander away from the app to something that he had always enjoyed more—videos and learning. He was finally over his infatuation with real estate and could think about his YouTube channel.

CIVIL SERVICES BECKON

Roman wrote the UPSC preliminaries in 2013 and by the time the mains and interview results were published, it was 2014. 'I still remember the date I got my final results—it was on 12 June 2014. I had cleared it and secured an All India Rank [AIR] of 18.' The celebrations had been in full swing when he got a letter to report for the civil services foundation programme at the Lal Bahadur Shastri National Academy of Administration (LBSNAA) in Mussoorie, scheduled to start on 1 September.

Although Roman and Gaurav had parted ways in 2008, when they had joined different colleges, they had kept in touch about their YouTube channel Unacademy and creating videos for it. Gaurav had even asked Roman to make some videos on how to crack the medical entrance exams. But Roman had not followed through. Gaurav had been creating a few videos ever since 2010, but was busy with Flatchat. Now that Roman was free from competitive exams and academic burdens, they decided that he would create UPSC-focused videos on

Unacademy. In June and July 2014, Roman provided content for a few videos, which were then dubbed over by a voice artist. These videos did not turn out great and it was decided that Roman would go to Bengaluru in August to spend more time with Gaurav and create more videos.

'When I was in Bangalore, I got a call from Ravindran sir who is the director of the famous IAS coaching institute Vajiram & Ravi, based in Delhi. He had invited me to give lectures to their students. So I decided to return to Delhi for that. It was a very big coaching institute and had more than 15,000 students enrolled. In my lectures, I would mention videos I had been creating on the Unacademy channel and would tell the students to subscribe to the channel,' Roman told me.

The month of August would test Roman's commitment and productivity to no end. He would give lectures at Vajiram & Ravi in Delhi, travel with Gaurav to Jaipur to give a TED Talk at the Jaypee University of Information Technology (JUIT), meet Sameer Guglani of Morpheus in Chandigarh. Still, he managed to publish 15 videos on the Unacademy channel before heading to LBSNAA on 31 August.

THE IAS LIFE

Nestled in the beautiful Garhwal Himalayan range, the LBSNAA campus inspires awe and pride alike from anyone who is fortunate enough to get an entry. A new chapter was unfolding for Roman, but his days at the academy were poles apart from those of his fellow candidates. He was riding the waves of opportunity on the back of his academic excellence but unlike other trainees, his heart still did not know its destination.

The day at the academy began at 6 a.m., when the trainees

were taken for morning exercises. Between 7–8 a.m., everyone chilled out, took a leisurely shower, and donned crisp formals before heading for breakfast at the mess. After an hour-long breakfast, they would attend the academic sessions from 9 a.m. to 4.30 p.m. Roman would instead sleep from 7–8.50 a.m., suit up in 10 minutes and head directly to the classroom. Why? Because he was creating videos for Unacademy till 3 a.m. and needed to catch up on his sleep. 'I was perhaps that one officer who had the least number of meals in our mess. I would stock up on Wai-Wai noodles and biscuits so I didn't have to waste time eating,' Roman adds with a chuckle.

The academic sessions covered the basics of district administration, project management, dealing with various stakeholders, etc. Afterwards, trainees would rush out to socialize. As the saying goes, IAS marriages are made not in heaven but in Mussoorie. IAS officers are notorious for marrying fellow officers and the after-class hours were the perfect time to find suitors. However, Roman had his priorities clear. Whatever time he was able to sneak away from the classroom and personal phone calls was poured into making videos for Unacademy. No matter where he was—on a trek to the Himalayas or on the beaches of Andaman—he kept recording three videos every week for the next year. The only break he allowed himself was in the evenings when the academy held musical performances. The guitarist in him could not resist humming and strumming a few chords during those cultural nights. Even then, he would keep creating content long after everyone was asleep.

The challenge for Roman was not just time management, it was facing the undercurrent of dissent from his fellow officers as well. No one liked the fact that he was creating videos and posting them publicly. Since he wasn't doing anything illegal, nobody could stop him, but eyebrows were raised. It only

made Roman want to rebel. He would create even more videos after receiving warnings disguised as well-meant advice.

Meanwhile, he was becoming better at decoding YouTube growth hacks. At times, he would record tactical videos advising UPSC aspirants on 'How to Read the Hindu Newspaper in 90 Minutes', 'Common Mistakes/Myths about UPSC', 'How to Prepare for UPSC' and so on. In some of his topical videos on 'Art & Culture', 'Environment & Ecology', he would discuss sample questions. As luck would have it, many of the questions he shared in his videos ended up appearing in the UPSC Preliminary Examination in September 2014. The word spread that Roman's videos covered the questions which had been asked in the exam and overnight, the number of views on his videos shot up. Within two months, the number of Unacademy channel subscribers had grown from 8,000 to 24,000.

THE UNSEEN INDIA

December 2014

It was -15 degrees Celsius. Roman stood at the Indian Army camp in the Rajouri and Poonch districts of Jammu and Kashmir, gazing at the vast expanse of the Pir Panjal mountain range. His cheeks were burning not just from the needles of frozen air but also the memories of last night's shelling on the India-Pakistan border, at the Line of Control (LoC). He clung tightly to his parka in order to prevent his teeth from chattering. He had spent the last 10 days with ambitious young officers like himself who had joined the Indian National Army after cracking the Combined Defence Services (CDS) Examination.

'While IAS officers got to sit in comfortable, air-conditioned offices, these people had to face terrorism, conflicts and harsh living conditions to protect their country. A few months after

we had left the camp, I got to know that the officer who had trained us had been martyred. Those 10 days were the most humbling experience for me,' Roman reminisces. And the most adventurous too. He got to fire a complete round of AK-47 bullets during his training and visited the locals whose families had been distributed between India and Pakistan.

These training sessions were a part of the Bharat Darshan tour that takes the IAS trainees across the length and breadth of India for two whole months. 'I had spent most of my life in Rajasthan and Delhi. And here I was, travelling the length and breadth of the country, across states and Union Territories, from Jammu and Kashmir to the Andaman and Nicobar Islands. Not just travelling but seeing the real India and the issues that the people face.'

After the first phase of his LBSNAA training had concluded, he was posted as assistant collector in Jabalpur in May 2015.

THE VIDEO ITCH

July 2015

On that eventful day, Gaurav woke up in a charged state. Another idea had found its inception in his mind and it felt more compelling than anything he had previously thought of. As soon as he got ready, he called Hemesh and set up a time to meet.

Hemesh had become used to Gaurav's impromptu calls and flowing stream of ideas. They would discuss so many of them, end up finding a loophole in the idea and forget about it. There was no reason for Hemesh to believe that today would be any different.

That day, Gaurav was excited about videos. After all, he and Roman had already been creating videos on YouTube for some

time and with Roman's academic success, their Unacademy YouTube channel was about to cross 100,000 subscribers. But Gaurav was not talking about putting up more videos; he was thinking of creating an app that would enable like-minded people to create educational videos just as Gaurav and Roman had been doing.

Gaurav was convinced that a complete video could be made by using the smartphone alone. 'You need only three things for a good video—content, voice and interaction with the content. We realized that it is all possible through a smartphone. I could upload the text content, highlight the important portions on the touchscreen, take pictures and even record my voice.'

Gaurav often gives the example of Twitch. Started as a video game broadcasting service, the website exploded in popularity in 2013 as it gradually added features that facilitated interaction among the spectators watching the live stream. People could host video game tournaments and game fans could live-stream it anywhere in the world at a click of a button. During the finale of Valve's *Dota 2* world championship, streamed in August 2013, Twitch recorded 4.5 million unique viewers, each of whom watched an average of more than two hours. By 2014, Twitch had become the fourth largest source of peak Internet traffic in the US. Considered ripe for plucking, Twitch was acquired by Amazon in a $970 million deal. Shortly thereafter, YouTube created its own gaming category, allowing gamers to live stream their games on the platform. What Gaurav was thinking of was a way to create a similar experience for students in India. Unacademy could be the platform designed specifically for education with community features.

Hemesh was aware of another video app whose popularity was shooting through the roof at the time. Dubsmash, a German app that lets users create videos in which they lip-

sync over their favourite songs, was trending in the top 10 free app downloads on the App Store. The app boasted of 50 million downloads already and had gone viral even in India. The primary reason for Dubsmash's stellar success was the ease with which anybody could create a video on it. Boasting an exhaustive database of audio clips, Dubsmash allowed the user to pick a trending sound and record a 'dub'.

It did not take much time for a techie and millennial like Hemesh to grasp the magic in what Gaurav was saying. 'Historically, I had noticed that whenever a technology makes the creative process easier, it gets mass traction. People flock to it and start creating.'

Gaurav was suggesting that there were enough educators/ teachers in India who would love to teach online. What stopped them was the fact that the educational video creation process was cumbersome and time-consuming. 'If we could make that easier, it made sense that more users would come to create videos,' Hemesh concurred.

Hemesh wasted no time and coded a prototype over the weekend. Although bare-bones in structure, it was a functional iOS app that allowed the user to upload pictures, and annotate those pictures while recording a voice-over. In the end, the user got a video that they could share with others. When he showed it to Gaurav, Gaurav made a quick video to explain some concepts in Java. The app worked and Gaurav was excited!

They then showed it to Roman, who was now posted as assistant collector in Jabalpur but was actively creating YouTube videos for the Unacademy channel. Roman tested the prototype by making a quick demo video. He also noticed the speed and efficiency gain made possible by the course creation app. Gaurav was convinced that the idea had merit and the technology could work.

So, on that Monday in July 2015, Gaurav and Hemesh had decided that this was an idea worth pursuing. In August, both of them quit Flatchat and Commonfloor. When Gaurav told Sumit that he was leaving, Sumit's immediate question was 'Why?' But when he heard that Gaurav is leaving to start his own venture in the edtech space, he made his peace with it. 'I would have been concerned if he was joining any of our competitors. But he was leaving to start up. I too had been held back when I had wanted to become an entrepreneur and I would never do that to anyone else.' Not only did Sumit accept his decision, he also wrote the first check for Gaurav as an angel investor.

The prototype that Hemesh had created would give birth to Unacademy's educator app in the coming few months. Next, it was time to persuade Roman to join the team full-time. That meant asking him to quit the IAS. It is every bit as stupendous as it sounds.

QUITTING IAS

Roman and Gaurav sat with their parents around the big table at the Spice Court restaurant in Jaipur. Their eyes met in nervous awkwardness.

Finally someone blurted out the obvious thought that was eating them all alive: 'So, you want to leave the IAS?'

'That's what Gaurav and I wanted to discuss,' Roman started to say but the look on his parents face made him stop. It was Gaurav's turn.

'We want to start our own company. Unacademy is growing and we need to do it now.'

'I am not doing it because I hate working in the IAS. I am doing it because I like the idea of building Unacademy.'

'And Unacademy is that thing where you create videos...?'

Soon, the questions and answers reached their crescendo of incredulity. Eyes were rolled and tears were held back.

The dinner ended with no conclusion to the subject of Roman leaving the IAS but at least the subject had been broached. Multiple discussions later, his parents finally gave him their blessings. The real challenge was not persuading the parents. It was developing his own clarity that had taken all this time.

It did not happen overnight. It could not have.

You don't wake up one day and decide to quit a career in the IAS after cracking an exam as prestigious, exalted and competitive as the UPSC-CSE. The clarity that ultimately led Dr Roman Saini, UPSC AIR 18 and ex-AIIMS, to quit his position as assistant collector to create a 'YouTube for education' had taken over three to four years to develop.

Gaurav and Roman used to meet on and off during their college days, whenever either of them was visiting Delhi or Mumbai. Later, Gaurav had shifted to Bengaluru and sent him the public relations (PR) release once Flatchat had raised capital. When Roman cracked the IAS exams, he flew down to Bengaluru to stay there for a month and work on Unacademy videos together. Roman would stay with Gaurav whenever he was in town and ended up meeting Hemesh, other team members and even some of the investors. They met again in Chennai and several other cities when Roman was doing Bharat Darshan as part of his IAS training. When Gaurav took to Instagram to share an old picture with Roman on 4 June 2021, he captioned it: '14 years of friendship, fights, trips, debates, building things and more'—aptly summarizing the bond between them that transcended not only distance but also differences.

Gaurav had often asked Roman to come to Bengaluru and work with him. However, with cracking one exam after

another and building a career in the civil services, Roman's life had been heading in a different trajectory. With Flatchat, it had been unclear what Roman's contribution could be. But once the YouTube videos started to become popular and his following on social media began to skyrocket, Roman was set to enjoy his new-found celebrity status online. When Gaurav had told Roman that he would be leaving behind Flatchat and starting afresh on an idea that was all about creating videos and learning, Roman had to finally make a choice. He had given himself all the time to immerse in the IAS life. But even when he was at LBSNAA, a place that people would kill to go to, he had cared more about creating videos for Unacademy. The more he reflected on it, the clearer it became. He knew what he needed to do.

When I asked Roman what made him jump such a big ship, he told me matter-of-factly, 'It made sense.' It is hard to believe that those three words can bear the onus of a decision as life changing as the one he made in 2015. Not that he would regret it at any point. But in September 2015, when he was finally putting in the papers, crossing the Rubicon to leave the service and head to the chaotic land of start-ups, history did get created. One of the youngest IAS officers of his day, Roman Saini had made front-page news the moment he did the unthinkable and the entire nation had taken notice.[2]

With Roman by their side to lead the content efforts, Hemesh suggested to Gaurav that they should also meet Sachin Gupta. Sachin had been Hemesh's batchmate in college and had been working at Cisco, Bengaluru, when

---

[2]Gosain, Manish Pratim. '24-Year-Old Quits IAS to Turn Free E-Tutor', Times of India, 10 January 2016, https://timesofindia.indiatimes.com/india/24-year-old-quits-ias-to-turn-free-e-tutor/articleshow/50516074.cms. Accessed on 13 October 2021.

Commonfloor acquired Flat.to. Hemesh had stayed at Sachin's place for the first few weeks after moving to Bengaluru. In 2015, Sachin was working with Goibibo in Gurgaon. 'He was one of the best engineers I knew. I thought he could lead the engineering efforts while I could focus on the product in our new start-up. So, Gaurav and I discussed the idea with Sachin and asked if he would like to join us,' Hemesh told me. Sachin had his reservations but ultimately Hemesh convinced him that it was a once in a lifetime opportunity. This is how Sachin became the fourth co-founder.

The founding team was now complete and looked unbeatable on paper; Unacademy had arrived.

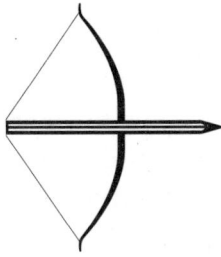

TWO

SUPERPOWER 1: BOLD PIVOTS

Unacademy's Most Important and Unconventional Decisions

I t was a good story in the beginning—democratize education via YouTube and make learning free forever. By the end of 2017, Unacademy had raised venture capital (VC) of $18 million and had onboarded marquee investors such as Sequoia in its latest Series B round.[3] The investors were now looking for some answers about how they would ever make money on their bets.

Unacademy eventually found its product-market fit via a novel and unique business model in January 2019. The path till this point had been anything but straight and they had passed through a graveyard of experiments. But, that is the nature of experimentation. As Jeff Bezos wrote in his 2018 annual letter to shareholders, after the spectacular fiasco of Amazon Fire Phone that precipitated a $170 million write-down in

---

[3]J., Anand. 'Sequoia, Three Other VC Firms Invest $21 Million More in Unacademy', *VCCircle*, 17 July 2018, https://www.vccircle.com/sequoia-three-other-vc-firms-invest-21-million-more-in-unacademy. Accessed on 17 February 2022.

Amazon books,[4] 'As a company grows, everything needs to scale, including the size of your failed experiments. If the size of your failures isn't growing, you're not going to be inventing at a size that can actually move the needle.' He went on to add, 'The good news for shareowners is that a single big winning bet can more than cover the cost of many losers.'[5]

Unacademy would shuffle and pivot uncomfortably until reaching its big win. Interestingly, many of its experiments were not exactly failures. Then why and how did the company decide to change course? Let's take a look.

LOSING BIG IS BETTER THAN WINNING SMALL

The vision was to create a tool that would work even in villages so that anybody, absolutely anybody, could teach on Unacademy. That was the vision for which Roman had quit the civil services, and Gaurav and Hemesh had quit Flatchat. They had not chalked out any business model yet. But it's never bad to start thinking of making some money, right? After all, you have to pay the bills!

About three months into starting Unacademy full-time, Roman had created a few UPSC tests and notes. Unacademy conducted a small experiment by launching Wizest—a page where they listed such digital resources for sale. Gaurav told me, 'We tried to monetize those tests via third-party platforms like Instamojo. In a short while, we had started earning nearly

---

[4]Kovach, Steve. 'Amazon Is Taking a $170 Million Charge for Unsold Fire Phones', 24 October 2014, https://www.businessinsider.in/stock-market/amazon-is-taking-a-170-million-charge-for-unsold-fire-phones/articleshow/44920884.cms. Accessed on 13 October 2021.
[5]Bezos, Jeff. '2018 Letter to Shareholders', 11 April 2019, https://www.aboutamazon.com/news/company-news/2018-letter-to-shareholders. Accessed on 13 October 2021.

a lakh per day in revenue. This made everyone comfortable in a way.' Any founder can tell you what the sight of the first revenue credited into your bank account feels like—intoxicating.

'I noticed that whenever I walked into the office, everybody would be talking about Wizest. They would be discussing things like "What else can we upload?" and "How can we sell more?" This is when I realized that no one was thinking about Unacademy anymore.' Gaurav could see his team being pulled into the trap of instant gratification—a tendency to gravitate towards actions that can lead to immediate rewards. It is a trick played by our brains; short-term rewards give a boost of 'happy hormones' like dopamine and endorphins that make it hard for us to resist such traps. But fine-tuning Wizest had only been a way to maximize the current revenues.

Gaurav adds, 'I believe what game you play is more important than winning in the shortterm. I extrapolated the numbers and came to a conclusion that even if we win this "*test wala game*", it was ultimately the smaller game. We were not going to build an iconic product based on these tests. This is not why we had quit everything to start Unacademy.'

Gaurav had done something similar at Commonfloor. When he had convinced Sumit that chat based apps are the way to go, Sumit had agreed to turning Flat.to into Flatchat. To everybody's surprise, Gaurav decided that he wouldn't just launch Flatchat, he would also completely shut down Flat.to. Flatchat may not have materialized the way he wanted it to but he was still convinced that the direction one takes is always more important than the revenue one makes.

'I did not want to win the small games. I was okay with losing big but I did not want to win, or even play, small games. So, I went into the office that day and announced that we would be shutting down Wizest. People were baffled. Some

of them were sad, but then they understood when I explained why we cannot afford to waste our energies on it. From the next day, we were focused on building Unacademy—what we had originally set out to build.'

BEING A CONTRARIAN

Shailendra Singh's eyes light up whenever he sees a founder ignoring the conventional wisdom and following their own convictions. As managing director at Sequoia Capital, he has been investing in tech start-ups in Southeast Asia for more than a decade. In the process, he has helped Sequoia India become the biggest VC firm in India.

Both are fervent tweeters and in the finite start-up universe on Twitter India, they were bound to cross each other's path. Shailendra kept coming across interesting tweets from Gaurav. They would like each other's tweets, comment on them and it wasn't long before one messaged the other to express admiration for his content. They don't remember who initiated the conversation but it led to a coffee meeting. This occurred sometime after the summer of 2017. By this time, Gaurav had met his fair share of VCs, faced plenty of rejections and had managed to raise $6 million. If he had thought this would be another typical VC meeting, he was in for a surprise. And if Shailendra had thought that Gaurav would pitch to him like a typical founder, he was in for a bigger one.

Gaurav took to the whiteboard and drew a timeline. He started telling the story of Unacademy and how his passion for making videos had led him to start an edtech venture. He thought that it was time to talk about metrics but Shailendra kept probing to learn his story. He was more interested in Gaurav and why he was doing what he was doing. Then, they started discussing the vision. Gaurav told him that he

wanted to build the biggest learning platform in India. 'Why only India? Why not global?' Throughout his short but eventful entrepreneurial life, he had heard VCs grind him on business models, on asking him to focus and think small.

So Gaurav took a moment to gather his thoughts but the only thing he could manage to blurt out was, 'What?'

Shailendra reiterated, 'You should think bigger.'

Gaurav thought that the person in front of him was being unreal. But he also knew, in that very moment, that he wanted to partner with Shailendra Singh.

They kept talking and would meet again. After a few conversations, Shailendra spotted the one characteristic in Gaurav that he had seen again and again in many of his most successful investments—being a contrarian. The Oxford Dictionary defines 'contrarian' as a person who opposes or rejects popular opinion. Gaurav did not want to create more content, he wanted to enable *others* to create content. He did not want to grow by aggressive selling; he wanted to figure the right way to monetize and was in no hurry to do so.

Shailendra recalls his first impression of Gaurav, Roman and Hemesh, 'I thought these guys were super interesting with original authentic ideas. They were not copying anyone, they were doing things the way it made sense to them. The funny thing is, Gaurav did not even use a deck, even when he pitched to our team later on. He gave us a demo of the product and everything was free-flowing. Most of the numbers I got from him were screenshots on WhatsApp.' He added, 'I felt that he was extremely ambitious but also very insightful. He had this deep desire to build outstanding, iconic products. There was no doubt in my mind that I wanted Sequoia to back them.'

But here was the problem. Investment committees in fund houses have their own thesis about who to invest in. One of the criteria they take very seriously is 'How will this start-up

make money?' Shailendra knew the first thing his team would ask him was about Unacademy's revenue model. They had launched the educator app barely two months ago and had no clear thoughts on monetization. He, personally, was not so worried about Unacademy's business model, or lack thereof. He has a term for it internally at Sequoia—'distribution-led businesses'. These are products which are able to find disproportionate distribution. 'When I see a strong, product-focused founder who has managed early distribution of the product, it is a powerful combination for me. Gaurav was obviously product-obsessed but also, there were these strong distribution hacks that he had created. For example, a lot of high-quality teachers were teaching, product NPS was high, retention was high and Google trends showed increasing brand awareness.' He had made up his mind.

Incidentally, Kunal Shah (founder, Freecharge and CRED) was acting as an advisor at Sequoia that year. Kunal had already been in touch with Gaurav and had even mentored him now and then. Kunal was also convinced that Sequoia should invest in Unacademy. Together, Shailendra and Kunal championed the case for Unacademy in front of Sequoia's team. When the inevitable question popped up, Shailendra said, 'Look, the worst case is that they make money through advertising. I know ads are not a large market. I'm not saying that this is the business model, what I'm saying is that if nothing else works, maybe they'll do other things. But I think the distribution first characteristics are clear and such companies can make other products that can monetize. Distribution means that they won't have to spend a lot of money to then convert people to being paid users.' The investment committee gave in to Shailendra's and Kunal's conviction. However, Sequoia was not ready to fill in the whole round and Shailendra invited SAIF Partners to invest the rest.

That is how Unacademy raised a Series B funding round of \$11.5 million led by Sequoia India and SAIF Partners in September 2017. Gaurav could not help but feel that he had found a lifelong mentor and a champion.

MONETIZATION EXPERIMENTS

In its early days, founders were committed to keeping the courses on Unacademy free. So, they tried to monetize in different ways. One of these ideas was to let the learners dedicate a token of appreciation for any educator they might have found helpful. Unacademy would take a cut on these token payments. Other ideas included letting teachers decide if they wanted to charge for their course and take a cut on it. None of these options worked out.

Free videos had helped the company scale up to 6 million monthly views but another problem kept cropping up. Whenever an educator became popular on Unacademy, offline institutes would poach them. It was becoming harder and harder to discover people who not only knew the subject matter but were also camera-friendly.

Up until this point, Unacademy was primarily an educational content company that was the face of UPSC preparation. After all, this is where Roman's popularity had led it to. The Unacademy Android learner app had been launched in February 2017 and focus had shifted to putting more content on its own website and app instead of YouTube. Roman announced on his social media accounts that he was looking to hire UPSC educators and a few passionate followers applied. Abhishek Srivastava was one of them. He had cleared the Staff Selection Commission-Combined Graduate Level Examination (SSC-CGL) and was posted as an accountant in Bhopal, Madhya Pradesh, but he was also

teaching General Studies at the popular coaching institute Career Launcher. He joined as an educator but found out from his conversations with Roman and Gaurav that they were looking for someone who could work with them and find more educators. Despite his family warning him not to leave a stable government job, Abhishek followed his hunch and instead joined this up and coming start-up. There were hardly 10 people on the Business team when Abhishek joined as a manager for the UPSC examination category. There were a few other examination categories (whenever I use the term 'category' in this book, it would refer to an examination as a business vertical on the Unacademy app) including banking, SSC, railway examinations, state Public Service Commission (PSC) exams, etc.

Another person who had joined just prior to Abhishek was Disha Agarwal. An MBA graduate from Management Development Institute (MDI), Gurgaon, Disha had one year management trainee experience at PepsiCo. Having relocated to Bengaluru after marriage, Disha started as an intern because Gaurav was still figuring out how to utilize her. She had started reaching out to educators for non-PSC examinations who could create content on the Unacademy app. Sometimes it meant reaching out to people she knew in her own circles or cold emailing 300–400 YouTubers. Sometimes people agreed for free, sometimes they were compensated if they could reach a certain number of views on the platform. 'It was a period of intense experimentation,' Disha told me. 'One of our experiments was called the Crusader Programme, in which we reached out to college students and offered them stipend and certificates if they created a minimum number of videos. Another was called Teachathon in which several teachers would create content and those who garnered the highest number of views would be awarded. It is hard to say

if there was one thing that worked because everything was happening simultaneously.'

Disha impressed Gaurav by the way she shouldered any responsibility given to her. As a result, Gaurav not only onboarded her full-time into the company but also started giving her more leadership tasks. She started heading the content team and various category leaders like Abhishek reported to her. This would become a repeatable pattern at Unacademy. Gaurav would test the employees and see if they are ready for more responsibilities. The ones who were able to handle the job well would be promoted. This way, Unacademy would have a good pipeline of leaders being groomed internally who could be then asked to step up as and when necessary. Disha appreciated the trust and empowerment she received. 'I had no leadership experience prior to joining Unacademy, so it was great to see that Gaurav was giving me these opportunities. He would monitor how I was coping and trust me with more work. Later on, another leader who was handling the learner success projects quit and I got to lead that team as well.'

All the courses on the Unacademy app, in those days, were pre-recorded using the educator app. The educators would create a short course that comprised a series of eight- to 15-minute videos. The limit of 15 minutes ensured that the educators did not ramble.

Educators were being paid per video which also meant the company had started burning cash. So, now, the inevitable question was—'What next?' All the founders would convene every day and discuss ideas. It was clear that the road to longevity would involve having quality educators on the platform, a vision that has only strengthened multifold over the years. Gaurav, Roman, Disha and the others in their team would come together and discuss which educators to try to

approach next. Gaurav would finalize the deal terms that would be offered. He would have clear ideas on what was to be written in the bio section of the educator and other such details.

FROM RECORDED TO LIVE

Gaurav met Shailendra and Kunal often in those days. As he was experimenting with different revenue models, he would brainstorm with the people he trusted and looked up to. This was the time when Sequoia Capital had made a few high-calibre edtech investments in Chinese start-ups including VIPKid. Shailendra had seen the vigorous rise of online live classes and suggested that Gaurav should try out similar live classes at Unacademy too. Gaurav mulled over it and agreed that it could be 'interesting.'

When he got back with his team and discussed the idea with them, everybody agreed that offering live courses from some of the top educators could be a good way to monetize the platform. For example, a top educator of UPSC courses could create a whole course on Indian Polity and the same could be advertised to all the students interested in UPSC classes. These classes would be conducted live as opposed to pre-recorded content and would allow the students to clear their doubts and interact directly with educators for the first time. The company believed their users would be happy to pay for such value-added features and premium content. The 'paid live classes' product became the Unacademy Plus Version 1 and was launched in October 2017 (not to be confused with the current Plus model that runs on subscriptions). One of the earliest courses was created by Roman himself. His 40-hour UPSC course on Current Affairs was priced at ₹12,500 and 500 students ended up enrolling for it. As the model appeared to

be promising, Unacademy started focusing on hiring more educators who could create high-quality live courses for sale on Unacademy.

'Kunal and I were shocked because within four or five weeks, Gaurav told us that they have launched live classes,' Shailendra told me. Taking novel ideas and running with them would become Unacademy's hallmark execution style in the years to come, as Shailendra would soon discover.

Around April 2018, the company also toyed with the idea of a 'One Rupee Special Class' promotion. The promotion allowed the student to watch one video of a paid course at the cost of a single rupee. The idea was to lower the entry barriers by letting more users get a taste of the paid classes; making them pay something (even if only one rupee) brought them out of the mindset of scrolling for free. They had to enter the payment information on the app which made them less resistant to pay for the full course in case they liked this class.

Throughout 2018, the company focused on educator acquisition. Abhishek's team smartly spotted up-and-coming young teachers like Sudarshan Gurjar who had their own dissatisfactions with the offline world. Arti Chhawari was a bachelor's student who was enamoured by history. She was referred by someone to the Unacademy team and once Abhishek's team got in touch with her, she came on board as an educator for Art and History and quickly became popular because of her flair for storytelling and clever use of visual aids.

Any educator who wanted to teach on Unacademy was asked to release five to 10 free videos to get started. Abhishek's team would track two metrics—overall views and successful views (counted only when a learner watches the video for more than five minutes). Educators who had a high ratio of successful videos would be then taken into the paid category. Grooming such not-so-famous teachers turned out to be quite

rewarding in the long run as Sudarshan and Arti would go on to become the number one and seven educators (by watch time), respectively, in the UPSC category.

Ready with a preliminary business model in place, Roman doubled down his efforts in bringing what the company would call 'star educators'. These were famous educators who had their own online following among students, such as Mrunal Patel. When Roman had been studying at AIIMS and preparing for the UPSC-CSE, he would spend hours on mrunal.org, a CSE preparation-focused website run by Mrunal. Mrunal had graduated from L.M. College of Pharmacy, Ahmedabad, and attempted the CSE in 2009. Although he cleared the preliminary examination, he was not able to clear the mains. He did not reattempt it and instead, joined Sardar Patel Institute for Public Administration (SPIPA) as a faculty member. SPIPA was established by the Gujarat government in 1962 as the apex training institution of the state. Apart from training the various categories of officers in the state, SPIPA is famous for its Civil Service Study Centre which imparts training to the youth of Gujarat aspiring to join the civil services (IAS/IPS/IFS/Group 1 & 2). This is where Mrunal had started teaching.

Mrunal's heart was set on breaking the hegemony of big coaching centres in Delhi who were charging a hefty fee for helping students prepare for the UPSC-CSE. He started blogging whatever he knew about UPSC preparation, often taking jibes at what he referred to as 'the coaching mafia' in Delhi. He posted past papers, mains answer writing tips, strategies and other miscellaneous information relating to the CSE for free. The idea was to allow anyone to start from zero and be able to crack the hallowed examination without evaporating their savings. The website grew in popularity and Mrunal started monetizing it via advertisements. He also started a YouTube channel where he actively posted current

affairs and other videos. His channel has more than 1 million subscribers as of 2021. When Roman had cracked the UPSC-CSE in 2014, Mrunal had featured his interview on his website as well. They knew each other via their common love for the UPSC as well as teaching.

Ever since Roman had quit the civil services, he had been trying to persuade Mrunal to become an educator at Unacademy. Till 2017, Mrunal kept rejecting him. Now that the founders were convinced that credible educators were their key to breaking the glass ceiling, Gaurav and Roman decided to make an offer that the educators simply could not refuse. They went all in. Roman booked a flight ticket for Mrunal in 2018, requesting him to come to Bengaluru and see what they were building. Mrunal agreed. The three of them were locked in a conference room for three to four hours and by the time Mrunal came out, he had made up his mind to join Unacademy. 'We assured him that he could keep running his blogs and help out students as he had been. We discussed our vision in detail and I guess it made sense to him. He could see that we also wanted to help as many aspirants as possible and make it affordable for them. If he could make money by teaching on our platform, he would be able to use that money to help many more people out there,' Roman told me. Mrunal's devoted followers and students also came to the app. Today, Mrunal is among the top three educators (by watch time) for the UPSC category on Unacademy.

Getting these star educators meant not only paying a hefty signing fee but also luring them with revenue share. Burned by its experience on YouTube, where its educators were regularly poached by offline coaching institutes, Unacademy also made them sign one- or two-year exclusivity contracts which prevented the educator from teaching on any competing platform and also specified that the recorded videos could

be streamed for up to two years on the Unacademy app.

Earlier, the educators were being paid per video for the free classes. Unacademy, now, introduced a 30–40 per cent revenue share model for the paid live classes so that the educators had skin in the game and were motivated to attract more paying users.

These efforts combined with the timely acquisition of a YouTube channel called WiFistudy in October 2018 (details in 'Traction Trumps Everything'), which boasted 9.1 million subscribers and a combined view of 1 billion eyeballs, created a good momentum as Unacademy reached 200,000 daily active users. In December 2018, Unacademy had earned a monthly revenue of ₹3 crore from its paid live courses!

There were a few problems though:

1. If a student did not like an educator after buying his/ her class, there was no option for a refund.
2. Unacademy was also becoming dependent on the loyalty of these popular educators who could leave any time after the contract, taking their students with them. In this aspect, it would be plagued by the similar headache that ails most offline institutes.
3. Popular educators were getting the bulk of the students while beginner educators struggled to catch any student's attention, further lowering their incentive to improve.
4. By paying à la carte, the student had to shop around for each subject as opposed to offline coaching classes that offer all the subjects under one package.

Gaurav became mindful of these issues that could raise their ugly heads in the long term. He set up another meeting with Shailendra.

UNACADEMY PLUS—NETFLIX FOR EDUCATION

December 2018

Shailendra knew Gaurav was rarely short on words but his furrowed eyebrows were telling him a different story today.

'I told you na, I am not feeling good about this. We are losing the platform advantage if we start depending on a few educators,' Gaurav said to him.

'Why don't we try a subscription pack and bundle all the teachers in one pack?' Shailendra asked.

'What do you mean?' Gaurav was puzzled.

'Instead of selling one course here and there, why don't we make a JEE subscription pack and a NEET subscription pack instead?'

'Wait—like Netflix?'

'Yes, you could say that. What you promote then is Unacademy JEE offering, Unacademy NEET offering or whatever other offering. This way, teachers are not selling or marketing themselves. They are all a part of this one package.'

Gaurav thought for a few moments before saying, 'That wouldn't work. The teachers would not agree. And we are doing ₹36 crore ARR now. What you are talking about is completely different.'

'I think you should think about it,' Shailendra said.

When Gaurav came back, he could not sleep. *What if Shailendra is right*? What he said was correct. People don't go to Netflix for one movie in particular, they go there because they can access hundreds of awesome movies all in one place. Why can't Unacademy do the same for education? One subscription for all classes—yes, it made so much sense!

His internal tussle continued. The biggest thing holding him back was the rising revenues they were witnessing in the

existing Plus product. They finally had a glimpse of a business model that could work. If he started the subscription, it may destabilize their current business. Maybe he should launch the subscription model product on the side and test it out. But he had this visceral feeling that he would not be able to sail on two boats at the same time. He discussed it with Hemesh and Roman, who shared their views, but in the end, it was Gaurav's call to make. And he did make up his mind fairly soon.

Shailendra received the update from Gaurav a few days after their last meeting: 'I am going to do it and I am going all in. So, we are shutting down the current product. I wanted to let you know that we may not be making any money for the next few months.' Gaurav sent similar updates to all other investors, adding that Unacademy would be launching a new Plus product which would be exclusively subscription based.

'I could not believe it,' Shailendra chuckled. 'I didn't expect him to put a total stop to the first product, you know. I was just giving him ideas but he went all in and I think that was the pivotal moment for all of us. He could have said, and what I had expected was that he would assign a few engineers on it and try something out in the next five months. I am telling you, 95 per cent of the founders would have done something like that and you wouldn't blame them for it. No one thought he would get it done the way he did.'

But then, Gaurav is Gaurav. He made his whole team rally behind the new idea and they decided to go for broke. As soon as Gaurav announced it internally, to all the leaders, that they would be killing the existing business and moving to a different model, the Business team started informing the educators. Barring those who were making big money on revenue share in their courses and were apprehensive and reluctant to change, most of the educators agreed to cooperate.

Gaurav and Roman personally talked to the popular educators and convinced them to come on board. In four crazy weeks, Unacademy had made its boldest bet yet and the team had defied all the odds against it to meet the impossible deadline (details in 'Velocity as a moat').

On 29 January 2019, Unacademy became the first edtech company to launch a subscription for live courses (referred to as Unacademy Plus from here on). It had 400 educators launching courses in 12 different exam categories. A UPSC aspirant could pay ₹36,000 for a year of subscription that gave unlimited access to all the UPSC educators' live and recorded videos. The pricing for banking and SSC examination prep subscription was ₹5,000 per year and that of Railway examination prep was ₹4,500.

While the singular focus on launching the product had consumed him so far, the reality sunk in once the Plus model went live. Gaurav would not sleep for days to come. No one in the edtech sector was offering subscriptions. He had shut down a perfectly functional product that was generating ₹3 crore in monthly revenues. Would his gamble pay off? Or, had he just made the stupidest mistake in the history of start-ups? Only time would tell.

WE HAVE ARRIVED

Gaurav looked at his dashboard intently. The revenue from the first 30 days of Unacademy Plus was ₹1.8 crore—nowhere close to the December figure for the previous product. He called up his mentor and board member, Bhavin Turakhia.

'It was a mistake, Bhavin. We did only ₹1.8 crore,' his voice was sinking.

'Would you chill? It's only the first month,' Bhavin comforted him.

When a podcaster had asked Gaurav what his biggest strength was, he had replied, 'It's my obsession. I am more obsessed than others.' And his biggest weakness? He said, 'It's my obsession, I don't know how to let go.'

Those two months after launching Unacademy Plus would feed the shadows of his obsession and anxiety like never before. He would regularly call investors and mentors in order to seek solace.

Some respite came at the end of the second month when he noticed a revenue of ₹2.5 crore. It was the third month when they finally crossed the previous peak and ended up doing ₹4.3 crore! The music didn't stop. By the seventh month, Unacademy Plus crossed a million dollars in monthly revenue (₹9 crore) and had clocked over 50,000 paid active users. There was no looking back.

Gaurav finally got good sleep that night.

'They have just blitzscaled from that point on,' Shailendra told me. 'And look, ideas are cheap. I give out ideas all the time but the credit goes to the founders who can evaluate if it has merit and then execute it. Gaurav backed the idea with everything he had and that is what made it successful.'

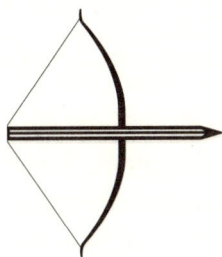

THREE

SUPERPOWER 2: TRACTION TRUMPS EVERYTHING

How Unacademy Grew So Fast

Gaurav wiped the whiteboard clean and started another sprint of brainstorming with Roman and Hemesh. Soon, the whiteboard was full again.

Every start-up faces a make-or-break moment. Unacademy's moment came in September 2017. Unacademy's growth had stalled. Content views had not grown beyond 6 million monthly eyeballs since the last three months. The founders were restless because they could not afford to lose momentum.

'This was also the period when Gaurav contracted a chest infection and was hospitalized. Health was bad, growth was not happening—it was a gloomy environment. I was making 10 videos a day but nothing was helping. We would lie awake the whole night and brainstorm on the whiteboard for six to 10 hours. There were tireless discussions—*yeh course banaate hain, iss educator ko leke aate hain. Poora whiteboard bhar jaata tha. Pachis points likhte the, phir mita dete the* (let's make this course, let's get that educator. We would write 25 points that would fill the whole whiteboard, then we would delete those and start again),' Roman told me. 'Growth should

never stop, that was the only thing that mattered to us,'—he summarized the key to Unacademy's resilience in one line.

This was one of the lowest moments for Unacademy but unlike most start-ups, it rebounded from rock bottom to a period of triumph, and never looked back. The Unacademy founders have, time and time again, dipped into their reserves of grit and resolve to keep moving forward. What ultimately ensured Unacademy's unprecedented success was a result of the innovative ways in which the founders had created traction in various stages of its existence.

TRACTION-MARKET FIT

If there is one holy grail other than the product-market fit that start-ups chase, it is traction. However, traction can be both a leading indicator of product-market fit and a reflection of it. 'The term "product-market fit" describes the moment when a start-up finally finds a widespread set of customers that resonate with its product,' says Eric Ries.[6]

Identifying this fit, however, can be tricky. The traction is relatively easier to target, especially when you don't know what your product is or can be—as was the case with Unacademy when it started. In an oft-quoted statement, Justice Stewart defined pornography as, 'I know it when I see it.'[7] The same applies to traction. The baseline of what constitutes traction might vary from business-to-business (B2B) to business-to-consumer (B2C) products, but the underlying truth remains

---

[6]Grifiin, Tren. '12 Things about Product-Market Fit', *Future*, 18 February 2017, https://future.a16z.com/about-product-market-fit/. Accessed on 17 February 2022.

[7]Lattman, Peter. 'The Origins of Justice Stewart's "I Know It When I See It"', *The Wall Street Journal*, 27 September 2007, https://www.wsj.com/articles/BL-LB-4558. Accessed on 17 February 2022.

intact—traction is growth. Traction is what makes the investors want to invest in you, traction is what makes your team want to work with you, traction is what makes you keep going.

Angel investor Sanjay Mehta writes[8]:

> Raising capital is tough and most founders hear that 'It is a pass' but do not get enough insights into why the deal was passed. There may be multiple reasons to pass the deal, team, market size, product etc. but everything gets ignored if there is traction in business. Investors chase traction.

In my last book, *No Shortcuts: Rare Insights from 15 Successful Start-up Founders*[9], I profiled a Silicon Valley start-up, Like a Little, which was essentially a copy of another flirting platform for college students in the United Kingdom (UK). The very idea reeked of the problems it could run into—objectifying women, cyberbullying, etc. Y Combinator, an American seed money start-up accelerator, had called the founders of Like a Little for an interview based on some other idea they had proposed in their initial application two months ago. When the founders told the co-founder of Y Combinator, Paul Graham, that they had pivoted to this flirting platform, Graham had found the idea superficial and repelling.

He asked, 'What makes you think we would want this?'

---

[8]Mehta, Sanjay. 'Founders Should Live and Breathe Traction, for Startups That's Everything', *Inc42*, 13 October 2020, https://inc42.com/resources/in-pursuit-of-traction-founders-should-live-breath-traction-for-startups-traction-is-everything/#:~:text=Founders%20Should%20Live%20And%20Breath%20Traction%2C%20For%20Startups%20That's%20Everything,-Sanjay%20Mehta&text=If%20you%20build%20it%2C%20they%20will%20come.&text=The%20most%20exciting%20phase%20in,dream%20is%20now%20a%20reality. Accessed on 13 October 2021.
[9]Tripathi, Nistha. *No Shortcuts: Rare Insights from 15 Successful Start-up Founders*, SAGE Publications, 2018.

The founders replied, 'Because we have two million users.'
He said, 'In two months?'
The founders replied, 'Yes.'
The founders were right. Not only were they accepted by Y Combinator, they ended up attracting funding from the who's who of the Valley, such as the VC firm Andreessen Horowitz, venture capitalist Ron Conway and internet entrepreneur Mark Pincus. Every problem gets ignored when you have traction.

So, the question essentially is: how do you get traction?

Gaurav Munjal often pondered over this question. And, then he stumbled upon the book *Traction: A Startup Guide to Getting Customers*[10] by Gabriel Weinberg and Justin Mares. The book, a popular reference in the start-up fraternity, describes 19 different traction channels and offers a bull's-eye framework to find traction.

Gaurav, like many other people, is an avid reader. But unlike many other people, he is exceptional at applying what he learns. This book convinced him that different stages of a company's growth require different traction channels. Unacademy's success would depend on how effectively he could discover and unlock these channels at different stages. He would have to experiment with different channels and see what worked best for Unacademy.

In due course, he vigorously experimented with different channels, found success in some, learned from them and more importantly, discovered newer ones that Weinberg and Mares had themselves missed.

---

[10]Gabriel Weinberg and Justin Mares. *Traction: A Startup Guide to Getting Customers*, S-curves Publishing, 2014.

MAKING THE FRONT PAGE

When Roman finally decided to quit the civil services and become an educator-cum-entrepreneur in 2016, he challenged decades of tradition and shocked many Indians. The real work began once the founding team was in place. The Unacademy founders were aware that they now needed to prove that they could deliver on their lofty vision. The first step was to go beyond the YouTube fandom and put their name out there in the real world.

Roman's decision was unprecedented, controversial and made for a great story. The founders recognized that it was a significant opportunity to announce Unacademy's arrival with a big bang but they did not have the means to spend on PR. Gaurav talked to a few journalists and cracked a deal with a reporter from *The Times of India* to give him exclusive access to their interviews if he could get them on the front page of the largest circulated English newspaper in India. The hustle worked and *The Times of India* printed this on their front page on 10 January 2016[11]: '24-Year-Old Quits IAS to Turn Free E-Tutor'. The news article went on to describe how Roman wanted to see students get past the various academic hurdles that stand in the way of youthful ambitions.

The narrative had struck quite a chord with the youth as the news kept trending on Twitter and Facebook for days, giving a tremendous initial recognition to Roman Saini and the Unacademy team. Their resourcefulness and clever use of unconventional PR had got the ball rolling.

---

[11]Gosain, Manish Pratim. '24-Year-Old Quits IAS to Turn Free E-Tutor', *The Times of India*, 10 January 2016, https://timesofindia.indiatimes.com/india/24-year-old-quits-ias-to-turn-free-e-tutor/articleshow/50516074.cms. Accessed on 13 October 2021.

INFLUENCER MARKETING WITH BEDI AND THAROOR

Unacademy had been doing 100,000 monthly views when Roman and Gaurav started posting their videos more regularly in 2015. When they invited other people to start teaching on the Unacademy channel, it gave a voice to many creative people who started teaching whatever caught their fancy. From teaching how to play a musical instrument to how to speak French, the content was getting more diversified. However, the bulk of the views were still coming from Roman's videos. His popularity, and more importantly, his credibility of cracking the toughest entrance examinations made him the face of Unacademy. He was a big influencer when it came to the UPSC and medical exams segment.

The founders realized that they needed more influencers to get further traction. Instead of paying the influencers, the founders decided to approach the academicians in their own network. Needless to say, Roman's network was the most star-studded one.

Having been trained at LBSNAA, Roman had met many celebrated officers like Raghuram Rajan, Aruna Roy, U.K. Sinha and Harsh Mander. Between him and his fellow trainees, they could connect to the most powerful leaders in India within a couple of degrees of separation. It helped that his story had been read by IAS rank holders and aspirants alike.

Roman started approaching a few influencers personally and urged them to record a video for Unacademy viewers. Kiran Bedi was one such influential personality who obliged. Roman went to her house in Delhi and helped her record a small video in April 2016. She was even gracious enough to post about Unacademy on her Facebook page, describing

it as a great way to learn, for people who could not afford expensive coaching classes.

This was not the first time Roman had done this. Just before he had resigned, news broke out that a woman now held AIR 1 in the Civil Services Examinations—Ira Singhal. 'I found out that it was her birthday. So, I got a cake and went to meet her at her home. I had also taken my laptop and pen tablet. I told her that we would love to post her videos on our channel. I suggested that we create a video about study tips for UPSC or anything like that.' But, people are always sceptical of videos. There is something about coming in front of the camera that fills people with self-doubt. Ira was no exception. She kept saying, 'No sir, I have never created videos and I don't think I have any study tips either.' This is where Roman's persistence paid off. 'I told her that I will help her and I was not leaving until she created three to four videos. *Mai to wahin baith gaya tha* (I just sat there waiting). She saw that I was not going anywhere, so she created a few videos that we posted later. This was the first time an IAS topper was sharing her advice on YouTube like this. It was watched by lakhs of viewers.'

Another celebrity influencer who Roman was able to convince was Dr Shashi Tharoor. 'I got one of my batchmates to introduce us.' Such clever use of relevant influencer marketing gave a credibility boost to Unacademy's image in the early days and saw it go from 100,000 monthly views to a million a month by January 2016. Soon thereafter, the founders closed an angel seed round of $500,000 and a pre-Series A round of $1 million.

THE VIRAL FOUNDERS

YouTube is not the only platform that was embraced by Gaurav. A typical millennial, he has always had a knack for

using social media to amplify his voice. Early in 2015–16, Gaurav had started writing answers on Quora, a popular American question-and-answer website. As per a *Quartz* article from 2014[12], Quora was more popular in India than in any other country outside the US, where it was founded. Further, it claimed that Quora was the most heavily browsed in Pilani, Roorkee and Kharagpur—the hub of engineering students. Quora offered an uncensored peek into interesting people's lives and minds. No wonder, the student populace on Quora loved reading about the first-hand experiences of academic achievers and entrepreneurs like Roman and Gaurav. With Commonfloor acquiring Flat.to and investing in Flatchat, Gaurav became one of the earliest and youngest successful entrepreneurs to write on Quora. He noticed that his answers were getting the ultimate validation in terms of views and likes. For instance, he answered a question 'How do I convince my 17-year-old-son not to be an entrepreneur?' on Quora in March 2015, that has 660,000 views and 28,900 likes till date.[13]

Once Roman cracked the UPSC-CSE, many Indians on Quora started asking questions about him. Gaurav ended up answering few such questions including 'What is it like to be friends with Roman Saini?' Then, people started asking more

---

[12]Walia, Shelly. 'Indians Have Found an Online Haven Where It's OK for Them to Know It All', *Quartz India*, 6 November 2014, https://qz.com/india/291739/indians-have-found-an-online-haven-where-its-ok-for-them-to-know-it-all/. Accessed on 13 October 2021.

[13]Gaurav Munjal's response to Quora question 'How do I convince my 17-year-old-son not to be an entrepreneur?', Answered in 2018, https://www.quora.com/How-do-I-convince-my-17-year-old-son-not-to-be-an-entrepreneur-He-spends-his-time-reading-books-on-business-building-things-robotics-and-coding-He-is-looking-for-an-internship-at-a-startup-I-want-him-to-focus-on-school-Am-I-wrong/answer/Gaurav-Munjal. Accessed on 17 February 2022.

questions, such as 'What is Roman's daily routine?', 'How did Roman crack UPSC in his first attempt?' and so on. This is when Gaurav encouraged Roman to start sharing his experience on the platform as well. Roman had already created an account on Quora a couple of years prior to this but it was only after Gaurav's nudge that he started taking it more seriously.

It did not take long for Gaurav to recognize the potential of Quora as a content marketing tool. Unacademy's target audience—Indian students—was already hanging out on Quora. There was no better place to strike a conversation with them. Both Gaurav and Roman started posting answers daily and soon featured among the top 10 writers on the platform— not just in India but globally. They did not miss a chance to mention that they were building Unacademy and would link their websites to all the answers. This created a surge of traffic to the Unacademy website but most importantly, made it a household name for every Quoran (a term used to describe an active user on Quora). For those years when Gaurav and Roman wrote prolifically on Quora, it remained one of the top traffic sources for Unacademy's website.

Noticing the importance of viral social media posts first across YouTube, and later on Quora, the duo started posting on other platforms too, including Facebook and Twitter. They would embrace and learn anything that could help them reach out to their users. In those days, Roman's popularity was soaring and he was invited to share his experiences through guest talks at IITs, NITs and many other prestigious institutes. These talks gave him excellent access to the students in an in-person setting. Here, he had a chance to interact with the students face to face instead of talking to them from behind a screen, and he made the most of it. His talks were typically attended by 500–1,000 students and the topic of Unacademy always came up. Roman

would encourage these young students to start teaching and creating content on Unacademy. Hearing their idol share his story of defying conventional wisdom and embracing the path of entrepreneurship resonated deeply with these students and hordes of them came on to Unacademy in a bid to consume and create educational content. 'I did a lot of speaking engagements in those days because the response was excellent. We found many educators through those talks who are still teaching on our platform,' Roman told me.

Both of them continued to contribute answers to Quora actively till 2017. By then, they had amassed 360,000 followers, 35 million answer views and top writer badges for the year 2017. Roman posted his last answer in December 2018, whereas Gaurav kept writing intermittently till January 2020. The reason for waning activity of the founders has as much to do with their increasing preoccupation with scaling the business as it is with the awareness of diminishing returns. Any more writing on these platforms or spending time in speaking engagements was only contributing to trivial increments in the business growth. It was time to explore newer user acquisition channels.

Gaurav added, 'We also stopped attending start-up events because they were not going to help Unacademy beyond a point. Most people give talks out of a sense of vanity and ego so that they can feel good about themselves but it does not help the business. What's the point?'

WE ARE NOT JUST UPSC

Paul Graham writes[14] that the best thing for a start-up to measure is the growth rate of revenue.

---

[14]Graham, Paul. 'Startup=Growth', September 2012, http://www.paulgraham.com/growth.html. Accessed on 14 October 2021.

The next best, for start-ups that don't charge initially, is active users. That's a reasonable proxy for revenue growth because whenever the start-up does start trying to make money, their revenues will probably be a constant multiple of active users.

By September 2017, Unacademy had no monetization plans and therefore, revenue was not a useful metric to track. Instead, it was focusing on the number of views on its videos and active users on the app. The news was worrisome. It had been nearly three months since they had been stuck at 6 million monthly views. This is when Gaurav, Roman and Hemesh pulled all-nighters to discuss growth strategies on the whiteboard. One of the key observations was that most of the views were coming from the test preparation courses. While quirky and fun courses were interesting, what users were really flocking to were videos that talked about cracking entrance examinations in India. This is why Roman's courses were so popular, because Unacademy users wanted to emulate him and do well in tough examinations like NEET and UPSC. Instead of browsing the app for entertainment, they were browsing for targeted guidance and strategies. Inevitably, Unacademy was attracting students who had specific goals in mind, such as cracking a particular examination.

However, the content on Unacademy was still limited to three government examinations—UPSC, Staff Selection Committee (SSC) and banking. The founders came to a conclusion that they could not expand any more on the current test preparation categories they were focusing on. They needed to make videos for more examinations to expand their catchment area and attract new users.

Mayank Garg had graduated from IIT Patna in the summer of 2017 with a major in Electrical Engineering and had no interest in coding. Being picky in his job search, he had either

rejected companies because the role did not appeal to him or the companies had rejected him because they could not fit him in their open positions. During his bachelor's, he had dabbled in coordinating technical fests, had represented India in Harvard College Project for Asian and International Relations 2015 (HPAIR), had done a research internship at Maurer School of Law in Indiana University and few other internships in India. If there was a pattern he was trying to find towards his destiny, it was still eluding him three months after graduation. Staying with his parents in Delhi, his time to find a job was running out. So, when he heard from one of his seniors who had been working at Unacademy that the company was hiring and Gaurav was visiting Delhi in October 2017, Mayank jumped at the opportunity.

'I am meeting some friends at Garage Inc. in Hauz Khas in the evening. Why don't you come there only?' Gaurav told Mayank.

Wait, isn't that a pub? Mayank thought. Yes, it was. *But hey, I finally have an interview*! Mayank took fresh copies of his resume and after a mental debate over what to wear for an interview in a pub, Mayank reached exactly on time.

Gaurav was hanging out with two other friends and waved to Mayank to join him. It was like a scene straight out of a movie. Gaurav and his friends were chatting about bitcoin and Mayank, who had no clue about any of that, kept nodding in between. Gaurav finally asked him what he had been up to, if he had earned any money before this and so on. Mayank kept responding, waiting for him to ask about something from his resume. He was least prepared for Gaurav's next question.

'Do you drink?'

'Um...yeah, I do but I have to go home and I can't drink before going back home. It is not allowed.'

Gaurav ordered three beers and a pineapple juice for

Mayank but when the waiter came, Gaurav asked him to put the beer in front of Mayank. Just when Mayank started to slide the beer away from himself, Gaurav threw a googly. 'Chug the beer and the job is yours.'

Mayank smiled awkwardly and Gaurav smiled back.

'I am not saying you have to drink. That is your call. But if you drink it, I will give you the job for sure.' Gaurav went back to chatting with his friends.

And just like that, Mayank did chug that beer and Gaurav offered him a three-month internship on the spot.

'That's it? I have a job?' Mayank couldn't believe it. No one can say what had hit him more—the beer or the adrenaline rush of the moment.

Gaurav would later tell him why he had been hired. 'Since I had no experience or expertise, all he wanted was to see my attitude. He had already made up his mind to hire me but when I drank that beer, he thought I was willing to go all in. And he admired that.'

When Mayank joined Unacademy's Bengaluru office two days after that unforgettable night, Gaurav put him on an important task—he made him the in-charge for the IIT-JEE test preparation category. In those days, Mayank got unprecedented access to Gaurav, Hemesh and the core team every day for a couple of hours when they would discuss ideas for expansion. From an unemployed fresher to working closely with Unacademy founders in the company's formative years, Mayank got the experience of his lifetime.

He approached the established coaching institute faculty in Kota, the Mecca for JEE aspirants. After a few conversations, it was clear to him that these educators were much more expensive than what Unacademy had been used to so far. UPSC, SSC and banking exam educators were still willing to teach on their platform because of Roman's presence.

However, IIT-JEE, CAT and other mainstream categories were tough nuts to crack since Unacademy had no realistic credibility in those. The offline coaching industry was valued well over $40 billion at this point. Top educators in Kota (for IIT-JEE) and Delhi (for UPSC) were in huge demand and were being paid anywhere between ₹50 lakh to several crores in salary. The pandemic had not yet forced them to recognize the value that online classrooms could bring. If you wanted to convince a teacher as famed as Vineet Loomba for example, you had to pay the price, sometimes five to 10 times of what Unacademy was paying.

Eventually, the team made up their mind—they will pay top money to India's best educators for teaching on Unacademy. Mayank, armed with fuller pockets, went back to the negotiation tables with the big guys in Kota. Amidst many rejects, there were a handful of successes. Unacademy got its first set of Kota gurus—Kailash Sharma for physics and Vineet Loomba for mathematics, and Mayank was promoted from an intern to a full-time category leader.

Within the next few months, Unacademy had expanded to 10 examination categories including popular ones like IIT-JEE, NEET PG, CAT and more. This was the beginning of Unacademy becoming the online face of test preparation coaching in India.

YOUTUBE AS A TRACTION CHANNEL

Even after Mayank had onboarded some of the famous educators for IIT-JEE, the views on the app were still not shooting up. 'We had created a nice pipeline of good teachers but what we needed now was students.' These were also the days when Unacademy was predominantly a UPSC-focused app. The Unacademy YouTube channel was also full of UPSC

preparation videos. Everyone in the company was living under the shadow of this one category, and any team that was dealing with non-UPSC related content was reeling under a feeling of underconfidence. 'There was this mindset in our team that we cannot attract big distribution channels or more users in other categories. But I went out and said that I wanted to experiment. I said even our YouTube channel does not work for me. It had mostly UPSC, SSC and banking videos. How do I bring in JEE aspirants to this channel?' The clean slate that Mayank was carrying with him turned out very useful. He came with no encumbrance of experience or biases. He was given a task to make the IIT-JEE category popular and he started thinking.

'I reached out to a lot of YouTubers. I closed this educator named Sachin Rana who was teaching chemistry for the IIT-JEE on YouTube. He had roughly 12,000 subscribers on his channel back then.' This meant that they did not have to pay as much to onboard Sachin. 'We pushed his first course on 2 January 2018 on our app.' What followed shocked everyone in the company. 'His video garnered 5,500 views on our platform. No one had got so many views in the IIT-JEE category before! In fact, that was the highest ever that a debut educator had reached on our app, in any category. Everyone was wondering how this could happen in a random category,' says Mayank with a smile.

You are not remiss in wondering why 5,500 views were such a big deal. It only goes to show how small Unacademy was and how deeply it was entrenched in the government examination category back then. What Mayank had proved was that they can do better in other categories, too.

Sachin Rana, who was a third year undergraduate chemistry student at IIT Bombay in 2017, had been posting chemistry videos on YouTube for fun. He was not an

established teacher from a top coaching institute. The fact that his videos were doing better than renowned educators reinforced the changing landscape of education. When it came to online teaching, the educators' ability to engage the viewers mattered as much as their subject matter expertise. Previously, the team had worried that if the content quality did not consistently deliver across all the videos, the users would leave as fast as they were arriving. But Sachin Rana's case had given them a new insight. These educators, who had great online presence, were a great lead magnet—a way to attract new users to the Unacademy app—but once the users landed there, they could discover other courses put up by expert faculty which had a lot more substance. In this way, the company had uncovered a new traction channel—YouTube.

Previously in 2016, once the Unacademy website and later app had been launched, the company had reduced its attention on YouTube—the very platform that had brought it into existence. YouTube was big in India and was growing bigger by the day. Globally, it was the second-biggest search engine after Google. Mayank's experiment with YouTubers like Sachin Rana made the founders realize that perhaps it was a mistake to overlook YouTube. In 2018, they started exploring ways to bring their mojo back on YouTube. However, the battle had changed from what they had last seen. There were a lot of young YouTubers like Rana, who were teaching niche topics and subjects on their own YouTube channels and had a few thousand subscribers. Whenever relevant and feasible, Unacademy would employ such YouTubers to teach on its app instead of its YouTube channel, as it had done in 2015. Some of these YouTubers adapted well to Unacademy's demands of quality and evolved into expert faculty themselves (as happened in the case of Rana who is currently among the top-10 educators for IIT-JEE Chemistry on Unacademy).

However, there was another way—a far more interesting and innovative one—with which they could leverage YouTube.

Unacademy started asking these long tail of educators to endorse Unacademy on their individual channels. They designed black T-shirts featuring a minimalistic, clean Unacademy logo and made the educators commit to wearing these T-shirts while recording their videos. The effect of this approach was that the viewer did not see Unacademy as an intrusive advertisement that would pop up in the middle of their video watching experience. The impression viewers would get was that the educators were supporting and recommending Unacademy. 'If you go and search for Unacademy on YouTube, you will not only find Unacademy channels but hundreds of other channels where educators can be seen wearing Unacademy T-shirts,' Gaurav told me.

An educator with 20,000 subscribers would agree to such brand campaigning for a sum as small as ₹8,000. Compared to spending lakhs on an influencer for posting a promotional video, this enabled Unacademy to bring immediate brand recognition when hundreds of such educators started appearing with Unacademy T-shirts on their YouTube feed. These were highly targeted channels since they were teaching the topics relevant for Unacademy users. Any person browsing such videos on YouTube could no longer miss Unacademy's name.

With barely any big marketing expenditure, Unacademy had gone on to raise a Series C funding of $21 million in July 2018, while it still had $15 million intact in its bank account. The founders' experimentations and obsession for finding newer traction channels were beginning to show results. Unacademy went up from 6 million to 20 million monthly views in the next six months.

BUILD OR BUY

In early 2018, Dinesh Godara had been looking for investors. Dinesh had started a second-hand books marketplace called famousfunda.com when he had been an engineering student at Rajasthan Technical University. He had become so adept at Google search engine optimization (SEO) that he was earning ₹3–4 lakh from monetizing his blogs, more than 50 of them at the time, via Google AdSense. Another successful website in his portfolio was a test preparation blog called onlineindiaeducation.com that ranked in the top 500 Indian websites (by traffic) according to Alexa India ranks. By the time he had graduated in 2013, YouTube had caught his fancy and he had started a YouTube channel called WiFiStudy, which helped users prepare for government exams such as UPSC, SSC, banking, railways, etc. One can say that his journey mirrored Gaurav Munjal's in his college days since both of them were early adopters of social media and were attracted to education-related content. The resemblance runs deeper— both of them hail from Jaipur and their YouTube channels, Unacademy and WiFiStudy, would cross 2 million YouTube subscribers on the same day on 30 May 2018.

One area where Gaurav had zoomed past Dinesh, however, was in entrepreneurial experience. He had the experience of starting Flat.to and of raising funds for Unacademy. 'Everyday on the news, I would read about all the money that Unacademy had raised. But if you look at WiFiStudy, it was completely bootstrapped and yet, we were growing faster than them on YouTube,' Dinesh told me. To keep fuelling the rapid growth, Dinesh needed investors on board. So, he started contacting venture capitalists on LinkedIn. He told them that WiFiStudy was growing faster than Unacademy without any investment and was looking for funding. Having

had no previous experience with fundraising, Dinesh became a LinkedIn Premium user and started contacting investors at random. As it happened, one of the investors he had pitched to had also invested in Unacademy. Soon, news reached Gaurav that another YouTube channel from Jaipur was looking to raise money and he was mentioning Unacademy's name in its pitches. Gaurav, in his trademark unabashed gusto, called up Dinesh and said, 'I heard you are looking for investment. I am in Jaipur, let's catch up.'

Unacademy, having decided to refocus on YouTube, was doing its best to regain its position as India's biggest edtech channel. However, WiFiStudy had been hard to beat when it came to YouTube views. Gaurav did not like the prospect of competing with them, especially if they ended up raising VC like him. The best-case scenario would be if the Unacademy YouTube channel could be made bigger than WiFiStudy's, but in case that did not happen, what would be the next best thing? Gaurav had a clear answer—if you cannot beat them, buy them out.

Gaurav had called Dinesh in April 2018 and proposed to meet up at the Marriott in Jaipur the next evening. 'I was not aware of how things worked in the start-up ecosystem. *Ek baar ke liye mai darr gaya ki mujhe shayad Unacademy ka naam use nahi karna chahiye tha* (For a moment, I became scared, wondering if I shouldn't have used the Unacademy name),' Dinesh told me with a chuckle, reminiscing about that meeting. However, he did gather himself and talked to Gaurav candidly. He told him that WiFiStudy was looking to raise $1 million at a valuation of $10 million to do something big. Gaurav offered to acquire his company in that meeting itself, but Dinesh declined. So, Gaurav offered to invest in WiFiStudy and Dinesh could not say no to that. Gaurav asked Dinesh to come to Bengaluru and pitch to his team so that they could

finalize the terms. 'He told me that once his team listened to my pitch, he would tell me within 24 hours whether or not he would invest. *Wahin baithe baithe, usne meri flight ticket bhi book kar di* (He even booked my flight right there). It was all happening so fast *ki mujhe kuch samajh bhi nahi aa raha tha* (that I couldn't understand what was happening).'

Two days later, Dinesh and two of his team members flew down to Unacademy's office in Bengaluru and presented to the core team including Hemesh. The pitch went well and Gaurav told Dinesh that he was interested in working together. He even made Dinesh meet the Unacademy board members including Shailendra Singh from Sequoia. After this meeting, Gaurav gave WiFiStudy a term sheet for investing $1.5 million for a 15 per cent stake. He added a clause so that whenever WiFiStudy would raise funds from another investor, Unacademy would have the first right of refusal. Dinesh was not too keen on this clause and delayed signing the term sheet for a long time. However, they both kept in touch and in Dinesh's words, 'Tuning *acchi ho gayi thi hamari* (We had become attuned to each other's ways).' Over time, exhaustion had started setting in on Dinesh's fundraising efforts and the conversation had moved from strategic investment to a full-acquisition deal. It was on 29 October 2018, that the deal was finally closed. With over 4.5 million subscribers and 70 million monthly video views, WiFiStudy was one of the largest educational YouTube channels in the world when Unacademy acquired it for a cash and stock deal rumoured to be valued at $10 million.

The acquisition turned out to be a goldmine for Unacademy. By September 2019, WiFiStudy had crossed 10 million subscribers on YouTube, making it the first Asia Pacific channel to do so. It topped the list of the most subscribed edtech platforms globally and its co-branded

videos were contributing to 15 per cent of Unacademy's revenues. In doing so, Gaurav had discovered a new traction channel that is often unheard of. 'When acquisitions work well, which is rare, they can be a massive traction channel and that is what we saw with WiFiStudy.'

Unacademy would double down on the acquisitions route in the coming years—Kreatryx for its Graduate Aptitude Test in Engineering (GATE) preparation content in March 2020, Codechef for building its presence in the coding category in June 2020, Mastree for K–12 content in July 2020, PrepLadder for medical entrance examination content in July 2020, Coursavy, which was a UPSC preparation mentoring company, in September 2020, NeoStencil for penetrating more learners in tier 2 and 3 cities with government and law examinations content in December 2020, TapChief for professional mentoring in February 2021, Handa ka Funda for CAT preparation content in March 2021 and Rheo TV for live game-streaming platform in July 2021.

AFFILIATE MARKETING

When Unacademy launched its Plus subscription model in January 2019, nobody knew what would happen. No other edtech company was relying on Netflix-like subscriptions and Unacademy was way out of its comfort zone.

Gaurav had set a goal of reaching 10,000 paid subscribers in four months. The big question for him was: can the company achieve this without burning a lot of cash? Instead of choosing to spend on marketing and advertisements alone, he came up with the idea of leveraging the 3,000 plus educators they had on their YouTube channel and app. They announced to their educators that they would pay a 30 per cent affiliate commission to any educator who brought them a paid

subscriber. The amount was non-trivial and a great way for the educators to monetize their followers on social media. For example, an IIT-JEE teacher could potentially earn ₹7,000 when the user bought a one year subscription.

Hemesh's team set up a way to allow customers to enter a discount coupon code when making the payment for a subscription plan. Each educator was given a unique discount code which allowed Unacademy to track who had referred this particular customer. The educator would simply advertise the code on their social media accounts and their followers would be incentivized to use it because they could get a 10 per cent discount by using such a code. The users were happy because of the discounts, the educators were happy because of the 30 per cent commission fee, and Unacademy was happy because it got a new subscriber.

Affiliate marketing strategies worked extremely well because Unacademy crossed 17,000 subscribers in less than three months and 40,000 subscribers by July 2019, without burning a hole in the company's cash reserves.

UNACADEMY PRODUCTIONS

With renewed focus on YouTube, Unacademy had split its YouTube channel into multiple channels, each focusing on a different area, including Unacademy JEE channel for IIT-JEE preparations and 'Chamomile Tea with Toppers', a channel which featured *Koffee with Karan*-like interviews of various exam toppers. Once WiFiStudy was acquired, Dinesh Godara became a part of Unacademy and started overseeing the Brands team which was managing WiFiStudy and Unacademy JEE channels. Now, the focus was to improve the quality of their content and keep growing.

Roman started expanding his content team in the summer

of 2019. 'In those days, the way that edtech companies worked was like this. They were creating central studios for their teachers. The teacher would come and record the videos, and the company would help edit and process their videos.' This is also how WiFiStudy and Unacademy channels were operating until then. But it was inefficient. Roman explains, 'For an educator, it meant wasting a lot of travel time to come to the office, then to wait until the previous educator had finished his recording and so on. The bottleneck is that only one person can use the studio at a time in such an arrangement.' After travelling all the way to the office and then waiting, educators were not at their most energetic self. The lethargy, if visible, could ruin the videos they ended up recording. 'It also becomes a breeding ground for internal politics among the teachers,' he added.

While other edtech companies might have been more forgiving, Unacademy founders were looking for any and every way to make themselves stand apart from the crowd. They came up with an idea to give every educator their own studio at a place of their convenience, which was usually right in their homes. 'It saved on an educator's travel time and cut down on a lot of the administrative work that the educators would end up doing at the central studio or offices,' says Roman.

Unacademy formally kick-started the Studio team whose sole purpose was to enable educators to create highly refined videos for YouTube that would look more aesthetic and attract more views. 'We would procure the camera, microphones, lighting, everything and set them up fully so that all the educator had to do was record the videos. We also trained them so that they were able to use all the technologies and tools effectively. I remember our team making a presentation for the educators at 2 a.m. so that we could bring them up to speed.'

The first of such studios was created in Delhi. There were even cases when two educators would be living in the same apartment. Unacademy would build them each their individual studios in such a case. Initially, each set-up cost ₹11–12 lakh but with higher volumes and more efficiency built in, the cost was brought down to ₹7 lakh for later installations. With these efforts, Unacademy content had crossed 100 million monthly views and 10 million subscribers by the third quarter of 2019.

After the COVID-19 lockdown in 2020, a lot of educators moved back to their hometowns. So, Roman's team helped them create studios in towns like Bhubaneswar and Mirzapur. By November 2020, 47,000 educators were teaching on Unacademy in over 14 Indian languages across 5,000 cities. The collective watch time on Unacademy's YouTube channel and app was touching 2 billion minutes per month.

From those eventful nights in September 2017, when the future of the company itself was shrouded in darkness, the founders had found their way to summery mornings. The sun was just rising on the horizon of Unacademy's bright future.

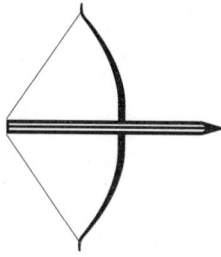

FOUR

SUPERPOWER 3:
TECH FIRST AND FOREMOST

How the E-Product Was Built

Any MBA would define successful companies as the ones that maximize value for their shareholders. Gaurav Munjal feels that there is another kind of successful company—the one that grows by bringing forth innovations that change the industry itself. 'No edtech player in India was offering subscriptions when we launched Unacademy Plus. Within a couple of months, everybody had started doing subscription plans.'

To be this kind of a successful company, one needs to be independent-minded. If a company is too busy watching over its shoulders to see what the competition is doing, it cannot think of fresh ideas. From the first day when hardly anyone understood what Gaurav, Roman and Hemesh were trying to build, to a time when bigger players are emulating its moves, Unacademy has come a long way.

The one superpower that one cannot ignore is its undeterred focus on the product and technology. Not only has it improved its product by leaps and bounds, there is a constant striving to make it better every single day. Apart from

making its users cared for by doing this, it is building a brand that can find its status among the most prestigious technology companies to work for.

BECOME A TEACHER IN ONE CLICK

Roman had been making videos on the Unacademy YouTube channel much before he cracked the IAS exam in 2014. Even as an IAS officer in training, he was creating videos in his spare time. Once the three co-founders had quit their current positions and started full-time on Unacademy, YouTube was the natural focal point. Gaurav and Roman started cranking out more videos. Roman, the young AIIMS doctor who had cracked the IAS in his first attempt, had a godlike following on social media. He would talk about UPSC subjects and how to crack competitive exams in his videos. Gaurav would create videos on engineering concepts.

This was not Gaurav's first rendezvous with the video world. Back in his college days, he had created videos to explain engineering computer graphics concepts to his friends. 'I already had my Dell laptop. I bought a whiteboard and recorded a simple video to explain a concept in computer graphics,' he recalled.

They had created roughly 500 videos until 2015. Apart from Gaurav and Roman, Ravi Handa was putting up videos on CAT preparation. By December 2015, they were getting 1 million views per month. The biggest problem till then was that while the Unacademy channel had decent views without any marketing, only three people had made videos—they needed more. 'The best minds in India were not even teaching online. We kept thinking that if they started teaching, what a difference it would make!' Gaurav told me.

Roman was the viewer-magnet. His videos had helped the

Unacademy channel go from 10,000 subscribers to 100,000. But to go beyond, they had to get more educators and more content. Most of the education companies at this point take the route of hiring more educators, cover more subjects and create more videos on the channel. They can then monetize by selling their content on tablets and charge a high price.

This is where Gaurav was clear that he wanted to build a platform company and not a YouTube channel. Unacademy's charter was to enable thousands of educators. But, getting 1,000 educators to create content was a costly affair. The pen tablet that Roman was using to create his content used to cost ₹8,000 or $120. If they had to buy such tablets for 1,000 educators, that alone would cost $120,000. Until then, the company had raised $500,000 from a few angels. They didn't have the financial wherewithal to spend 25 per cent of the funds on buying 1,000 pen tablets for their educators.

So, how could one empower 1,000 educators? One way was to buy and ship a tablet and laptop to each educator. The problem with this approach, apart from the financial non-viability, was the inconvenience. While Gaurav was tech-savvy, other educators including Roman did not find it easy to master the devices. Roman had to use three or four software to get the videos right. He would use Camtasia for screen sharing, another app for recording the audio and some other photo editing apps for creating thumbnails. These software are not for the faint of heart, they take upto 6 hours to learn. The team realized that the educators, most of whom were non-techies, were not going to be inclined to spend that kind of time on creating a video.

The other way was to use technology smartly. If there could be an app that made the whole video creation process easier, more educators could start teaching. All they had to do was send an email to the educator for downloading the

app instead of shipping the pen tablet. Hemesh's prototype was simplistic and had proved their concept but it needed to have a lot more functionality and robustness to be used by thousands of educators.

The urgency of an educator app was increasing day by day. As Gaurav and Roman fuelled content creation and the buzz around their fledgling company, Hemesh laid the groundwork to deliver on the promise of creating India's biggest edtech platform. He took up the onus of front-end design and product details while Sachin Gupta worked on the back end. They hired a couple more engineers as well.

Eventually, Unacademy released a beta version of an Android-based educator app that Roman started using right away. The founders added a 'teach' button on their YouTube page which would allow people to fill out a form and volunteer to teach on Unacademy. Roman remembers receiving 2,000 requests. He made sure to call more than a thousand of them individually over the next few weeks and onboarded 200–300 educators to create more content.

In those early days, the educator app levelled the field for anyone who had a passion to teach the topics that interested them, whether they were tech-savvy or not. By building a product, Unacademy started acquiring new educators at a fast pace which resulted in higher volumes of content and a lot more organic traffic. Eventually, even those who were not full-time teachers began using Unacademy to start teaching. Someone would create a video to teach an English lesson, while another would upload a video explaining how to play a musical instrument. But, most of the videos were still catered towards UPSC-CSE preparation.

Roman likes to give the example of Dheeraj Singh Chouhan who hailed from Saharanpur, Uttar Pradesh. Dheeraj had ranked twenty-seventh in the SSC-CGL 2015 examination,

an exam similar to but smaller than the UPSC-CSE. He did not have access to even 2G internet network and was not fluent in English. Yet he was able to teach on Unacademy using the educator app. On the first day that he was posted in a remote village in Chhattisgarh, someone approached him with a box of sweets and told him, '*Sir aapka course dekh ke hamare bacche ka selection hua hai* (Sir, our child qualified his exam and was selected only because of your course).'

By the middle of 2017, more than a thousand educators had created 40,000 lessons on Unacademy. All because of the educator app.

GIVE US THE POWER (POINT)

When Hemesh and his fellow engineers had started creating the educator app, there had been no other similar apps available in the market. There were desktop apps for video recording and processing such as Camtasia but there had been nothing designed specifically for the education segment. There was no precedent to emulate. The engineers would often follow their instincts and build the features that made most sense to them.

'We had to think from scratch about how the interface should look, how we should store content, how we should stream the video,' Hemesh told me. The first version of the educator app enabled the educators to take pictures of their whiteboards and record their voices. They could then add further interactions with the content such as annotations, etc. The app did not have the functionality of recording the educator's face yet. In subsequent iterations, the capability to let the educator record a 30-second selfie video was added to make the video feel more personal.

The team continued working closely with the educators

once they started using the app. This is when they started getting feedback and began to know of the educator's frustrations. The educators found it cumbersome to use the whiteboards! What they wanted was to be able to use good old PowerPoint slides. Given that most engineers associate PowerPoint slides with managers, consultants and other jargon-throwing professionals, they had skipped adding support for slides. However, they made sure to rectify this.

'So then we added a new feature to import PowerPoint slides which turned out to be a very popular feature and most of our educators ended up using that all the time,' says Hemesh with a hint of rueful surrender.

BEAT THE 2G BLUES

On 10 December 2015, the Unacademy.in website was launched for students (or learners in Unacademy's current parlance). Their YouTube channel was growing fast and the founders wanted to direct the traffic to their own platform. For the next year or so, the focus remained on the website and away from YouTube. They even decided to release new videos exclusively on the website.

The engineering team started to work not only on the educator app but also the viewing platform on Unacademy.in and a learner app that would go live much later in February 2017. In early 2016, Hemesh had just three engineers in his team. Although the product was functional at that point, the demands from the website and app were only increasing. Improving the browsing experience on the website, adding more features for the educators, creating notifications—the work had only begun. He needed now, more than ever before, somebody he could trust by his side.

It was during this time that the world of Flatchat was

reaching its endgame. The company that Gaurav and Hemesh had lovingly built was left behind at Commonfloor which was in turn acquired by Quikr in January 2016. In a few months, it had decided to shut Flatchat down. So, Gaurav and Hemesh started helping their Flatchat developers find jobs in other companies. In March 2016, they asked Flatchat engineer Alok Maurya to join them at Unacademy.

Alok had been Hemesh's junior at Motilal Nehru National Institute of Technology, Allahabad. They had both been part of the college web team at the office of the dean of academic affairs. Their responsibilities included handling the personal and academic data of all the students and maintaining the web servers in the institute. They even developed the fee payment system in collaboration with the State Bank of India. Hemesh had even invited Alok to intern at Flat.to and later join full-time at Flatchat.

Alok was well-versed with the quiet but determined way of Hemesh's work. He had also witnessed Gaurav's mojo in starting up. Once it became clear that there was no future for Flatchat, he agreed to join his friends at Unacademy.

As soon as Alok came in, Hemesh assigned him the biggest task he could think of—solving the problem of poor video experience. They were frequently getting complaints from their users in smaller towns. After all, many of their users who were watching UPSC-CSE preparation videos hailed not from the metros but from smaller towns and villages. 'People were complaining that they couldn't stream our videos and that they would take forever to play. From December 2015 to March 2016, this was the single-biggest technical issue.'

Unacademy had been using a third-party video player which worked miserably in low bandwidth situations. Unacademy had no control over how the player functioned. Hemesh noticed that any video in the 720p (1280×720 pixels)

format typically consumed anywhere between 5–6 MB per minute of bandwidth. So, a one-hour 720p video would require the end user to stream 300–400 MB of data.

At this point, mobile data was not cheap either. As per a report by Mary Meeker, 1 GB of data used to cost ₹225 in the first quarter of 2016.[15] Of course, Jio would swoop in and enchant millions of Indian mobile users with data freebies in September 2016, but that revolution was yet to come. With high data costs and low bandwidth availability in their target segment, Unacademy could no longer rely on an external video player.

On searching for a viable solution in the industry, they found that most of the other players were only serving large video formats. Perhaps it was acceptable to them but Hemesh was convinced that the Unacademy app must work well even on low-end devices. He would not compromise on the UX.

The solution that they came up with was to design Unacademy's own video player and Alok was placed at the helm of this critical project. Videos were being created on the educator app which allowed educators to upload slides, add voice-overs and write on the canvas (the editable area in the app similar to a whiteboard in the classroom where the user can scribble using the touch or point devices) and then, combined all these components in an mp4 video format. This video would turn out to be bulky and expensive to stream.

What Alok came up with was a way to stream the required information in terms of raw events instead of the full video. Each interaction was recorded as an event with a timestamp. 'We were recording raw events separately in our back end. For example, the timestamp at which the audio would need to be

---

[15]Meeker, Mary. Internet Trends—Code Conference, Kleiner Perkins Caufield Byers, 1 June 2016.

played would have to be marked or written on the canvas. We realized that we did not have to send the full video, with all the components already combined, to the user's browser. What if we simply sent the raw components and stitched them together on the browser itself when the user requested a video?'

This thoughtful re-engineering brought down the size of the same hour-long 720p video from 300 MB to 40 MB. Not only did it help address the user complaints, it also brought down their server processing and storage costs once it went live in April 2016.

The team had learned a new lesson—if you want to do something better, do it yourself.

ALWAYS BE HIRING

Saurabh Maheshwari had been Gaurav's classmate in the sixth standard. Saurabh had then gone to the Vellore Institute of Technology for his bachelor's, after which he had joined a technical consulting company where he acquired the chops for Android application development. Later, he went on to lead the technical team at Hitwicket, one of the earliest made-in-India mobile games. This same Hitwicket won Prime Minister Narendra Modi's AatmaNirbhar Bharat App Innovation Challenge in August 2020.

Even when working on Flat.to, Gaurav would message Saurabh every once in a while to ask if he was willing to leave his current role and join him. Saurabh would keep saying no and the event would be replayed in the next few months. Gaurav can be quite persistent when he wants, especially when he sees he has a chance. He has a secret superpower that people who have ever dealt in a transaction with him know. 'I never have a problem with someone saying no. I

don't see it as a rejection,' he explains. He goes on to add, 'But yes, you should know where to draw the line. You cannot harass someone.'

When Saurabh was finally willing to look for new opportunities, the first person he contacted was Gaurav, who had now moved on from Flatchat and started Unacademy. That is how Saurabh became one of the first engineers to join Unacademy in 2016.

DESERTERS DON'T SINK THE SHIP

2017 was a momentous year for Unacademy founders. On one hand, the company was starting to find its footing in the edtech space. The educator app which had been in private beta mode till then was made publicly available. Anybody could install it and start teaching on Unacademy. Their video views had shot up from 10,000 to 6 million a month. Hundreds of educators were now teaching on their platform. Although still far from figuring out its monetization model, the company was being taken more seriously and new investors were willing to bet on this non-IIT team. In January 2017, the company had raised $4.5 million Series A round, led by Nexus Venture Partners and Blume Ventures. In the following six months, it raised a Series B round of $11.5 million in which Sequoia entered its cap table.

On the other hand, Sachin Gupta's path had been drifting away from Unacademy. With his personal responsibilities coming into picture, he had been unable to devote the time and commitment expected from a founding member. Realizing that he could not fulfil the demands made by the company at such a pivotal stage, he had decided to relinquish his position and move away.

This was also the time when Gaurav had been getting ready

to tie the knot with his girlfriend Reema Behl. The founders made a 10-day trip to the US. They first went to San Francisco in December where they met a bunch of investors and then celebrated Gaurav's last few bachelor days. The shock of their lives awaited them when they got back to India. Three of their six engineers had decided to quit Unacademy. In the same month, the company was parting ways with Sachin as well.

With his impending nuptials in February 2018, Gaurav relied on Hemesh to hire quality engineers. The team entered into firefighting mode. Given the urgent nature of the problem, they resorted to a referral strategy with steep rewards. They designed and posted on social media, a referral plan in which anybody who gave them a lead would immediately get an Amazon voucher worth ₹200. And, if their referred engineer got hired, the referee would also get a brand-new iPhone. This allowed the team to receive 200 leads, 10 of whom were hired in the next few months. The team had managed to pull itself out of the soup for now but it was a valuable lesson learned—don't leave yourself vulnerable.

NEVER STOP IMPROVING

The Unacademy subscription model, Unacademy Plus, was launched on 29 January 2019, with 400 educators teaching different courses within 12 exam categories. The focus had shifted from pre-recorded courses to live classes streamed to thousands of learners. The content had to be delivered instantaneously.

Although with Alok's optimizations, the educator app worked well for pre-recorded courses, the live courses had their own technical complexities to deal with.

With the Unacademy live classes, Hemesh had aspired to a performance similar to Zoom, the video teleconferencing

software program. Zoom has made it possible for companies to work remotely, children to receive education remotely and for people to socialize remotely. Zoom had introduced a live video experience unlike any other. YouTube live streaming or similar services prior to Zoom would all feature a 10- or 15-second lag time between the real and streamed video experience. Zoom improved the experience by reducing this lag to 200 milliseconds.

However, Unacademy classes cater to much larger audiences than a typical Zoom meeting. On average, an Unacademy class is watched live by 500–5,000 learners. Later, Unacademy also featured guest lectures by celebrities under its 'Legends of Unacademy' series in 2020. The class taken by Virat Kohli and Anushka Sharma saw a peak attendance of 60,000 learners in real time.

To handle such attendance, Alok and Hemesh worked on further bandwidth optimizations on the video player and created a new player for live classes. The key strategy was similar—instead of serving the full videos directly, they would make a raw compilation of different components. These components include the video of the educator who is speaking, the slides that they are referring to and a canvas where they can write. The video forms the bandwidth-heavy component but it is not the primary focus for the learners. While it is good to see the educator's face as they speak, learners pay more attention to the slides and the canvas.

Let us take an example to understand how streaming works. Let us take the hypothetical case of Aditya, an educator on Unacademy. He sits in his room as he teaches the course. The camera shows his face and a portion of his upper torso. While he teaches, only part of his face moves but the other components on the screen, such as the slides and canvas, remain more or less stationary. The first frame of the video

will record the whole scene but the subsequent frames in the video can only capture Aditya's face which is the moving part (which means capturing fewer pixels and thereby, consuming lower bandwidth). This is a gross simplification but helps explain why videos on whiteboard or stationary backgrounds can be streamed more optimally because lesser moving parts mean lesser data to be transferred. They do not require a high sampling rate. On the other hand, Netflix cannot stream a movie like this because it is a motion picture and the devil lies in its details. In simpler words, more movement in front of the camera means more data to be captured and therefore, more bandwidth is consumed. Such videos end up being larger in size and take more time to load.

The team decided to go with a picture-in-picture display where the primary display is of the slides and a smaller window shows the speaker's video. By showing the educator only in the small window, they could reduce the resolution required for the educator's live video to consume less bandwidth. After some experimentation, they realized that the educator frame could be reduced to 180p (320x180 pixels) without impacting the UX. The overall video stayed in 720p format and could be streamed at a 1-2 Mbps download speed, making the live classes run without buffering and accessible to learners with low bandwidth connections.

Looking for ways to further enhance the UX, the Unacademy team sent all their educators green screens, in the form of a plain green cloth, to be used as their backgrounds while streaming their classes. The Unacademy software detects the green pixels and removes them, thereby making the background transparent. Further, the software overlays the clean silhouette of the educator over the slides, creating a smoother watching experience for the learners.

HIRE FOR STRENGTH, NOT FOR LACK OF WEAKNESS

When Shubham Kumar Boundia had been working as an associate product manager at Ola, he had coordinated with Honeydeep Singh Sabharwal who was in charge of HR at Ola. In March 2019, Shubham noticed that Honeydeep had moved to Unacademy, and was actively hiring.

A graduate of the Indian Institute of Technology, Banaras Hindu University (IIT [BHU]), Shubham was an ambitious engineer looking to make his mark in the start-up world of Bengaluru. Unlike the unidimensional, coding-proficient engineers, Shubham enjoyed working with people and took an active interest in the subjects of finance and business. He had led the Marketing team for his college's TEDx events and completed a diploma course in microfinance and entrepreneurship from BHU.

He had just finished one year at Ola when he decided to test the start-up waters once again. He dropped a casual message to his old colleague Honeydeep. Little did he know that Unacademy was on a hiring spree after having raised close to $40 million. The founders were looking to assemble a core Management team and expand aggressively in Engineering, Finance, HR and every possible department. Honeydeep jumped on the opportunity and promptly scheduled Shubham's interview.

Shubham arrived for his interview and met Hemesh for his first round. He kept waiting for Hemesh to ask him the typical product management questions on design thinking and frameworks but the thing Hemesh was interested in was this: he wanted to know why Shubham was looking to leave Ola and come to Unacademy if he was happy there.

This theme would often play in Hemesh's interviews. He wanted to bring the most driven engineers to Unacademy.

More than their skills, he would be interested in their attitude. Attitude is a loosely thrown word that we use when we don't know the specific thing that appeals to us. Attitude is one's way of thinking or feeling, but what Hemesh specifically was looking for was what motivated this person. Shubham didn't disappoint him when he said, 'I want to maximize my learning every day. I can either learn slowly by doing or learn quickly from good peers.'

The conversation flowed easily and Hemesh told him about the product and the problems they were working on. Hemesh soon discovered from his responses that he was somebody who understood numbers much better than design. This did not surprise him because Shubham had worked as a product analyst at Ola before moving into product management. What Shubham discovered was that Unacademy was a 'product and design-first' company where he would be able to thrive as long as he could add value to the product. Starting to build his career in product management, this was precisely what he was looking for.

Shubham and Hemesh's thinking also aligned well. Shubham would join the team full-time and when he would start hiring for his own team, he would follow Hemesh's philosophy—'The best way to operate is to throw people in the ocean. They will figure out how to swim and save themselves and if not, they were not a good fit anyway.'

Hemesh assigned Shubham to work in the growth team where he could wield his analytical skills in solving problems related to optimizing the sign-up funnels, checkout processes, payments and conversions. It did turn out to be the perfect opportunity for Shubham, as he would soon realize. In his two-and-a-half-year-long stint at Unacademy, he would go on to receive two promotions and become the leader of product for the growth team.

In another instance, when Hemesh was interviewing another product management candidate, he asked him about his opinion on the Android versus iOS debate. The candidate showed Hemesh some iPhone features that Hemesh, despite being a dedicated Apple user, had not noticed. As the discussions progressed, Hemesh became convinced that the candidate had an obsession for details and understood what made a UX great. Accordingly, he was put on the core product's design team, taking care of the live classroom experience for Unacademy learners.

For the most part, Hemesh's cautious approach worked well. After all, he was more wary of hiring the wrong people than missing on hiring a good candidate. Gaurav also harboured marked impatience when it came to working with people who did not punch beyond their weight. As with any start-up founder, they thought Unacademy's needs were unique and more special. They obsessed over finding the culture fit in these new hires even as the very definition of the company's culture was still evolving. Hemesh was particular that a candidate should be self-driven and have the right intent behind joining Unacademy. If their responses did not convince him on these fronts, he would reject even those who were technically skilled.

On one occasion, Alok had disagreed with Hemesh's assessment of a candidate. Alok had interviewed Sai Krishna for Android development and had been impressed with his technical understanding. However, Hemesh had some doubts about Sai's ability to fit in the Unacademy culture. According to Hemesh, Sai did not have clear goals for his career. Would he manage to gel with the small team at Unacademy and feel motivated to work long hours? The two discussed the matter at length and seeing how keen Alok had been on extending an offer to Sai, Hemesh had given in. At least in this instance, Alok

had been right. Sai performed extremely well and emerged as one of the best Android developers in the company. He was always open to listening to his co-workers even when they held a different view, and this would go a long way in avoiding a common pitfall that small start-ups run into—'languishing in their own echo chamber'. Anybody who has worked with Hemesh raves about his open-mindedness. Gaurav is also generous in giving his people the freedom to experiment, a trait that has been crucial in shaping Unacademy.

Such incidents soften the sharp edges around the hiring process. The team started to understand that candidates came from different conditioning, backgrounds and circumstances. Not every engineer had the clarity to know what they wanted to do or the luxury of working solely for ambition. Candidates who came from tier 3 towns, shouldering the responsibilities of supporting their families were no less qualified than those who had mastered the start-up alleys of Bengaluru.

Like many other Indian tech entrepreneurs, Hemesh found wisdom in Silicon Valley's way of doing things. Ben Horowitz's mantra, 'Hire for strength, not lack of weakness', resonated strongly with his meticulous nature. His interviews would run long, and he would ask probing questions to discern what the candidate excelled in. 'I believe that if you can detect people's strengths, it is easier to hire them because you know how to maximize their potential,' he says. Whenever he recognized that their skills were more suited to another role, he didn't hesitate in assigning them positions where they could best apply their core strength.

In the early days when they were going from zero to one, this sort of trial-and-error approach served the team's needs fairly well. They did not rush into hiring and until January 2020, the technology team consisted of only 35 engineers. This kept the attrition rate low as well. It was observed that people either

left in their first three months because they would realize that the company was not for them or they stayed for years. Another major reason for which engineers left was to start their own companies. In such cases, Hemesh did not try to stop them. In fact, Gaurav has invested as an angel investor in many start-ups started by ex-Unacademy engineers.

BRING ME THE MONEY

While the COVID-19 pandemic wreaked havoc on people's lives the world over, Unacademy was positioned to fill the gap left by the national lockdowns. Social distancing norms made it impossible for coaching classes to continue offline operations. The buzzing town of Kota that was home to 1.5 lakh students preparing for India's toughest competitive exams[16] before the pandemic found itself deserted in 2020. Very few coaching classes were able to offer satisfactory online classrooms. These students were now stuck at their homes, anxious uncertainty looming in their future.

Unacademy saw its subscriber base shoot up overnight. More and more people wanted to enrol and learn from the educators on the online platform. After all, it was better than studying by themselves or waiting for offline classes to resume. Many of them opted purely for financial reasons as well. A typical IIT-JEE coaching class in Kota charges ₹1.2 lakh in tuition fee. Combined with basic living costs, a student ended up shelling anywhere up to ₹2.5 lakh for his two years education and preparation. The Unacademy subscription for the IIT-JEE preparation course would cost them ₹35,000 and

---

[16]Iqbal, Mohammad. 'The Dark Side of Kota's Dream Chasers', *The Hindu*, 29 December 2018, https://www.thehindu.com/news/national/the-dark-side-of-kotas-dream-chasers/article25861203.ece. Accessed on 15 October 2021.

allow them to take classes from a selection of 100 educators, including well-known, established ones such as Kailash Sharma and Vineet Loomba.

As the product leader for the growth team, it was Shubham's job to help convert free users on Unacademy's platform to paid ones. But panic ensued when a string of payments started failing on the app. At one time, more than ₹1 crore worth of payments was outstanding and failing in transactions. The growth team studied the error messages sent from the banks on these failed transactions and discovered that the majority of them showed 'Daily limit exceeded'. A closer scrutiny of the problem revealed the underlying issue—many of their users had Rupay cards which had a daily spend limit of ₹25,000. Most of the courses on Unacademy cost more than this. In fact, the UPSC subscription was priced at ₹90,000. They realized that the user intended to make the payment but was unable to.

Shubham reached out to Unacademy's banking partners and confirmed that the daily limit imposed by the banks was the primary culprit. However, there was not much Unacademy could do about bank rules. So, the team gathered to brainstorm and came up with the following three points:

1. The volume of transactions was only going to increase as the company grew and attracted more learners.
2. With every error, the company was bleeding revenues and losing valuable customers.
3. The banks were not going to change their rules.

'Designing solutions is the easiest part of product management. Identifying the right problem and prioritizing which one to solve is the biggest skill that a product manager can bring to the table,' says Shubham. 'It was clear we had identified the right problem to solve and now all we had to do was work

backwards to find that solution.'

Like a pedantic product manager, Shubham ensured that his team didn't become biased towards any solution until they had come up with a clear problem statement. The team formulated their desired goal as 'Anybody who wants to learn on the Unacademy app and is willing to pay the subscription fee should be able to enrol in it.'

'Now you work backwards and identify what is stopping the users from achieving this. You then realize that they are willing to pay but cannot use existing mechanisms. You identify that it is not an affordability issue but an availability issue. So what can we do about it? Can we distribute the payments by splitting the order value? But if I split across two or three orders, how much time do I give the user to make all the payments? Should I give subscription access on the first payment or the last?' Shubham bares his thought process.

In this case, the restriction that the payment had to be completed in one go was what was becoming the failure point. Unacademy came up with three solutions:

1. Letting the user pay in monthly instalments. But this approach was not the best for their accounting books because it would delay the realization of revenues to a future date and could lead to recovery issues.

2 Letting the user split the payment in multiple transactions and give access to the subscription right after the first payment is completed. However, their research showed that it would also create recovery issues because the person may choose not to make the leftover payment. In this case, it would become a paid trial and the company wanted to stay away from that possibility.

3. Letting the user split the payment in multiple

transactions or what the company calls 'payment pathways' but hold the payments in escrow and activate the subscription only when full payment is completed. If the user does not complete the payment within seven days, they get the full refund. This solution worked well for both the learner and Unacademy. Also, it was easy to market because the user did not have to pay any penalty if the full payment could not be made for any reason.

This third approach became the Holy Grail for the payment problem. The solution was rolled out in a record 1.5 months and Unacademy continued its ascent on an enviable growth curve.

DARK NIGHTS

On 3 May 2020, Hemesh woke up to the worst nightmare of his tech career. A cybersecurity firm named Cyble had disclosed that Unacademy's database had been breached by cyber attackers and roughly 20 million records of their user information were being sold on the dark web.[17] For the uninitiated, the dark web is a part of the Internet that cannot be accessed by average users like you or me. The dark web allows private networks to communicate and conduct business transactions while remaining anonymous and untraced. Cyble also reported that the latest user records in the repository dated back to January 2020, thereby suggesting the possible date of the actual hacking episode.

---

[17]Ahaskar, Abhijit. 'Millions of Unacademy User Accounts Exposed in Data Breach: Report', *mint*, 6 May 2020, https://www.livemint.com/technology/ tech-news/over-20-mn-unacademy-user-accounts-exposed-in-data-breach-report-11588775083410.html. Accessed on 17 February 2022.

'It was tough to accept that something like this had happened to us. We were using stringent encryption methods, PBKDF2 algorithm with a SHA256 hash, making it highly implausible for anyone to access the learner passwords. Of course, we had been careful and followed the best practices for keeping the user data secure but that obviously had not been enough,' Hemesh told me. There was not a moment to lose. He had to get the situation under control. He hired an external information security agency to help the company with an incident response plan, a set of instructions designed to help companies prepare for, detect, respond to and recover from network security incidents. Such agencies help affected companies with preparing an appropriate response and handle the regulatory and legal aspects of the breach. Hemesh assessed the extent of the damage and released a statement for the press.

But much of the work was to be done in-house. Within the next 15 days, he had hired a senior security specialist with 20 years of experience. They hired 10 more engineers to create an internal security team whose entire job was to find and fix the vulnerabilities, come up with stringent access control policies, build a robust logging mechanism, conduct regular security scans, research and implement the latest security fixes and so on. The incident brought home the realization for Hemesh that Unacademy was no longer a tiny start-up. It had grown to the point where it was not only attracting users but also the evil eyes.

CALLING FOR ADULT SUPERVISION

In the summer of 2020, Hemesh arrived at the thought that they needed a different hiring plan. His conversational style of interviews and personal intervention could no longer work.

The business was growing too fast and the demands on the product were ever increasing. His team, full of go-getting young talent, needed adult supervision.

Mahesh, who was leading the technical hiring for him, found an interesting candidate on LinkedIn in July 2020. A seasoned engineer with two years of experience at Sun Microsystems and 10 years at Akamai, Umesh Bude had been taking a break after a brief stint at OYO. He had planned to take time off for himself and travel the world but COVID-19 had ruined his plans. He had been stuck at home when Mahesh reached out to him.

Umesh had clear priorities for his professional life. A man of few words, it mattered to him that his values aligned with those of the company he worked for. He was staying away from social media and e-commerce start-ups because he couldn't identify with their purpose. As he heard an Unacademy recruiter talking about the company's drive to democratize education, he found himself quietly nodding along. He believed in the mission that the company stood for. The other thing that he was looking for was to work for a company that valued its engineering and product.

'At Sun, I had worked on the JVM [Java Virtual Machine] which runs on 60 per cent of the computers that are being used all across the globe. Similarly, Akamai powers close to 30 per cent of Internet traffic. It is a good feeling to know that every time these people use their device or Internet, my code gets executed. I feel like I have made an impact.'

At Unacademy, he would be impacting the lives of the learners who would be watching their lessons from the remotest corners of India. But what sealed the deal for him was how his interviews were conducted. Hemesh asked him three things:

1. How do we improve the learning experience?
2. How do we make our educators more effective?
3. How do we expand our team without destroying our culture?

Hemesh told him that most of their users were from tier 2 towns and used low-end devices. On an average, they would end up spending 60–90 minutes on Unacademy's app to watch classes. How could they make sure that their devices wouldn't overheat when they spent an hour on the app?

The fact that most of the conversation had been about the product and users instead of revenue and sales, comforted the doctrinaire techie in Umesh. He opened up warmly to Hemesh and shared his experiences and ideas. After all, he had worked with the world's leading technology companies that built and sold their products. He, in turn, had successfully built global teams from scratch for such companies.

Convinced of the technical and cultural fit, Hemesh hired Umesh as his vice president (VP) and head of engineering. Their journey had started on a promising note.

PEAS IN A POD

Although the team had 60 engineers in 2020, it still operated much like a 20-member team. Hemesh, Alok and most of the other engineers were in their 20s and had never created large teams for any company. This was the case for most of the founders and early employees of the Internet start-up generation. 'Move fast and break things,' the mantra eternalized by Mark Zuckerberg, works well until broken things really start becoming unfixable. A young buzzing start-up can quickly become chaotic and accumulate technical debt. Hemesh,

unlike many other founders, was able to sense that it was time for them to streamline the process. His timely intervention in hiring Umesh would help Unacademy avoid the trap.

Umesh's first initiative was to revamp how engineering teams were structured. In a small company, the tech team can be divided by skill sets—back end, front end, data science, quality assurance (QA), etc. But this model breaks down once a team reaches the capacity of 40–50 engineers. When there is a 15-member front-end team working on five different projects, there is no clear ownership left. No one knows who is accountable for what.

Instead of dividing by skill sets, Hemesh and Umesh adopted a scaling model known as the 'pod' structure. A pod is a small cross-functional and multidisciplinary six- to eight-member team designed from the customer journey point of view. Each step of the customer journey becomes a pod—a self-contained unit with clearly defined mission and vision statements. They created 10 pods after closely inspecting the Unacademy learner's journey. Each pod had its own designers, product managers and engineers, and would be managed by an engineering leader. For example, the 'Awareness' pod's purpose is to get more and more learners on the platform. The 'Accelerate' pod is responsible for converting free users into paid customers. The 'Core Learning Experience' pod deals with the live class experience whose goal is to create a world-class learning experience. The 'Learner Experience' pod handles the post-sign-up experience of the user and so on.

Each pod acted like a start-up on its own. The pods were designed in a way that prevents one person being assigned multiple pods. This was important because it helped in keeping the mission very clear for each individual. It also removed any cost of context switching, that is the cost incurred due to the

tendency to shift from one unrelated task to another. Each pod followed its own build-test-deploy cycles. The beauty of the pod model is that it is extremely scalable and hence adopted by many tech-heavy companies. Each pod can determine what resource is missing and hire accordingly. This single-minded focus on their own mission allows the pod members to be uber effective.

The downside of such a model, however, is that it creates a separation between people who otherwise may have common interest and could bond together. For example, front-end engineers across the organization did not get to interact with each other since they worked in isolated pods. To combat this, the team introduced the concept of horizontal pods known as 'tribes' which are loosely bound and do not have any project mission. For example, the data science tribe allows data scientists from different pods to connect with each other.

ONE TO HUNDRED

The other heavy-lifting project for the team was to make the hiring process scalable. For hiring at scale, the team had to be clear on two things:

1. What is the competence and skills required at each level?
2. How can they assess those things?

The first one led to the creation of a matrix for defining hard and soft skills required at each level. The second called for designing a clearly defined process for each interview round.

Table: Unacademy's internal guide for allocating topics across different rounds in the technical interviews

Role	Screening	Round 1	Round 2	Round 3	Round 4	Round 5
Software Engineer (Back end)	Coding	Coding Computer Science (CS) basics	Problem Solving CS basics	Problem Solving CS basics	Culture fitment Past experience	NA
Senior Software Engineer (Back end)	Assignment	Coding CS basics	Problem Solving Low-level design CS basics	Problem Solving High-level design Deployment and infrastructure knowledge Troubleshooting	Culture fitment Business acumen Mentoring Code/design review Past experience	NA
Engineering Lead (Back end)	Assignment	Coding CS basics	Problem Solving Low-level design High-level CS basics	Problem Solving High-level design Deployment and infrastructure knowledge Monitoring, Alerting Troubleshooting	Product management Business acumen Requirement definition Project management Data-driven decision-making	Culture fitment Managing ICs Stakeholder management Past experience

The teams started thinking of painstaking details to make the process clear and robust. They defined how many rounds of interview would be done for a role and what each round would focus on. The next step was for leaders to coach everyone in the team to become a better interviewer. They started a practice where newbies could shadow the senior members when they would conduct interviews. After all the rounds were completed, a debriefer round would be conducted among the different interviewers where they would debate the candidature of the interviewee. Here, they encourage members to question and counter question aggressively. The final question they would discuss was whether this candidate would raise the bar or lower it within the company. This practice is also borrowed from the West where FAANG companies (namely Facebook, Amazon, Apple, Netflix and Google) conduct a bar-raiser interview round to assess the desirability of a candidate. Unacademy has picked what has been working well in other companies rather than innovating the hiring process. 'Trillion dollar companies are built on these principles, so why not use them?' Umesh asks. 'After all, what matters is how well we are able to execute it.'

Once the processes were established, Hemesh started thinking about how to keep the culture intact in this phase of rapid expansion. Rather than leaving it to the discretion of each interviewer, he decided to systematize the culture fit assessment by defining the key success factors at different levels of seniority. Currently, the engineering team has eight levels of hierarchy under Hemesh. Levels five and six constitute the engineers. Level seven constitutes the engineering leads. Levels eight and nine constitute the engineering managers. Levels 10 and 11 comprise directors and level 12 consists of the VPs.

While each level was expected to exhibit common attributes such as ownership, team spirit, the ability to deal with ambiguity and so on, anyone at level seven or above had to demonstrate an additional ability to mentor new employees. Anyone above level eight was expected to exhibit team building and leadership skills as well as the tendency to support innovation.

With Softbank's funding, Unacademy became a unicorn in September 2020. The company would grow at a dizzying pace from then, quadrupling its engineering team size within a year. Unacademy's new practices were showing promising results. This did not mean that people were not quitting anymore, it just meant that their quitting did not leave the company struggling behind them.

A/B TESTING YOUR WAY TO SUCCESS

In the first few years, Unacademy was run like a typical resource-starved start-up that would keep juggling between features that made sense for the business and ones that users asked for—not necessarily in the correct order. But once the journey from one to hundred started, Unnacademy had the resources to do the things that bigger companies love to do—A/B tests! Not that it is a new concept but the term has been used heavily only ever since Facebook popularized the concept of growth hacking. Every funded start-up today has a team that focuses on growth. Gaurav doesn't like the term but his grudge is mainly pointed at the word 'hacking'. For him, it implies that growth is a short-term goal when in reality, growth is everything and not just a goal.

Irrespective of what you call it, Unacademy embraced having a team whose sole responsibility was to think of growth. The Accelerate pod became the team that created

its own army of product managers who run A/B tests and fuss over things such as sign-up funnels, checkout funnels and the colours of buttons. Shubham, who runs the product management for this pod, describes his role, 'Setting up a growth team is hard because you work on a lot of things that do not see the light of the day. Out of the 10 things we are working on at any given time, we may end up executing only two things.'

The growth team does a lot of user research. Based on the need and depth of information they are looking for, they may choose one out of these four ways:

1. Call and ask the user directly.
2. Conduct surveys, run questionnaires and then triage the solution—this works only when you have a huge user base and you believe survey responses are good enough. This is useful only for asking the user's opinion on yes/no questions but not as effective when one is trying to answer more open-ended questions.
3. Focus group discussions—a few learners are picked and invited to a zoom call. The team throws ideas at them and records their reactions.
4. One-on-one discussions with power users.
5. Screen recording sessions for testing new UI features— they give the users access to a test interface and record where they click and how confused the users are by the new UI features.

In the spirit of nimbleness, the growth team does not fixate on coming up with the perfect solution. They start with a solution and iterate to refine it. 'We would rather go to market with a solution that works for 90–95 per cent users and solve for the remaining 5 per cent later rather than waiting longer to come up with a solution that works for all the users.'

Whenever there is no clear answer, the growth team jumps on to their A/B tests. 'Any funnel you see can be done in different ways, showing the options to "filter" first and "sort" later, or vice versa. There is no white paper on these things, they are all subjective.'

One of the experiments run by the Accelerate pod was to test the placement of the sign-up form in the user funnel. The big question that haunts any app developer is where the sign-up form should be placed. Should it be placed right at the beginning of the user funnel or only when required? Conventional thinking suggests that one should delay asking for sign-ups and allow the users to browse freely as long as you can, but their experiments showed a 40–50 per cent jump in sign-ups for the group that saw the mandatory sign-up on the first screen versus the control group.

Shubham recalls how apprehensive he was of making this feature live. 'I was dreading the sign-up rate dropping drastically and I confess that this was counter-intuitive to me. When I think about it now, I feel it works this way because our app is very intent-heavy. We are not a lifestyle app that users browse for their leisure. When people open the Unacademy app, they are doing so with a specific intent to watch a class and they have already made up their mind to sign up. In intent-heavy apps like ours, we found it is better to ask users to sign up earlier into their app experience rather than later.'

While being different from lifestyle apps such as Zomato and Flipkart helps Unacademy get a faithful set of users, there is a distinct downside of the same. Unlike these lifestyle apps, Unacademy is not used by the common people. In fact, it's predominant users are K–12 students and people writing competitive tests. Let us see how that hurts the company.

BUILDING THE NERD GRAVITY

In his essay 'How People Get Rich Now'[18], Paul Graham compares the 100 richest Americans in 1982 to the 100 richest in 2020. 'In 1982, the most common source of wealth was inheritance. Of the 100 richest people, 60 inherited from an ancestor. By 2020, roughly three-fourth became rich by starting companies and one-fourth by investing.'

Never before in the history of the world have nerds ruled the roost as they do now. I personally witnessed this shift during my MBA days at the New York University, Stern School of Business in 2010. NYU was known to attract the finance whiz kids who wanted to build careers in investment banking and trading. But the collapse of Lehman Brothers and the housing crisis coupled with the rise of techies such as Mark Zuckerberg and Jack Dorsey had dampened MBA candidates' faith in Wall Street. A lot of ex-bankers were now in search of technical co-founders to build apps and get rich soon. For the first time, engineers could choose who they wanted to work with.

A similar shift crept into the Indian economy albeit a decade later. From parents looking for technical grooms for their daughters to MBAs wanting to get into product management as opposed to banking, popularity of technology careers is on an all-time high. This has also created a talent vacuum in the industry. More start-ups are coming up, demanding competent and talented engineers.

In such a competitive landscape, a start-up cannot survive on chasing talent. While Silicon Valley giants are paying $300,000 to $500,000 for top AI talent, India is scooping up

---

[18]Graham, Paul. 'How People Get Rich Now', April 2021, http://www. paulgraham.com/richnow.html. Accessed on 28 February 2022.

programmers with big hikes and shiny new perks. In July 2021, BharatPe offered BMW superbikes, the latest cutting-edge gadgets and lifestyle products, trips to Dubai for the Twenty20 cricket World Cup and early appraisals, in order to attract talent. As has been witnessed though, the talent that comes for perks also goes away for perks.

There is a more sustainable way of attracting talent as few other companies have figured out—become a place that is cool enough for engineers to hang out. But before we jump into equating cool to ping-pong tables, wearing shorts at work, beer Fridays and the cliches, consider the fate of many hyper-funded companies who could not survive despite doing this. Perhaps attracting talent is like dating. Jitender Kumar, director of engineering, comments, 'You can't really call yourself a true tech company unless you start acting like one from inside.'

Jitender is a new addition to the Unacademy engineering division. In his 9-year-long career, he has collected enviable brand names on his resume. He comes from Microsoft, Flipkart and Myntra—companies that any software engineer would die to work for. For him, it was a big pull that Unacademy's website and app reeked of a product-first focus in the company. It was also that Unacademy is just at that sweet stage of growth where he feels he can make maximum impact. When he joined Flipkart in 2015, the company was already stable and on a growth curve. He hopes he has boarded the Unacademy train at a better juncture. He was interviewed by Umesh, who was looking for people who would not only bring technical chops but also the ability to induce positive transformation at work. Umesh posed the same question to Jitender as he did to any candidate interviewing for a senior role, 'Have you ever been able to bring a positive change in your workplace at an organizational level?'

Jitender (known by the nickname Jeetu at work), apparently, had good examples from his previous stint at Myntra. He had worked on predicting the demand for clothing items and accordingly made recommendations to the suppliers for stocking up on the same. His work involved working with data scientists in the company. But here was the issue—the centralized data science team was stretched so thin between multiple projects that they had no time. Seeing that he had to look for a solution on his own, Jeetu ended up designing interfaces between tech teams and data science team so that the work responsibilities were clearly divided and distributed effectively, reducing the dependence on the data scientists. The details that he shared were enough to convince Umesh that Jeetu had actually done this. 'Change is very hard to bring. He provided beautiful insights that one cannot make up unless they have done it,' Umesh told me.

Engineers like Jeetu joining the Unacademy team bodes well for its positioning, after all, engineers attract engineers. If one thing worked very well in the early days of Apple, Google and Facebook, it was that engineers saw who was working in these companies and they wanted to join the party. Peter Thiel, who has been lauded for assembling what later became known as the 'Paypal Mafia', had this interesting theory that the best start-ups work like cults and that they can only be the best if they can excite engineers with their mission.

If there is anything that engineers abhor more than PowerPoint, it is those managers who know nothing about technology but continue holding strong opinions about what the technology team should work on. Any sales-driven company does not usually garner respect from the best of engineers. The real nerdy techies would rather work under a pushy leader like Steve Jobs, who gave them impossible problems to solve, than under a pointy-haired boss treating

them like a means to a business end. Engineers often don't give enough credit to any other department be it Sales or HR. So, what Jeetu is alluding to is valid. You cannot pretend to be a tech-driven company if you do not operate like one.

It was pointed out that Unacademy had a big disadvantage against lifestyle apps such as Flipkart, Uber or Zomato. This is so because it is hardly visible to the tech talent out there. Outside its learner and educator community, the Unacademy app is hardly used by common people. And this makes attracting quality engineers somewhat difficult. A hiring manager rues the fact that most of the engineers outside don't know how beautiful the Unacademy app is. 'If they did, they would want to work with us.'

Jeetu showed an interest in taking initiatives to make Unacademy an aspirational tech brand. It had twofold advantages—(i) it helped attract talent, and (ii) it fostered a sense of pride among people already working here. This is how a commune and a brotherhood among the techies starts forming, who can feel at home with each other. With this in mind, Unacademy kicked off the tech blog and weekly Tech Talks.

Tech Talks existed even before Jeetu had joined the company but they were a HR-driven event. An email was circulated before the talk, requesting the engineers to attend the talk. This was the worst way to get engineers to do something. At one point, management was mulling over incentivizing engineers to attend these talks via rewards. Someone commented, 'Why don't we just shut it then?' The team started exploring better ways to make them work.

Jeetu focused on two things—firstly, curating topics that attract the engineers to the talks and secondly, training the speakers to make them better at engaging the audience. 'If we are asking 100 engineers to spend one hour on this talk,

it is worth spending four hours prepping for it.' Engineers are not naturally good at public speaking. Jeetu would spend a couple of hours going over the material with the speakers and helping them deliver it more effectively. For the topics, he asked for suggestions in a feedback form after every talk. One such suggestion was showing up repeatedly and led to the talk on 'How do live classes and canvas work?' Sometimes, the topics spring up in impromptu cafeteria discussions such as the one on 'How do hackers hack?' and so on.

From 25 engineers attending the first talk to 45 attending the latest one, the nerds were starting to bond.

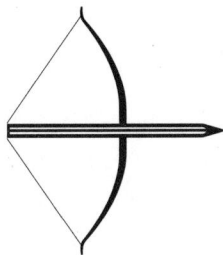

FIVE

SUPERPOWER 4:
PERFECTING THE PLATFORM

How the Company Makes Money While Keeping Its Educators and Learners Happy

2019 and 2020 were the defining years of the Indian edtech sector. In 2019, online education was a thing of the future. By 2020, it had become the only option. The players who had entered the arena before the novel coronavirus unleashed its deadliness were poised to make the most of the post-pandemic interest in virtual classes. Every company was trying to move fast, and make bets it thought would lead to more customer acquisitions. BYJU'S was the uncontested category leader in terms of revenues and their valuation had shot up from $5.5 billion in 2019 to $12 billion in November 2020.[19] It became the third Indian start-up after Paytm and OYO to achieve the exalted status of a decacorn (denoting a valuation of $10 billion or more).

Another edtech company, Vedantu (focused on the

---

[19]'Valued at $12 Billion, BYJU'S a Class Apart', *Financial Express*, 23 November 2020, https://www.financialexpress.com/industry/sme/valued-at-12-billion-byjus-a-class-apart/2134159/. Accessed on 13 December 2021.

K–12 segment), had launched its 'live' classes much before Unacademy, when it took one-on-one tutoring from physical to online classrooms in 2014. In the summer of 2019, it launched WAVE, an AI-enabled tech platform that claimed to monitor over 70 parameters of the student-teacher interaction such as modulations in a tutor's voice. In 2020, the pandemic had boosted its valuation to $600 million.[20]

While Vedantu had taken the route of AI to differentiate the product, Unacademy had instead chosen to focus on a business model that would give the most satisfaction to the learners. BYJU'S had predominantly focused on ramping up its acquisition and marketing spend to grow wider as well as deeper.

It is tempting to think that every edtech start-up was destined to hit it out of the park by the virtue of the post-pandemic interest in online education. But the reality could not be farther from it. Just a year down the line, Vedantu fired 100 sales executives without any notice in March 2021. As per *The Ken*, Vedantu's problems occurred because of a lack of clarity on their plan of action.[21] Even BYJU'S hyper-growth would be plagued with a plenty of bad press over its questionable sales practices in the coming year. For the financial year ending 2020, BYJU'S would not meet its profitability target of $150 million but at least, it had turned

[20]Samidha Sharma and Alnoor Peermohamed. 'Vedantu Eyes $100 Million from Coatue at $600 Million Valuation', *The Economic Times*, 30 June 2020, https://economictimes.indiatimes.com/small-biz/startups/newsbuzz/vedantu-eyes-100-million-from-coatue-at-600-million-valuation/articleshow/76701545.cms?from=mdr. Accessed on 13 December 2021.
[21]Banerji, Olina. 'Vedantu's Painful Growth Spurt in the Eye of an Edtech Storm', *The Ken*, 26 March 2021, https://the-ken.com/story/vedantus-painful-growth-spurt-in-the-eye-of-an-edtech-storm/. Accessed on 13 December 2021.

profitable in the previous year.[22] Speculations were rife in August 2021 that BYJU'S would acquire Vedantu. Unacademy had just found its product-market fit in terms of revenues when the subscription model hit the right notes with its users. Flat.to and Flatchat had never grown beyond 50 employees. Gaurav knew that he had not achieved his definition of success in those start-ups. So now, he was cautious, more than ever, to not let the music stop.

Unacademy would reach an ARR run rate of $140 million by September 2020 and become a double unicorn before the end of the year.[23] The devil, however, lies in the details of how the company pulled off this incredible feat in a super competitive market.

CREATING THE NETFLIX EXPERIENCE

Disha Agarwal was employee number 28 at Unacademy when she joined the company in May 2017. She had started heading a team called Content Diversification where her job was to ensure that Unacademy could expand into different kinds of examination categories. Another team called Revenue handled the operations part which included onboarding educators, managing the classes, etc. She started hiring diligently and helped expand the content team. Many early business

---

[22]Chengappa, Sangeetha. 'Why BYJU'S Did Not Meet $150-Million Net Profit Target in FY21', *Business Line*, 15 April 2021, https://www.thehindubusinessline.com/companies/why-byjus-did-not-meet-150-million-net-profit-target-in-fy21/article34323074.ece. Accessed on 13 December 2021.

[23]Singh, Rajiv. 'We Won't Settle for No. 2: Unacademy's Gaurav Munjal', *Forbes*, 15 April 2021, https://www.forbesindia.com/article/edtech-special/we-wont-settle-for-no-2-unacademys-gaurav-munjal/67453/1. Accessed on 13 December 2021.

employees such as Prajwal Rao, Shruti Singh, Neha Kaplish, Abhishek Srivastava and Punith Reddy reported to her. Further, she focused on creating an energetic camaraderie within the team. 'We worked really hard on the way. So we made sure that we party hard too,' she told me. 'We had given ourselves a target of closing 100 educators in December 2017. And we did that, and even small wins like that were celebrated with enthusiasm in our team. This is what kept us going and made sure we didn't burn out.' The content and revenue teams were 100-people-strong by 2019.

On 29 January 2019, Unacademy became the first edtech company to launch a subscription model called 'Unacademy Plus' for live courses. By July 2019, Unacademy had onboarded 500 educators on the app and clocked 40,000 paid active users. Today, Unacademy has 150 plus educators in the UPSC category alone.

From 'YouTube for education' to 'Netflix for education', Unacademy's product-market fit exploration journey seemed to have found a logical and successful conclusion. Just like you can stop watching a movie that is dreary on Netflix and switch to something right up your alley, learners could switch from an educator they did not like to someone they did, without any friction. Learners were happy and 'voting with their wallets', in Gaurav's words.

It is easy to call it Netflix, but until the UX ended up being as smooth or as seamless as discovering and watching content on Netflix, the name would remain wishful thinking. So, Unacademy set its focus on delivering the 'Netflix experience' to its users. This called for bringing more experienced leaders.

Ankita Tandon was interviewing the CEO of one of the biggest Internet consumer start-ups of the day at The Leela Palace in Bengaluru Gaurav and Roman were sitting at a table nearby. As soon as the CEO left, Gaurav approached

her. This was not their first interaction, albeit the setting was considerably different from the first one. Ankita had co-founded and grown DeliveryChef.in, one of the first foodtech start-ups in India to reach four cities between 2012 and 2014. When Gaurav was studying at NMIMS, Mumbai, she had come to give a talk on start-ups. Gaurav had pitched her the Flat.to idea back then and kept in touch later too.

He did not waste any words this time. 'Were you interviewing?' he asked Ankita.

Ankita tried to deny it when he said, 'That guy does not meet people casually for one hour. So, you must be interviewing.'

The conversation followed and Gaurav offered to drop her home. On the way, he explained how Unacademy was growing and looking to hire experienced leaders. This was his hiring pitch. Unacademy had just crossed the zero to one phase. He wanted Ankita to help grow it from one to 10 and beyond. He offered her a role that would allow her to lead the business (which consisted of Content Diversification, Revenue and Operations teams) at Unacademy and the combination of the opportunity, and Gaurav's persuasion was enough for her to say yes. Eventually, Ankita joined Unacademy in September 2019. All the content-related teams were merged under a single Business organization and Ankita was given the entire PnL responsibility.

Back then, there was a 50-people inbound sales team known as counsellors. Unlike typical sales teams, which are outbound in nature, they would call only those users who had spent a baseline time on the app and showed some intention of joining the Unacademy Plus subscription service. Counsellors would help such users understand what Unacademy was offering. They were forbidden to cold-call any user who had not watched any videos. These counsellors

were the customer-facing professionals at Unacademy, and given the company's obsession with detail, they had to be groomed well so that they could answer any customer query with confidence. Unacademy was offering courses for multiple examinations (category in Unacademy's parlance) even back then. For instance, UPSC was one category, NEET was another. Talking to the users meant being well-versed not only in the product plans but also in examination details or syllabi queries. Needless to say, counsellors' training was something that the company took very seriously.

Since training them was time-consuming, Unacademy decided to train a counsellor team only on the top categories, such as UPSC, IIT and NEET. These categories were the ones which drove most of their revenues. Ankita decided that the other categories would be monitored for number of subscribers and watch time, and once any category was identified as a 'breakout category', a dedicated counsellor team would be created for it.

Another challenge that impacted the business was the seasonal nature of examinations. Most of the enrolments ended up happening between April and the Hindu festival of Diwali, which is usually when students have finished their K–12 or college examinations and started preparing seriously for entrance exams such as IIT-JEE, NEET, CAT, UPSC, etc. Ankita discerned that the business cycle would have to align with the examination timings. It was crucial that the right courses were launched and promoted at the right time. She sat down with different teams including Marketing, Product and Operations, and together, they designed annual calendars which would keep the business synchronized with the examinations.

Although the users were happy with the wide selection of educators and courses they could now access for a flat fee,

there was still a major inconvenience. When the user signed up and joined the Plus subscription service, the experience was akin to jumping into a sea of content. One had to constantly keep track of who was teaching what and how many classes had already been streamed by an educator. The learner had to plan their own schedule and syllabus. It was like entering school mid-session. Of course, you could watch the recordings or join the course with another educator who was teaching the first lecture, but you were pretty much on your own.

Abhishek Srivastava's team, who was leading the UPSC category, took notice of this. He explains, 'If I had to break down the whole syllabus of UPSC, it came down to 19 subjects. It was tough for a learner to go and track so many subjects and so many educators. They could get lost in the process.'

Abhishek and Ankita thought of a solution. They introduced a concept of 'batches' which worked similar to offline classes. The batches clubbed various educators who would start and complete the examination syllabus in synchronization. Just like offline institutes offered droppers' batch (people who had taken a drop year to prepare), freshers' batch, crash course batch, etc., the batching tool allowed Unacademy to launch batches targeted toward a specific examination. For example, the NEET 2020 batch would offer courses targeting the NEET examination in 2020. The subscribers could still access any and all educator videos but they could join a batch that worked best for their schedules. 'This feature was a winner,' Abhishek told me.

Ankita worked with the Product and Business team to 'productify' the batch creation process. The innovation here was to keep the syllabus organized on a rolling basis. Educators would keep teaching from the first lecture to the last and then start the cycle again. The new batches would start the syllabus from the current lecture and club the previously

missed lectures at the end. This allowed the batches to run smoothly, irrespective of the date they were started. Hemesh's engineers created a dynamic batch tool which enabled the category managers to launch batches with ease. It also allowed onboarding subscribers to join the next batch irrespective of the time of the year they were joining. 'This broke the seasonality because now people could join a batch anytime throughout the year,' Ankita explained. Unacademy started promoting new batches and aspirants came flooding to the app in a bid to join the next one. As of August 2021, Abhishek was launching nine UPSC batches every week!

On the one hand, TestPrep (which included all categories related to cracking competitive examinations) business was giving incredible returns. On the other hand, Unacademy was setting its sights on the future by launching K–12 as a separate category. After all, the biggest companies in edtech were thriving on K–12. Ankita helped launch the K–12 category in April 2020 just as the lockdown was announced by the Government of India. She had smoothened out the details of category creation and created a basic playbook to the extent that allowed the Business team to launch a whole new examination category within 15–18 days. Ankita had set the business on to a winning start by making the product more user-friendly and prepping the teams to be able to scale in near future.

NO SALES, PLEASE

Till date, Unacademy has had no on-the-ground sales force. In business parlance, every sale is 'pull-based'. For example, if a student comes across an app and he initiates the purchase decision because he likes it, it is called a 'pull-based transaction'. On the other hand, if the Sales team calls a customer and makes them aware of a product leading to a

sale, it is a 'push-based transaction'.

Even from the early days of its monetization experiments, Gaurav was clear that Unacademy would focus on pull-not-push sales. This was also because he had never enjoyed the operations and sales-heavy nature of the real estate market in his Flat.to days. Subconsciously, he had known that he didn't want to be trapped in a company where sales and operations are the primary growth levers. He was, and will always remain, a product- and marketing-oriented person.

This is why the company did not rely on a sprawling Sales force from day one. But now that subscriptions were taking off and Unacademy was expanding into more examination categories, more counsellors were needed. A whole Sales organization needed to be built and Gaurav knew he could not delay hiring a head of Sales anymore. The HR team was given a personal briefing by Gaurav on what to look for in this candidate. He made it clear that anyone with a 'sales at any cost' philosophy should not be brought to him.

Their search led the HR team to Karthik Kailash, a promising candidate at Simplilearn with more than a decade of leadership experience at Standard Chartered Bank. Once upon a time, in his banking days, Karthik had seen the mammoth rise of fintech start-ups that proved to be tough competition for banks. That is when he had decided that he should ride the wave of digitization rather than being left stuck in traditional businesses. At Simplilearn, which is a training and certification company, he had warmed up to the potential of edtech. The industry was growing and Karthik led a 60-member team that oversaw the sales for its B2C business. 'Simplilearn created upskilling courses on industry-relevant topics. It was a founder-driven company and had a very small Sales team when I joined. I filled in the gap of a business

leader who understands how to expand the business and has experience with sales too.'

In his conversation with Gaurav, he was immediately captivated by his emphasis on customer obsession instead of sales. 'At Simplilearn also, we did only inbound sales. So, when Gaurav told me that he doesn't want cold-calling or forced sales, it resonated with my values,' Karthik told me. The rate at which Unacademy was growing made it easier for him to decide. As soon as Karthik joined, he knew the first step was to prepare the Sales team to be able to rapidly expand. This meant that he had to first create the proper organizational structure. Until then, the 50–60-member Sales team was managed by two associate directors. Karthik, with help from Ankita and the HR team, created an assistant vice president (AVP) sales role below which came the directors, associated directors, managers and, lastly, the counsellors or the sales associates. Unacademy was now ready to expand its sales force.

When this mass hiring started, Karthik was mindful of hiring the right kind of counsellors who would follow the company's 'ethical sales only' philosophy. To ensure this, he created two checkpoints in the interview process. One, if the candidate came from any company whose sales policies were known to be aggressive and unethical in the market, he looked for the candidate's motivation to interview with Unacademy. 'We saw many cases where the candidates were saying that they did not feel good following the sales tactics on their previous company and that is why they are looking to switch,' explained Karthik. Such candidates were welcomed. Two, Unacademy would give scenarios to the candidates to evaluate their mindset. 'For example, we would tell them that the company is running a XYZ offer. This is the incentive you can earn if you do X number of sales. Then I ask them what

offer would you give to the user to sell the product. If they say anything dubious like "I will frame the offer in a way that the user would be more likely to sign up," we would probe further. If we feel that the candidate is trying for a quick sale and not caring for the end user or is willing to keep the user in the dark, it would be a clear no.'

The other task that Unacademy focused on was to formalize the training process for the counsellors. Right after joining Unacademy, a counsellor would undergo eight to 10 days of training. 'This training helps them get familiar with the intricate details of the examination they would be supporting and what our product offers. For example, they will be trained to memorize who our top educators are, what kind of features are available on the app, etc. Then, we would train them on the etiquettes of how to talk to the learners. Lastly, we would help them understand learner personas. For example, our IIT-JEE learners could be freshers who have two years to prepare, or a "dropper" who has already written the exam once and has only a year to prepare. The concerns of these two personas are very different. Therefore, it was important that we train our counsellors on how to talk to different users.'

Once the counsellor finishes training, they are asked to do three mock calls in which they are presented with different kinds of learner scenarios, following which the trainers give them feedback on how they performed. Finally, they go through a last mock call known as 'the graduation call.' This is where they are ultimately tested on everything that they have been trained on. If they pass this, they are brought on to the floor where they can start taking real calls. In case they fail the graduation call, they are given two more attempts on the same. If they don't clear these either, they are sent back to training and have to start from scratch.

'We care about following through on the promises we make

to our users, therefore it is important to us that our employees are highly informed. Our instruction to Sales is very clear—tell them what we are offering; nothing more and nothing less. We make sure this is strictly followed and are aware that lying to the user could result in termination of contract,' an employee from the learner support told me. There have been instances of people getting fired for calling users from a personal number and promising things they shouldn't have.

But the number one rule to adhere to is: no cold calls. He adds, 'It is proven that if you sign up today on Unacademy, you actually won't get a call. The call goes out only if you signed up, watched a few free classes or signed up for any free tests because that means that you may have intent to use Unacademy Plus.'

Once the lead is identified, a counsellor is assigned to call the user. The first conversation is to establish the user profile and build a rapport; subscription plans are pitched only after this. The counsellor also helps identify the best plan and duration for the subscription. The Business team audits and monitors these calls very seriously because it knows that this is the customer-facing aspect of their product.

Karthik paved the way for the Sales team to scale. By February 2020, it was 200-people-strong. So far, each salesperson was working from the office in Bengaluru but with the growing demands of the business, Karthik and the HR team knew that location was becoming a limiting factor. They could only hire so many people in Bengaluru. Besides, the novel coronavirus cases in China were wreaking havoc and it was becoming clearer that the virus might transcend all geographical barriers soon. The only questions were how soon and how bad the impact would be. 'Our processes and CRM [customer relationship management] systems were already on the cloud. People used to work from home once in a while.

So we thought, why not go entirely remote in case of the Sales team?' Karthik told me. He pitched the idea to Gaurav in a meeting in February 2020. A remote Sales team would help scale hiring and would be safer for the employees in case the novel coronavirus affected India too. Gaurav said yes. In the next month, Karthik tested the remote pilot with the existing 200-member team. When the work continued seamlessly, the company turned the Sales team into a remotely working organization 1 March 2020 onwards. Once the COVID-19 lockdown was announced on 24 March, many companies were scrambling to make their employees start a fully remote work life. But the Sales team pilot had already prepared Unacademy well to transition to this new way of working.

FAIR PRICING, NO DISCOUNTS

Another area where Karthik sees Unacademy standing apart in its sales practices is its stance with respect to discounts. 'Gaurav doesn't believe in discounts for short-term gains; not unless they add value. He believes in pricing the product fairly and if that has been done, there is no need for discounts. That was largely refreshing for me to see because every other company where I had worked before used discount-based pricing.' Let us understand what this means.

Companies typically offer two-tiered discounts. First, usually an upper limit is set, and the Sales team is allowed to offer discounts based on their discretion keeping this upper limit in mind. Such discounts can go up to 30 per cent, giving a lot of power to the Sales team. For instance, a salesperson might call the user to initiate a pull-based or push-based transaction. If the user is still not interested, the salesperson can incentivize the user with further discounts. We have all heard of such pitches, 'Since you are a special customer, I

can get the price further reduced by 20 per cent but it's valid only for today!' Second, a few companies offer discounts for retention. The company might have a refund policy which allows the user to ask for a refund if he or she is not satisfied with the product. At this point, the retention discount kicks in and the user is offered continued use of the product for a discounted price.

'Unacademy does not subscribe to these methods. We are transparent about our prices. The only discount that users can avail is the educator referral codes, which is a way for us to track the referrals. Beyond that, we don't offer any discounts,' Karthik explains. This has another hidden benefit for Unacademy. Its learners have come to appreciate Unacademy's transparency and remain assured that they are not being cheated. Secondly, its targeted users have grown accustomed to its pricing. They know that waiting for discounts is not going to work. So, if anybody wants to enrol, they enrol right away instead of looking for a sale down the line.

EX-OYO WIZARDS

May 2020

Gaurav was growing restless. On the one hand, Unacademy Plus was growing more robustly than what he could have expected. On the other hand, the pandemic was unleashing a way of life never imagined before. Once the pandemic hit India, Unacademy's focus on 'helping crack exams' as a business could not have been more well-timed. It had taken years for Indians to embrace e-commerce, and edtech players had expected the same—they knew that parents and students would, someday, warm up to the merits of online classrooms

but no one had thought that it would happen so soon and so abruptly. Some players were prepared for it and those who weren't would miss the ride of a lifetime.

Unacademy's learner base was no longer just those students who had gone to study at places like Kota but also those who could no longer go to local coaching institutes in their own hometown because of the lockdown. Although people say there are a ton of resources for studying on the Internet, test preparation requires a level of structure and rigour that cannot be found in the wild landscape of the World Wide Web. The sheer number of MOOCs, videos, e-books, forums and social media pages make it extremely hard to find the exact content that would work well for an individual. The problem is not as much of availability as it is of discovery.

Unacademy's app, with its laser focus on examination preparation, made it an ideal learning resource for those learners whose future was suddenly left at the mercy of a virus. These students had no clarity on when the exams would be conducted, how they would be conducted and what changes to expect. Unacademy's educators would not only discuss the course content but lend support to them by putting up videos on exam updates, strategies for studying at home, etc. Needless to say, Unacademy's subscription model was thriving. If the company's mission statement was to make Unacademy better than the offline coaching experience, they were inching closer.

Gaurav has always been focused on the big picture and believed that good things were coming; he was convinced that business would grow five times very soon. It was as if Unacademy's journey had been leading up to this one moment and he was resolved to make the most of this unexpected opportunity. He could see that the business would need bifurcation of the verticals soon because the TestPrep

business was growing like wildfire and they had just started the K–12 segment. Gaurav told HR that he needed more business experts. The HR team was constantly scouting leaders who understood the Internet business but also brought a certain maturity and ownership in terms of the PnL.[24] One such position was that of a chief of staff role. The only charter for that role was for the candidate to possess an ability and intellect to work closely with the CEO.

One shortlisted candidate for this position was Vivek Sinha, who would go on to become the chief operating officer (COO)—a post that had been left glaringly open—in less than 12 months of his tenure at Unacademy.

Vivek comes from a small town in north Bihar. Laden with the responsibility of raising three children, Vivek's father could not afford to send him to Kota to study for IIT-JEE. His siblings were often home schooled as his father, working for the state government, got frequently transferred. Vivek studied and found a way into the Mechanical Engineering department at NIT, Jamshedpur. More interested in learning leadership and strategy, he took business development and operations roles with big conglomerates such as the Lodha Group and Reliance Industries. In 2015, he moved to Gurgaon and took an entrepreneurial bet in the e-commerce space focused on the home interior and improvement segment and raised a quick Series A round of $5 million. His timing proved inauspicious as 2016 saw the markdown of Flipkart's valuation by Fidelity and vertical e-commerce crumbled. He had to let go of his 200-member team. 'Sometimes, you work for 14 hours a day and give your blood and sweat and even then it doesn't work,' he reminisces.

---

[24]In investment banking, PnL Explained is an income statement with commentary that attributes or explains the daily fluctuation in the value of a portfolio of trades to the root causes of the changes.

Vivek was heartbroken but went back to work. An investor found him and his co-founders a place in MobiKwik just after the demonetization was announced. Demonetization had given the perfect fillip to fintech companies. MobiKwik entered a hyper-growth phase and he helped build a massive sales force of 1,800 people in no time. At one point in June 2017, his team was onboarding 10,000 new retailers per day on to the platform. This experience gave him unparalleled insights into running operations for an Internet business. Scaling the categories for the business, building an organizational structure to manage the expanding operations and working with product and compliance—he was grooming himself to lead fast-growing Internet start-ups. However, the company itself was under the pump with fierce competition from Paytm and upcoming payment solutions. 'Only deep pockets survive in the payment business,' Vivek explains. As MobiKwik struggled to compete with better-funded competitors, it entered into the lending business. This is when Vivek found himself out of place. 'I was not a finance professional who understood credit and risk. I understood scaling a start-up and building operations and sales. Lending was not where I could add value.'

He left the company to join OYO which was on a dream ride in 2018. He was hired as one of the first external VPs in the company and would go on to head the franchise business and later the luxury hotel joint venture between OYO and Softbank. Thanks to his previous real estate experience, he suddenly felt very much at home. 'I knew a lot of housing finance companies, real estate builders, etc. I could add a lot of value in the hospitality sector.' But, once again, the market timing proved unwise. The pandemic had put the brakes on OYO's growth trajectory and Vivek had to wind down his teams. On the side, he put efforts into another idea of B2B

e-commerce but investors said no. Vivek had excelled in his roles but external factors had intervened and the companies he was working for would suffer.

During this phase of self-introspection, the HR team from Unacademy reached out to him and set up a call with Gaurav. Vivek's confidence increased when one of his cousins back home in Bihar said, '*Haan bhaiya, humne Unacademy ka naam suna hai. Hum kabhi kabhi special classes bhi attend karte hain* (Yes brother, we have heard the name of Unacademy. We even attend their special classes sometimes).' Perhaps it reminded him of his own teenage days when he was not able to go to Kota because of lack of funds. Unacademy's product made sense to him. What also encouraged him was the fact that macro and micro factors pointed to a boost in the edtech sector. Having been burnt by wrong timing before, Vivek was wary of staying in the hospitality industry, which was obviously struggling. He agreed to a call with Gaurav.

'What is your favourite book?' asked Gaurav.

'*The Fountainhead*.'

'And second favourite?'

'*Shoe Dog* by Phil Knight,' he answered.

'Those are my favourites too. Why don't you come down to Bangalore and we can chat more then?'

The conversation intrigued Vivek, and he decided to research Unacademy and Gaurav. He read Gaurav's blog and posts on Quora. Gaurav had piqued his interest enough to make him take one of the first flights that took off after the first wave of COVID-19. 'My friends were calling me mad to be flying at that time.' He flew down to Bengaluru and met Gaurav for a few rounds of conversation. 'I found him to be absolutely forthright. He was to the point and frank. I wasn't just considering the offer on the table, but also the people I would have to work with. I thought *Gaurav ke saath kaam*

karke maza aayega (it would be fun to work with Gaurav).'

The head of HR, Tina Balachandran, recalls the episode, 'After Gaurav and I had talked to Vivek, it was clear that he possessed strong business reasoning skills and expertise. Since we knew OYO to be an extremely fast-paced, highly aggressive organization which had seen a stupendous growth path, Vivek's background was a fit. It was a no-brainer. The only thing we had not finalized was what role to offer.' Gaurav decided to give him an open-ended offer. 'We told him that we are signing him for a position in the CEO's office now but it could play out differently in the long run.'

Tina calls it Gaurav's way of stress-testing a candidate. 'He likes to see if you are open-minded and willing to step out of your comfort zone.' That is not the only incentive; Gaurav often looks at the big picture and takes his time to identify an employee's strengths before assigning them specific roles. Of course, not every candidate is open to this ambiguity in designation and it only helps him weed out the ones who are not 'fully committed.' Vivek earned brownie points when he was not fazed by this unusual offer. He was open to starting from an un-demarcated role and prove himself if required. As it happened, Vivek started working right away from Bengaluru and flew out to Gurgaon a month later to bring his 70-year-old mother, wife and infant daughter back with him.

As the first experiment, Gaurav asked Vivek to help scale the IIT-JEE and NEET categories in the TestPrep business. While these courses were rising in demand, there was still untapped potential and Ankita's hands were full. Vivek dived right in and his effortless leadership helped the teams break whatever ceilings they were facing.

'Ankita had led the business admirably until then. I thought I could help scale it to the next level because I had the advantage

of witnessing and driving similar growth in OYO. So I knew how to do some of these things,' Vivek told me. In particular, Vivek targeted the obvious areas of concern. 'Unacademy had one distribution channel back then. Everything was dependent on its YouTube strategy. That was a risk according to me. So, we decided to open up new distribution channels for the business. We started creating more affiliate channels such as influencers who would help promote our courses on their social media accounts. The campus ambassador programme was formalized, which allowed college students to promote Unacademy on campuses and earn commission for any sales generated via them and so on.'

Next, Vivek and Gaurav discussed how to use scholarships and other student engagement events to generate more traction. One of their most successful experiments turned out to be a test series called 'Unacademy Champions League', which was conducted in September 2020. It was a month-long scholarship test in which students participated in free tests every week in a bid to win Unacademy Plus subscriptions in the IIT and NEET categories.

Additionally, he streamlined operations and made it work like a well-oiled machine. Under his initiatives, proper teams were created for managing learner and educator satisfaction, taking care of educator payments and reference material creation among others. He also started the push which would make Unacademy transition from a mere marketplace between educators and learners to a comprehensive platform that provided a curated learning experience. Vivek focused on academic and curriculum orientation so that the courses were not entirely educator-dependent.

Lastly, Vivek breathed fresh life and discipline into the Sales team. By this time, the Sales organization was 500-people-strong. One of the most innovative changes

was to determine how sales leads would be assigned to the counsellors. Together, Vivek and Karthik introduced a metric called 'lead score', that is calculated based on factors such as watch time, time spent on the app, how frequently a user is logging in, etc. This score quantifies the intent of a particular user to join Unacademy Plus—higher the score, more likely he is to sign up for Plus subscription. Then, they created a system which prioritized the list of leads based on lead scores. Further, it was decided that higher-intent leads would be contacted by high-performing counsellors first, thereby increasing the chances of a sale.

One of the concerns with a fully remote Sales team was that it was easy to lose track of how the counsellors were performing. Vivek brought in ways to automate the processes and performance-tracking systems which helped the sales revenues to increase threefold per centre in a matter of months. While the efficiencies were being put in place, Vivek tightened the screws on quality control as well. He explains, 'Our competitors in the edtech industry often encourage the sharing of personal phone numbers, but it is a strict no at Unacademy. We made sure that our systems fully mask the customer's number whenever they talk to our counsellors. Our counsellors never have access to customer contact details.'

The way Vivek had been able to work across different teams to bring in systemic improvement earned him Gaurav's and the Business team's trust in no time. He was then given the charge of more categories next month. Vivek felt he could use some help. He reached out to ex-colleagues who had worked with him at OYO and shown potential. He hired the ones who had helped him in scaling up the Operations and Business teams. Akash Kalp was one such person. Vivek later hired more leaders to take care of smaller struggling

categories, making the TestPrep category Management team 200-people-strong by the end of 2020.

REIN IN THE CHAOS

'Unacademy was still a start-up. There were no robust operating plans or standard operating procedures (SOPs) in place. Business was being managed on excel sheets. We needed to introduce some method to this madness,' a category manager recalls. Another problem was that while they were running digital ads with the help of the Marketing team, the expenditure across categories was not well-defined. Different categories were running ads, often reaching the same user with different ads. This spillage was noticed because users were signing up for categories that were not supposed to be advertised. Let's say you are 20 years old and Unacademy runs ads that are targeted only based on age, Google will start showing you both UPSC and CAT ads in such cases.

Business teams built a rudimentary performance marketing set-up where they could optimize the ad spend more efficiently and design more targeted campaigns. They further experimented with the duration for which a particular ad was to be run. Previously, the company would float ads for an upcoming scholarship test just two days before the test. This was highly wasteful because Google takes time to learn how your ad is performing and who the right users for it are. By increasing the duration to 15 days, they started seeing much higher conversions on their ads. Later on, the Marketing team hired a performance specialist leader, Jagadeesh, who had digital marketing and customer acquisition experience with companies such as Ola and RedBus. Jagadeesh further formalized these processes and added mechanisms to track

click spam and injections. Together, they were able to increase the new user growth by four times while spending 30 per cent less on the ads.

Once it was clear that the company needed to promote new batches, free tests and any special event at least 15 days in advance, the Business team came up with a scheduling process. Every educator and their relationship manager was instructed to have the next three months of content planned in advance. Such foresight enabled precise marketing and sales efforts that helped the annual revenue run rate soar to $200 million for TestPrep and $18 million for K–12 by July 2021.

THE STARRIER SKY

For its Plus subscription model to thrive, Unacademy needed more 'star educators' who could produce top rankers in their respective exam categories. Roman had managed to attract such educators in the UPSC category but there was much to be done elsewhere. While Mayank Garg had onboarded a few popular educators from Kota when the IIT-JEE category was launched in 2017, they were not enough to drive Unacademy's aggressive vision in 2020. New category leaders put on their deal-maker hats and contacted Sarvottam Career Institute, one of the biggest coaching institutes in Kota for the preparation of Pre-Medical exams like NEET-UG and AIIMS. Initially, they tried to float an acquisition offer to Sarvottam which had seven directors at that time who had invested significant capital in establishing their offline institute in Kota as well as building an app for online teaching. Having so many directors delayed any sort of decision-making and they kept resisting the offer from Unacademy for a long time.

Ultimately, the team looked deeper into their books and created a compelling pitch. The team discussed with

them the potential revenue loss they were facing because of the shutdown of their offline coaching business. They told Sarvottam directors how Unacademy's offer can help them make more money and is potentially risk-free with a contract in place. In the end, most educators realized the ease and convenience of teaching on an established platform; when they run their own set-ups, they lose sleep over getting more students, worrying about competitors, etc. With Unacademy, all they have to do is the one thing they love, i.e. teach. All other headaches are borne by Unacademy. Burdened with internal clashes and COVID-19 losses, Sarvottam's board finally relented and joined the Unacademy platform after 3.5 months and 20 rounds of conversation. Today, their teachers are teaching exclusively on Unacademy.

Unacademy also closed deals with other giants in Kota including Vibrant Academy, founded by the educators from Bansal Classes and Nucleus Academy. All these educators have been known to produce top 100 rankers in IIT-JEE and Unacademy was now poised to emerge as the biggest player in the TestPrep business. Similar efforts and bigger deals enabled Unacademy to onboard 30 new teachers in the NEET category as well. Revenue doubled and the company was now generating 10s of crores per month via NEET subscriptions alone. To add to the satisfaction, Unacademy's revenue, 90 per cent of which at one time came from UPSC subscribers alone, was diversified by the last quarter of 2020. UPSC now constituted only 15–20 per cent of the TestPrep revenue.

In September 2020, Gaurav posted his ambitious vision on his blog:

> Just today, one of my Board members messaged me that we now have more subscribers in TestPrep than any other

online or offline institute. That's one way to look at it and that's not a bad way to look at it.

But here's another way:

Who I would really love to compete with is Netflix—they have 193 million subscribers. Now can we compete with Netflix and build 'iconic products' for learning and education that have more subscribers than them?

We certainly can and we certainly will. And we will play to win.

The game was afoot.

LEARNER HAPPINESS OVER REVENUES

The problem with aggressive sales is that it ultimately breaks the users' trust and they start abandoning the product. However, many companies crumble under the pressure of managing investor expectations as they scale and resort to quick-growth tactics. To ensure Unacademy does not fall to the same fate, Gaurav had to percolate the culture of no outbound-sales wide and deep into his employees' psyche. And the way he did it shows his far-sightedness and determination.

First, Gaurav made learner satisfaction the core metric for everyone in the company. However, Gaurav knew that employees do not follow what you say but what you do. Unacademy had conducted a scholarship event and the Finance team sent him the details of the payout to be made to the winner. Gaurav noticed that they had deducted the tax deducted at source (TDS) on the same. The Finance team tried to explain to him that it is the norm to do so. But he was adamant. He told them that the winner should get exactly what they had advertised in the scholarship test. If it means bearing the tax themselves and incurring extra expenses, so be it.

The company relies heavily on a tool called Slack which is used for internal communication. At its heart, Slack is a messaging app but designed for organizations to be more productive and efficient at communication. One can create slack channels which are akin to closed groups where your messages would be received only by the colleagues who are added on to the channel. Unacademy created a 'negative' Slack channel in which all leaders (people at or above level 6) in the company were added. The channel was used to report any negative review or feedback by a learner. Gaurav would himself check the channel regularly and ask the relevant stakeholder to follow up. Gaurav is so particular about any kind of negative learner experience that he calls out any employee who might have caused it. The end result is that everybody is accountable. As Vivek Sinha would tell me later, 'If we got a bad room review in OYO, I knew my job was not threatened. But here, if I don't keep our learners happy, I will be kicked out. And I will do the same to my reportees.'

Balaji Ramachandran, a young graduate of IIM Ahmedabad, joined Unacademy as a programme manager in July 2020. Having shown his mettle across sales, category leadership, supporting growth strategy, etc., he was asked by Gaurav to create and lead a 'Learner NPS' team. In this way, he became the de facto custodian of learner happiness, a title he wears with pride. 'Gaurav is a founder who cares about loyalty and not just valuation,' Balaji said. 'My team's number one priority is that no learner query should go unanswered. We are relentless in improving our product to ensure learner satisfaction. Lastly, I am empowered to keep any stakeholders accountable to learner happiness.'

Jargon aside, what Balaji looks at comes down to this: he is responsible for keeping a track of learners' happiness and taking whatever action needed to improve it. For this,

he collects the learner feedback via a rating tool on the app. 'Every 28 days, the learner gets a prompt where they can rate us anywhere from one to five stars and leave a comment. Each comment, especially the negative ones, is read by my team who then calls up the learner to understand the issue in more detail.'

They receive around 150,000 responses a month across all the categories and approximately 16 per cent fall into the negative rating bucket (anything less than four is considered negative). But it is not only about gathering feedback; what matters is what you do with it. One consistent negative feedback they received was that the educators were rescheduling the classes at the last minute.

Balaji had worked at Bain & Company, a top management consulting firm that trains its consultants to do extreme wizardry with data. Combined with Unacademy's fixation on data, Balaji's experience was put to the fullest use. He combed through the rescheduling instances and found that 18 per cent of classes were being rescheduled. On further investigation, he came to the conclusion that 20 per cent educators were causing 80 per cent of the rescheduling, which meant that those educators had simply fallen into a habit of cancelling at the last minute. He noticed that the company's current policy allowed educators to reschedule up to six hours before the class with no penalty. So, Unacademy came up with a new policy so that the educator had to give at least a three-day notice before rescheduling a class. Failure to do so levied a penalty of 1 to 2 per cent of the educator's base salary. 'It is a very small amount but we wanted to send a message that rescheduling should be the last resort and only in the case of an emergency.' They added an exception during Covid times when many educators had genuine reasons for rescheduling. Vivek announced the policy change in the next town hall and the results spoke for themselves. Within a week, the number

of classes being rescheduled had reduced to 15 per cent and within two months to 7 per cent! The number of learner complaints also, accordingly, went down from one in five to one in a hundred.

Another way in which Unacademy kept a pulse on the learner's happiness was by looking at the one-month and three-month subscription renewal rates. Unacademy offers subscription plans for one month, three months, six months, one year and more, depending on the examination. Given the nature of the courses and the time commitment required for preparing for any examination, most of the courses run for more than three months. People typically go for a one-month or three-month plan only when they are not sure about the product because the company offers significant discounts on long-term subscription plans.

'We treat our smaller duration plans as trial plans. Hence, their renewal rates give us concrete information on whether our courses are meeting learners' expectations or not.' This lead to an interesting discovery—most learners were looking for classes taught completely in English and some of the educators were falling into a habit of speaking in Hindi. Non-Hindi-speaking learners were not renewing in such cases. Sometimes, the feedback shows that the learners were not happy with the quality of educators in one particular subject— e.g., Geography for UPSC preparation. Such feedback helped the category leaders to onboard appropriate educators such as those who teach fully in English and those who are good at teaching Geography.

Balaji believes that short-term fixes are best implemented via policy and process changes, as shown in the examples above. However, long-term fixes can only come from the product. One such feedback was that learners were unable to find courses that suited them the most. As the number

of courses had increased multifold on the platform, learners were having difficulty discovering the right courses. When the team discussed this with the engineering team, Hemesh came up with a concept of saving 'learner preferences' (e.g., language, timing preferences) in the product. This allowed the app to filter based on the preferences and recommend the most appropriate courses (similar to Netflix's movie recommendation engine).

Unacademy had, so far, been able to keep its learners satisfied (as reflected in the consistent learner NPS rating of 95 per cent or more) and avoid any bad press. It was a big-picture move, informed by the knowledge that the key to success is customer loyalty and satisfaction.

WE EXIST BECAUSE OF THE EDUCATORS

In April 2021, Gaurav called in Aditi Arora and Vivek Sinha for a meeting. Aditi had recently moved to a programme management role in the Educator Relations team. Gaurav asked her what Unacademy was doing to keep their educators happy.

Salaries had never been a problem for popular teachers in Kota and Delhi—places where millions of students flocked to every year for studies. But not everybody could afford to move to these places and become a full-time teacher. Apps like Unacademy were finally encouraging people who loved to teach by giving them the flexibility to teach from anywhere. With attractive contracts that include fixed base salary comparable to the ones given by the established offline institutes, commissions from affiliate sales that can add up to significant bonuses and employment benefits including health insurance, Unacademy was giving them offers they could not turn down without remorse. The company had gone to the

extent of honouring contracts with very highly-paid educators even if they were not delivering as many views as expected.

But these were material incentives; Gaurav wanted to know what was being done apart from the obvious. Aditi told him how their relationship managers take care of the educator's needs. Most of the educators had a relationship manager to coordinate with and this manager coordinated to keep the educator informed on what kind of content or promotion to push on their videos but also helped them with any difficulty they might face.

'That's not enough,' Gaurav's response was quick. He was happy with the way learners were being taken care of and he knew that educators were equally important for the survival of the company. Learners cannot be happy until there are quality educators on the platform. And quality educators are being wooed by competitors every single day. 'We should have a separate vertical, a team whose sole job is to make the educators feel valued and happy.'

Gaurav even went on to propose a name for this job—Educator's Delight team. Aditi recalls, 'He basically said that there are always going to be other companies who can pay an educator more than what we are paying. Our educators should stay with us not for the salary but because they feel cared for. They should feel that no other company is going to treat them as well as we do. His intent was clear—"I want us turn our attention to the delight factor". He gave one more instruction. He said that each director and category manager would be responsible for the delight of educators in his category. He believed that taking care of educators is so important that it would work well only if it comes from the top. Managers have to ensure that their team is taking it seriously.' This was Gaurav's way of percolating the value top down in the company.

Gaurav takes inspiration from the Oberoi Group when it

comes to customer obsession. 'If a guest asks for a particular brand of tea once, then that tea brand is served to the guest every time the guest stays at an Oberoi property. And this is done top down—the managers make sure that the smallest of the details are taken care of,' he noted. He wanted to see Unacademy obsess over its educators in a similar fashion. Soon, job descriptions for 'Educator Delight manager' were floated out in which the company sought hospitality professionals who would contribute towards long-term retention of the educators via deep engagement.

Aditi developed a life cycle journey for the educators. Starting from receiving an offer to their exit, an educator at Unacademy goes through certain stages—onboarding, launching the course, launching new batches, getting paid, finishing a course, renewing a contract and so on. Aditi started deep diving into each stage to understand the potential challenges that the educators could face. 'A lot of these educators come from offline institutes. Teaching on the Unacademy app is a big change for them because it's all technology-driven and most of these educators, especially the ones who are a little older, find it difficult to adjust. So, I ask whether we are doing enough to help them transition seamlessly on our platform. I ask whether we are doing enough to resolve their concerns in a timely manner.'

Lastly, an ombudsman team was created so that the educators could escalate their grievances in case the relationship manager is unable to give them a satisfactory response. The team of delight managers also organize monthly events for educators in which awards are given out along with a celebrity performance. 'In May, we had Jubin Nautiyal, in June, we had Biswa Kalyan, the stand-up comedian. Most recently, we had Sunil Grover as part of our July awards. They perform and also interact with our educators,' Aditi told me.

The awards are given in multiple categories including a power solver award which is given to the educator who has conducted the most number of doubt-solving sessions, an educator of the month award given to an all-round performance, go-getter award for contributing to the maximum revenue on the platform and so on.

On a personal level, Vivek often sends video messages to the educators on important occasions like their birthdays, anniversaries, etc. Unacademy would sponsor luxury weekend getaways for a newly-married educator and gift hampers for a baby shower. Gaurav personally worked with Aditi to help come up with a design for a milestone trophy for educators crossing a threshold of views (similar to a YouTube gold button award). Further, Gaurav announced on 29 July 2021, that Unacademy would give stock options to their educators (teacher SOPs) which are similar to employee stock options (ESOPs). The company recognized that its success was largely based on its educators and it was leaving no stone unturned to keep their loyalties in place.

TEACHING HAS NEVER BEEN SO REWARDING

Many coaching institutes suffer when their star educators turn complacent. Unacademy tries to make the educator feel valued, but also keep them motivated to give their best every single day. The company started displaying a leaderboard so that the educators could see their relative ranks on performance metrics such as number of views, number of subscribers, total watch minutes, etc. This further motivated and incentivized them to do better.

There is one reward that every educator felt particularly proud of: receiving a 'knowledge hat' from a learner. A knowledge hat is unlocked based on how many minutes of

lessons learners watch on the app. For example, a green hat is unlocked if they watch for 500 minutes and a purple hat after watching for 5,000 minutes. But instead of making it only about the learner, Unacademy allowed the user to dedicate their hats to their favourite educator. This recognition from the learners meant more to the educators than material rewards because most of them teach out of the passion they hold for their respective subjects. Nothing can beat the joy of receiving a golden hat, which is unlocked after a user has watched lessons for one lakh minutes. One of the top educators, Mansoorali K., taught courses for the Kerala Public Service Commission (PSC) in Malayalam. He had a record number of 67,000 hats dedicated to him out of which 61 were golden. What it means is that 61 learners who had watched lectures totalling one lakh minutes on the Unacademy platform called Mansoorali their favourite teacher.

It is not surprising to see Unacademy using 'hats' as rewards. Gaurav Munjal, a big *Harry Potter* fan, incorporated his company under the name Sorting Hat Technologies Pvt. Ltd. Sorting Hat is one of the most well-known magical objects in the *Harry Potter* world; it is the hat that sorts new students into houses. In this way, the sorting hat decided the destiny of the wizarding world for generations. Perhaps, Gaurav also imagined that his company would play a role in deciding the destiny of future learners.

Talking to Mansoorali requires a translator if you don't speak Malayalam. He is an ex-superintendent of Kasaragod sub jail in Kerala whose real passion lies in teaching. He started writing the PSC examination at the age of 18 years. 'I cleared the constable examination without much preparation. That's when I realized I can crack any PSC examination with a little effort. And then it became a craze,' he had told a reporter from *The Indian Express* in 2018. Even after joining

the service, he kept appearing for the exam and securing top 10 rank. He was often called for guest lectures at the coaching institutes where his speeches would inject new enthusiasm in the students. He started his own Facebook page on Kerala PSC where he would post sample questions and study tips. Soon, he acquired more than one lakh followers. This is when, in 2018, the Unacademy team reached out to him.

Once he found out that he could get on a platform like Unacademy, and help hundreds of thousands of students crack Kerala PSC and get 'decent government jobs', he quit his service and started teaching full-time. More than helping ambitious students crack the exam, he enjoyed how his way of teaching made the boring subjects come alive for the test takers. 'People who had decided to quit studies, who were droppers, have been inspired through my teaching. I made subjects like General Knowledge simpler and easier to memorize for the students. I feel I am impacting many more lives now that I am teaching, than I could do during my service,' the translator communicated the thoughts of the soft-spoken educator to me.

The presence of an educator like Mansoorali boosted the presence of Malayalam-speaking learners on the Unacademy app and validated the potential of regional language content. However, most of the content is still geared towards English- and Hindi-speaking communities.

Although Unacademy as a TestPrep business was seeking to present an online alternative to offline coaching institutes, its technology was changing the industry. The educators who thrived on its online platform were not often the same people who were ruling the roost in offline classes. A physical classroom accommodated 250–300 students in a hall whereas online classes are attended by thousands of users. While offline classes allow students to interrupt and interact directly with the teacher, educators in the online classes are often staring

at the camera and cannot see if the learners are nodding or left confused. Needless to say, the camera-friendliness and comfort of the educator mattered a lot more in the digital world. This led to the rise of the suave millennial educators who not only understood the subject matter but could also teach it effortlessly in this new medium.

When Sudarshan Gurjar took a job with Tata Communications in Pune after spending two to three years preparing for UPSC, he could barely stand it for a week. '*Aap itni knowledge gain karte ho, toh uska use bhi to karna chahiye* (when you gain so much knowledge, you should use it too),' he reminisces about those days. He left his job at the end of 2015 and came back to Bhopal with no plan in mind. One day, he saw a pamphlet from a State PSC coaching institute. He called them up to enquire if they needed a teacher. That is where he started teaching for the first time, although it continued only for two months before the owner moved to Gwalior to join a prominent coaching institute. But those two months had unleashed the teacher in Sudarshan. He went to Gwalior and started teaching in this bigger institute.

Soon, his popularity had soared to the extent that batches were being scheduled around his availability. He was now handling 600–700 students across English and Hindi batches and went on to become the academic head within a year. As things looked up with a stable and well-paying job in hand, he got married in February 2018. In June, a fellow teacher told him that he was creating some videos for a company called Unacademy that conducts UPSC classes online. His interest was piqued and he asked his friend to put him in touch with his connection at Unacademy. As it happened, the Unacademy associate called him the very next day.

He asked him to create five lessons so that Unacademy could assess his content, voice and teaching quality. 'I created

five lessons in two days to teach a chapter on rocks. Biggest challenge for me was to make the slides because I was used to the whiteboard,' he told me. His videos were approved and the associate asked him to create 50 lessons (of eight minutes each) in the next 20 days. Sudarshan did it in three days. Then they gave him a target of 100 videos to be created over a month and he did it in six days.

By making the videos so fast, he caught the attention of Abhishek, who was heading the UPSC category. 'I was probably the only educator who had published 52 lessons within 24 hours. I remember working for 18–19 hours that day,' Sudarshan shares with pride. The learning curve for him was huge—after all, he had never recorded a video lecture before this. Unlike other educators, he had no social media presence. 'I started from zero. My dad was my first follower,' he added with a chuckle. But within three months, he became so active on social media channels of Unacademy that he got the 'perfect presence award' in October 2018. The company flew him to its Bengaluru office and Sudarshan never looked back.

Back then, he had been teaching for six to seven hours in offline classes and would then create videos for Unacademy in his spare time. Then his employer had objections—they wanted him to choose offline or online. 'It was risky but I decided to go ahead with Unacademy. They had given me this great platform and I was committed to teaching. *Maine kabhi majboori me nahi padhaya* (I have never taught because of any compulsion). I taught for seven hours the day I got my first vaccine shot even though I had to take two paracetamols.'

Sudarshan feels that the online platform has a lot of features which gives it an edge over the offline classes. He explains how often he uses the 'poll feature' on the Unacademy app when he is teaching world maps. 'I simply point to a country and ask the students to identify its correct name from four

given options. It helps with student engagement and they learn faster.' Polls also show instant leaderboards so that the learner can see their rank in the class. Sudarshan's knowledge is finally being put to right use and he couldn't be happier.

'*Jab aapko sab milta hai toh aap bhi accha karne ki koshish karte ho* (if you get everything you need, you also try to give your best). They gave me insurance and even extended it to cover my parents when the pandemic hit. I get congratulatory calls to celebrate my anniversary on the Unacademy platform. It is not about the gifts, it is about the gestures. That is what really matters.'

While Sudarshan was looking for stability and respect as a teacher, Prateek Jain, one of the star educators in the IIT-JEE category, became a teacher for the love of the subject physics. He was so enamoured with physics that he went to IIT Kanpur in 2017 to do a research assistantship under Dr H.C. Verma, the celebrated author, 'idol' and 'pedagogical God' for JEE aspirants. In between, he had been teaching physics at coaching institutes like FIITJEE to make some money. While he was doing well as a teacher, Prateek was also preparing for the Graduate Record Examinations (GRE) so that he could go abroad to pursue a PhD in physics. This is when he read the book *Rich Dad Poor Dad* by Robert Kiyosaki and his life changed. He felt he had this gift for physics and instead of spending another five years doing a PhD and not knowing where that would lead him, why not keep teaching?

So, he moved to Kota and was teaching in renowned institutes when Unacademy contacted him. He joined the platform in July 2019 and went on to become the number one educator in physics for both IIT-JEE and NEET categories. His confidence, use of millennial slangs and friendly vibe attracted students. His students have held AIR 6, AIR 10, etc., in these exams in the last few years. Prateek has been growing

so fast on the platform that he set up his own staff of nine support educators who help him create content and conduct doubt-resolution sessions for his learners.

Prateek is young and doesn't care about benefits like insurance. For him, the biggest perk is the location independence that comes with his job. He ended up going to Goa for a few months and teaching Unacademy classes from there. 'I am just waiting for the COVID-19 pandemic to be over so that I can go to Bali and teach from there.'

Unacademy is fine-tuning its relationships with the educators. Given that only two to three Plus educators out of more than 3,500 contracted by Unacademy have left the platform on their own volition, the company's efforts seem to be bearing fruits.

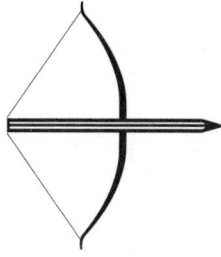

SIX

SUPERPOWER 5:
BUILDING THE GROWTH DNA

How the Company Built a Winning Team and Scaled from 500 to 5,000 Employees

Bhavin Turakhia (CEO, Directi) calls it the difference between chasing success and chasing mastery. 'When you are chasing success, you get the binary outcome of either succeeding or failing but when you are chasing mastery, there is no success or failure, there is only constant growth. Every month, all you are measuring is how further ahead on this problem or this topic or this subject you are than you were last month because it is a lifetime journey.'

Having met many accomplished entrepreneurs during my New York days and then in India, I have found that start-ups are the ultimate expression of the leading founder and his values. Gaurav's pursuit of personal growth has, unsurprisingly, seeped deep into the DNA of Unacademy.

Jerin Kesavan (head, Talent Acquisition) summarized it best, 'Gaurav grows on you. When you see him driven and working like that, he motivates the leaders around him to take on the same attitude. Everyone has blossomed into a better

version of themselves—Tina, Vivek, Karthik, all of us have become 100 times more effective at delivering things. When I had first heard that our goal is to hire 3,000 plus people in six months, I wasn't sure we would be able to achieve it. Now, I have been given a target of hiring 2,000 more people in two months and I get on with it without any second thoughts. We take the milestone and work backwards. There is no question of whether it will work or not; we will make sure it works.'

For Gaurav to complete his quest for creating the most valuable edtech start-up of the world, he needed to find thousands of similar minds and hands that were also determined to build Unacademy at record-breaking speed. But he also wanted to make sure that the expansion did not come at the cost of losing the core spirit of Unacademy. After all, he has seen many start-ups that have gone for a toss because they grew too fast. His thoughts were now converging to that one word, over which many high growth start-up founders lose sleep—'culture'.

HYPER-GROWTH MEANS EATING YOURSELF

In Scandinavian mythology, one finds the mention of Jörmungandr, the third son of Loki and Angrboða. Jörmungandr is a sea serpent that grew so large that it was able to surround the Earth and grasp its own tail. The myth led to a depiction known as ouroboros, which shows a serpent eating its own tail. In many cultures, it is interpreted as a symbol for the eternal cycle of life, death and rebirth. As the serpent eats its own tail, it grows but also destroys a part of itself.

In 2019, Unacademy's subscription business had started on a promising note. The company was 500-people strong at this time. The company had found its formula to create value;

the question was how to sustain and grow it further. Gaurav could see that the business growth, abetted by the pandemic, could be shouldered by this small team. As Unacademy sought to break into a higher orbit, the company would have to reinvent itself. He was right.

Unacademy grew from 500 employees to 5,000 in the next two years; for context, 2,000 out of this make up the Sales team. Google grew from 1,500 to 15,000 people in a little over three years. Twitter grew from 90 to 1,500 people in less than three years. Start-ups that find the product-market fit need and tend to grow rapidly. When any organization scales at such a breakneck pace, it is as good as literally having a different company every six months. The organization eats itself and is born anew.

Back in 2019, the founders were asking themselves— 'how do we hire faster? What kind of organization structure should we follow? Should we split the Business team into verticals? Who is responsible for the PnL? Should we split the Product and Engineering organization? Do we get an in-house recruiter?' And many more such questions. Gaurav started looking for a head of HR who could steer the ship with deft but agile hands.

'I have seen financial hardships as a kid when my father was the sole breadwinner in the family. When my twin sister decided to enter engineering, he could not afford to spend a lot on both our education. So, I decided to study commerce,' says Tina Balachandran. But, having limited resources since early childhood had taught Tina to fend for herself. 'I've been very independent because I didn't want to put any added burden on my parents. So, all my education has been self-sponsored—be it graduation or my MBA.' Tina found her way into HR when her dad saw a trainee position in HR at Accenture. He thought the field would suit Tina's gregarious

and sociable personality. He couldn't have been more right.

Accenture picked 20 trainees from across India and trained them on core HR skills. She did well in her training and was invited back full-time after completing her MBA from XLRI Xavier School of Management, Jamshedpur. 'Accenture gave me a great foundation when it came to structures, processes, policies, etc. I think it was a very forward-looking organization.' Tina spent 2010–2019 in different Chinese organizations including the giant conglomerates Huawei and Tencent, and a smaller start-up(ish) company called LeEco. She was the fifth person to join LeEco in India and helped them grow to 600 people within a year. Unfortunately, financial mismanagement at the headquarters forced them to lay everyone off and shut shop. 'I ended up managing the emotional setback of letting go of everyone I had hired and then winding down operations. But I learned a lot, especially, what a start-up should not do.'

When Gaurav approached Tina for leading the HR function, Unacademy's brand name was not what it is today. The more Gaurav pursued her over multiple conversations, the more she got intrigued. She did put forward two non-negotiable demands that she wanted Gaurav to address. One was that she cannot work in a bureaucratic organization. Two, she will be given the resources, both in terms of budget as well as autonomy, to hire and build the organization. This was coming from her experience with LeEco—she wanted to make sure that the start-up she works for can afford the resources needed to grow. Gaurav did not even need to think about it, and said yes.'

'I still remember one line, which he had said during my fourth discussion with him, "Tina, you will not regret your decision" and I think that said it all,' she told me. In the end, it was more about Tina joining Gaurav than joining Unacademy. It was December 2019 and a lot of work lay ahead.

HR IS MORE THAN DRAWING RANGOLIS

By April 2020, Tina had helped Ankita Tandon (existing director of business) and later, Karthik (VP of Sales) to scale the Sales team from 50 to 500 and started building the overall organizational structure to support the increasing headcount across all departments. She formalized the process of building the HR Business Partners (HRBPs). 'Early stage start-ups have a generalized team which runs your payroll, your induction, onboarding, hiring and everything. This structure does not work as the company grows because different teams have different needs. What I did is create a structure wherein each person in HR is mapped to a business unit. It's called business partnership.' This evolved into an organizational structure where each team (Tech and Product, Sales, Business, Marketing, etc.) got assigned one HRBP for talent acquisition requirements and one HRBP for other requirements. HRBPs function as 'internal consultants' to senior leaders, providing both strategic and non-strategic HR advice and support, depending on the specific needs of the business unit. This scaled well as the HRBPs attuned themselves to the needs of their particular team, making them highly effective at what they do.

Arushi Mudgal, the HRBP for Hemesh's Tech team, is a perfect example. She was handling Product and Tech HR at Myntra when the Unacademy team approached her for a position as HRBP. Tina had recently joined the organization and interviewed her. Next, she sent Arushi to meet Hemesh. Back then, the technology team was barely 35 members in total. This conversation was most unexpected. 'Honestly, I didn't know what Unacademy was when they called me for the interview. But when I talked to Hemesh, he asked me how I can improve the employee experience and growth in his

team. He asked me what frameworks can be used for internal movement of the employees. I have worked with many tech and product leaders but he was very different and I could see he would not expect me to only, you know, do rangoli kind of activities as HR,' Arushi told me.

Arushi was looking to work with start-ups that would empower her to innovate and 'really help people'. 'I was also exploring my field. I was seeing if the HR policies that we come up with are simply copied from Amazon and Flipkart or do they truly improve the lives of our people. I found Hemesh to be following the same approach. He was himself researching best practices and was really interested in making his team a good place for his employees. That was the main reason I said yes even though I had other offers from bigger companies.'

Arushi came in as HRBP for Hemesh's Tech and Product organization towards the end of 2019. Hemesh involved her in big decisions around creating an effective organization structure, strategies for hiring in leadership roles, etc. 'That gave me an opportunity to explore my field and to actually do something beyond what is written in HR textbooks.'

One of the key duties of the HRBP is to drive the entire life cycle of the employee in that unit. They are responsible for everything the employee goes through—right from pre-joining, onboarding, to performance management, succession planning, learning, engagement, etc. With Hemesh's involvement and empowerment, Arushi became an integral member of the Tech organization and helped scale it to 200 plus members in 2021. She even sits with the team and meets with Hemesh daily. This has enabled both of them to experiment with and create their own best practices. One of the engineers commented, 'Our HR is nothing like what you see in typical companies. It's not like we see them only

at the time of onboarding and exit interviews. Arushi works with us very closely.'

Arushi and Hemesh noted that the initial three months are very crucial for any new employee. If employees choose to stay beyond this period, there is a very good chance that they stick around in the long term. While the teams' 'throw in the ocean and see if they can swim' strategy worked well in the zero to one phase, Arushi observed that it was backfiring in the scaling up stage. Arushi came up with a plan to make this first-three-months journey a very good experience for the employee. At Myntra, she had come across something called the Amber tool. It is an AI-enabled employee engagement chatbot created by another start-up inFeedo whose aim is to help HRs find the unhappy and disengaged employees in the company. Amber is programmed to send a chat and feedback request to the employees at a predetermined frequency. Arushi set it to sending a feedback request once the new employee completes the first month at Unacademy and then every 45 days thereafter.

When the Amber bot popped up on this employee's screen, he opened it with annoyance. The tool showed five emojis from saddest to happiest and asked him, 'Please rate how you are feeling at Unacademy today?' He punched in the second-saddest emoji. The AI bot activated upon seeing a low response and asked follow up questions to determine the cause behind the employee's disgruntlement. After collecting his responses and depending upon the severity of the trigger, the bot sent an alert to Arushi and Hemesh. In this case, Arushi noticed that the said employee had been complaining about repeated meetings being scheduled after 8 p.m. She collected the information from other employees in that team and escalated the issue to the concerned managers. Thankfully, they were able to course-correct before losing this employee.

In other cases, Arushi could figure out that a particular pod's employees were unhappy. Upon probing deeper, she discovered that most of the members in the pod were those who had been with the team for a much longer duration. The handful of the new-timers in the team were feeling lost while these senior folks were feeling overburdened with shouldering extra responsibilities. It was tricky to rebalance the pod by moving around people because many of these old-timers were deemed critical for the team. Arushi and Hemesh discussed the issue and came to a conclusion that the only solution is to move the teams from being people-dependent to process-dependent. As Umesh Bude joined the team in the middle of 2020, wheels were set in motion to bring about such transformations. Successful experimentation with new tools like Amber is one of the many examples of Unacademy's forward-looking approach.

'Working with a leader like Hemesh changed my thinking as well. I started to think of new ways to use Amber,' Arushi told me. She noticed that most of the feedback they were getting on Amber was positive. She wondered how to leverage it. So, she reached out to the inFeedo team and discussed her ideas. As a result, Amber added a feature whereby if any employee leaves a positive feedback, they are given an option to post it right then on Glassdoor. Further, Arushi found out from inFeedo that Unacademy's engagement and response scores on Amber are one among the three highest tech start-ups in India. The scores reflect how much the employees engage, how frequently and how well their concerns are resolved by the HR, etc. Hemesh is keen on keeping a finger on the pulse of his employees' satisfaction, and together with Arushi, he is learning how to do it better every single day.

Another area where Arushi's team defies the typical HR convention is in applying first principle thinking. 'Most of

the companies do fancy engagement activities with their employees to post on social media. We have tried to think what would be most helpful to the employees. We continued expanding our team during the pandemic which means that most of the new employees were getting no face time with the rest of the team. In fact, we had grown from 50 to 200 in this time. Initially, we tried Zoom call events and all the fancy stuff, but then we saw that old folks were talking and the new folks were not interacting much. Also, Zoom calls were adding to screen-time fatigue and suddenly there was a drop in the number of the participants. So, we started another engagement event called TGIF. It is a three minute quiz that we do every Friday at 5 p.m., and I have not seen people go so crazy for a quiz before,' Arushi chuckled. 'We did an Olympic-themed quiz once and we got 30 replies on one question. It was insane because people knew they were over the time limit and not going to win but they still kept replying. We once did a meme contest and that was very popular too. In fact, people have approached me and appreciated that such a simple thing like a three-minute activity can be so fun. The key is to keep experimenting and understand your employees' pulse.'

Each HRBP, in a similar fashion, has been working closely with their business units to help Unacademy grow without losing its core ethos.

ENGAGE PEOPLE WITH SIMILAR VALUES

In 2018, Unacademy's HR shortlisted three candidates from the Indian School of Business (ISB) during campus placements. Now, it was time for the final round of interviews. Gaurav decided to conduct it personally over a Zoom call but instead of interviewing each candidate individually, he invited them for a group interview. Three years down the line,

Shweta Sivasankaran still vividly remembers the interview. 'It was the most extensive and intense interview taken by a CXO-level person on our campus. We were locked-in for more than two hours and my friends outside were wondering "what the hell was going on in there!" Usually, the last rounds are the shortest; here, it was the opposite,' says Shweta.

A Chemical Engineer by background, Shweta had predominantly process-engineering experience in the oil and gas industry in Singapore and a small campaign management stint with renowned non-profit organization, Oxfam, in the UK. Although she was shortlisted for a business development position right at the start, she requested Gaurav to consider her for a position in Marketing, which was her passion. So, Gaurav threw her questions around allocating budget for various activities and so on. He then asked her to take two minutes and draft an email which could be used in their educator outreach programme. In between the conversation, Gaurav told one of them to leave because he didn't look prepared enough for a role at Unacademy. 'That person had been agreeing to everything Gaurav was saying whereas the two of us were being vocal in our disagreement. I don't know if it was because of that, but it started getting pretty intense in there,' Shweta reflected on the interview.

Somehow Shweta maintained her poise in that marathon interview and drafted the email. Gaurav read it out and told her that it looked better than what they were currently using. 'But, he said it with such a straight face that I had no clue if I should be happy or not. It is so hard to read him.'

Unacademy became popular in ISB for conducting 'interesting' interviews. Next year, Gaurav asked an MBA student to call two educators at Unacademy and find out their pain points. The tricky part was that he did not give him any contact information. The person reminisced, 'I reached

out to my friends until I found someone who happened to know someone else. Then I spoke to a friend's cousin and somebody's uncle who knew someone who was teaching at Unacademy. It wasn't just about finding the contacts; we had to do all of it within 30 minutes.'

Testing them on the very tasks they would be required to do in their jobs, Gaurav was not only giving them a dry run of life at Unacademy but also a glimpse of its values. Next, he put them on the spot by asking them to evaluate each other and tell him which two people should be hired out of the five. He knew they would be uncomfortable saying anything bad about each other. He wanted to see how they would handle such a situation.

Most of these freshers, including Shweta, were not only impressed by Gaurav's questions, they left the interview in awe. It was not every day that they saw a company caring so much for two stakeholders that are most often ignored by edtech businesses—its learners and its educators. Shweta also appreciated that Gaurav was giving her a shot at marketing despite her not having a background in the same. She joined as a marketing manager after graduating in May 2018.

Spotting values is easier when the founders are personally interviewing any candidate. The greater the degree of separation from them, higher is the likelihood of missing the value-fit. In such cases, interventions are a good way to make sure every new employee is aligned with the organization's core DNA. In another example, when Gaurav called an employee within his first week of joining, it was the first time that the two of them were speaking. Gaurav asked him how many educators had he spoken to since joining? He responded, 'Two.' Gaurav replied, 'Only two? I have spoken to four this week.' Gaurav asked him the same question with regard to learner interaction. That phone call made it very clear to this

employee that he had not arrived at a run-of-the-mill start-up. 'Gaurav showed that there are two stakeholders that matter the most to him and the company. He, despite being a founder, had found time to talk to more educators and learners than me. After that, he did not have to remind me ever again. If you work at Unacademy you know that you cannot take educators and learners for granted.' Gaurav understands that leaders are busy and can't talk to learners daily but he wants to see that they are thinking of creating a process where they are engaging with the stakeholders and getting relevant insights.

Another employee adds, 'Gaurav is the most hands-on founder I have seen. He likes to get involved with the team. We get unplanned calls from him many times where he shares with us his idea and asks if we've already tried something similar.' He says he has talked to Gaurav directly probably 10 times more frequently than he has talked to the co-founders of any of the earlier start-ups he worked at. Such touchpoints between the leadership team and the founders have made it possible for Unacademy to sustain its focus and values despite rapid growth.

LEADERS WHO EMPOWER

Mayank Garg, the senior category leader, who brought the IIT-JEE TestPrep category to a strong foothold, was being given more categories to handle. 'In 2018, the JEE category was in the top five according to revenues and in top three according to the number of views. I could not see myself doing it any longer. I didn't want to settle into a business role where I'm just talking to teachers every day and scaling this part up. I was just 22, you know.' Different people long for different things. Mayank, who had taken a long break after graduation to pick a role that would excite him, did

not want to settle into a comfort zone. Every company has employees who get bored, but not every company knows what to do about it.

After giving it much thought, Mayank went to Gaurav one fine day in October 2018 and laid it out, 'I feel my learning is being saturated. I want to do something different.' Mayank did not know what he wanted to do or what this meeting would entail. He was prepared to leave the company if nothing bore fruit. Gaurav heard him out and replied, 'Give me a few weeks, let me figure something out.' Gaurav put him in charge of launching new YouTube channels for Unacademy. After all, Mayank had shown great success by finding JEE educators on YouTube. Mayank spent some time launching new channels, including the Chamomile Tea with Toppers channel, which garnered half a million subscribers in 2021. In December, Gaurav came up with something more specific, 'There are some openings in Product and we need someone who has good user and business understanding. Why don't you try it out for two to three months?'

That is when Mayank became a product manager in Hemesh's team in January 2019. Hemesh gave him a free hand. 'He asked me where I wanted to start and I said I want to work in the Live Classes team. He said okay. I felt I could make the maximum impact there. Also, it is the core product in the company.' Mayank applied the same first principle thinking in his new avatar that he had applied in his previous business role. 'There was no other edtech company in India that was really product focused. We had Vedantu, BYJU'S and others, but none of them were known for the product or the product experience or their live classes. So, I thought: how I could use this product and what it was missing.' Long story short, Mayank experimented a lot. One thing that became really successful and evolved into one of the most-used features on the platform

was 'polls'. Educators were teaching thousands of students in some of the popular Unacademy classes. One pattern that Mayank noticed was that almost all the examinations were multiple choice questions (MCQ) based. So, these educators were asking a lot of sample questions and taking quizzes in their classes. However, the only way for a learner to respond to the question asked by the educator was to type in A/B/C/D in the comments. Imagine hundreds of students trying to answer the quiz and the comments box getting flooded. The educators could never read their answers or respond to them. It was hard to determine how many people got it right.

So, Mayank came up with a simple tool that allowed the educator to create a poll so that the learners could just click on the answer they think is correct. The tool would aggregate all the responses, show who answered it correctly and also create a leaderboard. Now, each learner had immediate feedback on how fast they had answered and where they stood in the class! Many educators later raved about this feature. One of them said, '*Coaching class me toh aapko kabhi pata hi nahi chalta. Mahino lag jaate hain student ko ye pata karne me ki wo kitna accha ya bura perform kar raha hai. Online me toh ab fatafat jaan lete hai* (Such things are not possible in an offline coaching class. It takes months for any student to find out how well or poorly they are performing. In online class, they can find it out instantaneously).'

The fact that Mayank fit in so well in his new role also goes to show that Gaurav understood his strengths and enabled the internal movement in a way that was most conducive to Mayank's preferences as well as Unacademy's growth. Mayank credits Gaurav for understanding his knack for data and helping translate his Business team experience into product building. Mayank thrived in his product management stint for most of 2019 and 2020. Looking back, he most enjoyed

the time when the company was working in its growth phase where there were no clear roadmaps or structures in place. 'Until the end of 2020, there was a hustle in the whole team to build and ship things. We used to experiment big time. Great thing about Hemesh and the whole team was that we were not afraid of failure. We used to come up with ideas and discuss "okay let's build this". And "let's build this" didn't mean two months down the line; it meant "let's build this tomorrow"!' As Unacademy was transitioning to its one-to-hundred phase and building-processes were in place, Mayank's free spirit could not find a place on the team anymore. 'I am someone who needs freedom. If you restrict my degree of freedom, my output will go down. I started feeling saturated again.' Mayank put in his resignation to the surprise of many who had worked with him. Hemesh asked about his plans upon quitting the company. When Mayank told him that he was not joining any other company but rather taking time to perhaps start on his own, Hemesh did not try to stop him. They amicably parted ways in mid-2021.

While 'hiring for the right fit' or 'empowering promising employees' came naturally to Gaurav, Unacademy needed other leaders who could do the same. In Vivek Sinha, the future COO, it found one such leader.

Aditi Arora had meandered her way into Unacademy on tentative footsteps in June 2020. After a chequered career across finance, strategy and non-profit, Aditi was anointed as the category manager for the newly-launched CA examination category. The high-growth phase of the company back then left her little leeway and she was struggling to steer the CA category to meaningful results. This is when Vivek Sinha joined Unacademy. Initially, he was given the charge to help out the category leaders.

Aditi had apprehensions heading into her first meeting

with him. The category was barely growing despite her best efforts. She did not know what lay ahead. To her surprise, Vivek did not go into interrogation mode. He told her that he believes the CA category can grow much bigger and that she is the right person for it. He then asked her ideas on how she can achieve it. After understanding that the team had not yet secured any big educator for CA, he advised her to focus all her energies on getting the best educators first. Aditi came out of the meeting with a new spring in her step and direction in her head. 'It gave me so much confidence to see a seasoned leader like him say that he has confidence in something that I was working on, you know,' Aditi told me.

Vivek was not emptily boosting her morale, he was empowering and helping Aditi settle in her new role. Aditi went on to secure exclusive contracts with certain big educators for the Unacademy platform and found her momentum. Later, in October 2020, Vivek told Aditi, 'I am promoting you to senior category manager. It is not even a promotion, it is a designation correction because given your pedigree and experience, you should already have been hired at this level.' Aditi is not alone in believing that Unacademy's leaders have, many times, gone out of their way to show how much they value good work. They are not bogged down by policies when it comes to acknowledging or rewarding high performers.

Vivek remembers his own first few months at Unacademy, 'I was a very new person, so my incentives for performing well were to get more autonomy and recognition. I find Gaurav, as a manager, to be incomparable in giving recognition. I had worked very hard even with my previous employers, Reliance and Tata, but I see myself attaining another level at Unacademy. Why's that? That is because the company makes me feel valued.' And Vivek was not talking just about monetary incentives.

He had been able to breathe new energy into the Business teams with his way of working and the TestPrep business was thriving. It was projected that the Business team would hit its highest revenue yet, on a certain day in December 2020. The whole team stayed in the office till midnight on D-Day to see whether they would touch that number or not. Everyone's eyes were glued to the dashboard that showed the real-time statistics. It was five minutes to midnight when they hit the much-awaited figure. Everybody was ecstatic, revelling in the moment of their biggest achievement yet. This is when Vivek's phone buzzed. He recalls the incident in his usual measured manner of speaking but with a trace of a satisfied smile. 'At 12.05 a.m., I got a video message from one of our biggest investors and board members. The investor personally congratulated me and my whole team.'

'Frankly, that feeling was unbeatable. It was only possible because Gaurav took the pain to arrange it. This investor is a very busy man. Gaurav must have insisted that it happen, no matter the late hour. *Aisa kaun karta hai?* (who does this?) A company can give me expensive laptops or monetary awards but making me feel valued is something else.' Vivek adds after a reflective pause, '*Mai aapko difference batata hun. Baaki companies me agar koi 110 per cent de raha hai and koi 90 per cent de raha hai, toh unme difference aa jayega 10 per cent zyada increment ka, right? Uske liye jaan kaun deta hai? But Unacademy me aisa nahi hai* (I'll tell you the difference. If you give your 110 per cent in other companies and someone else is giving 90 per cent, the difference would be an extra 10 per cent increment, probably. Who cares for that? That is not the case at Unacademy). If someone is giving 110 per cent in Unacademy, then they can grow as fast in one year as their peers are in five years. That is how much we value commitment.'

When Vivek promoted Aditi out of cycle, he was following the same mantra. He also saw that Aditi had only a few junior people working in her team. He hired another of his colleagues from his OYO days, Akash Kalp, as a director. Akash further helped Aditi expand her team to 17 members. There is a fine line between guiding and micromanaging. Many leaders miss it. While Vivek was intervening and trying to show Aditi (and other category leaders) how to grow their businesses, he could have made them dependent on his expertise. Aditi reminisces about his direction in those days, 'He would tell us that "I'm going to tell you how to do things, but I'm only going to tell you once. And then it's your journey and how you use whatever I'm telling you. I will not hold your hand." I feel lucky that we got to work with him so closely in those days. He doesn't tell us to work on the weekends or work late. He genuinely doesn't expect any of that; but he wants to see the work getting done. That is all the commitment he needs. He has been a great example and none of us are surprised to see how well he has done in the company.'

Vivek's intervention and initial guidance went a long way in setting Aditi up for success as a PnL leader. Unacademy finally produced its CA topper like Komal Jain, who held AIR 1 in the CA finals, in 2020. Aditi, later, started the Educator Success team focused on catering to every need of the educators.

MISTAKES ARE FOR LEARNING

She was the brand manager at Unacademy when the company was launching its first print ad—a front-page advertisement in *The Times of India*. Even today, her voice quivers when recalling that episode. 'It was our first newspaper campaign and it was going out on Monday morning. I had done the print proofs and had sent it across to our team for double-checking

on Saturday. Nobody spotted any problems; so, we went ahead. But on Monday morning, I saw a message on our WhatsApp group. Somebody had sent a screenshot of the ad and circled the last line which was published in fine print. It said "Download the *Unacdemy* app". The second "a" in Unacademy was missing.'

Within the company, Gaurav is known for his attention to detail. He calls out if anyone makes a typo even in WhatsApp messages. Here was the company's first print campaign in India's most circulated English newspaper and the creative had an error! She panicked. She informed the other two members of her team and the three of them messaged their boss and the chief marketing officer Karan Shroff, individually, to acknowledge the error and say sorry. 'The three of us went to him as soon as he stepped into the office. He was quiet at first. Obviously, he was upset. But then he said that it is as much his mistake as ours. He said we win as a team and we fail as a team. All he wanted from us was that such a mistake should not be repeated.'

All of them were called to the CEO's office later that evening. By the time the three of them stepped inside, Karan had already been talking to Gaurav. 'I am sure the CEO wanted to take some drastic measures. After all, it was front-page advertisement, you know? What I could gather from our conversation was that Karan had already taken the blame for us. He had put it forward as collective responsibility. No action was taken.'

Karan remembers the episode with a chuckle. 'You know the moment I saw the error on our group, I was like *ab toh gala katega* (now we are finished)! But it was done. So, I sent the screenshot to Gaurav and messaged him, 'Gaurav, *mistake ho gaya* (a mistake has happened).' Meanwhile all three of them were messaging me that they had made a blunder. They

were calling me to apologize,' Karan told me. 'You know why I let it go? None of them blamed another person for the error. The person who had designed it, the person who had written the copy and the person who had sent it out—they all said it was their fault for missing it. It was a petty error. It shouldn't have happened; but it was done. The interesting thing is that it was a very young team. None of them knew each other well and they could have easily pointed fingers at one another but they didn't. That showed character to me. I was proud of them for that.'

When Gaurav saw Karan's message, he was livid. He communicated his displeasure in no few words to Karan and Karan accepted the fault gracefully. That day, Karan gave the newspaper to the employee who had sent it out. 'I told her *ye apne desk pe rakhna* (keep it on your desk), and remember this day. Never let this happen again. And I know she sees that paper before she sends out any ad campaign now. For me, failing is not the problem. It is about being able to learn from your mistakes, that is what makes for a winning attitude,' Karan told me.

METAMORPHOSIS

In one short year from the time she had joined, Tina had seen Unacademy make glorious strides. She didn't have to 'pitch' the company to prospective employees anymore; they came prepared with full knowledge of it. It was good to be in the driving seat, to get to choose from the most qualified of applicants. In response, they had made the whole process utterly streamlined. They rolled out offers as fast as possible and were closing in on a turnaround time of 30 days for any position below level 8 and up to 60 days for the levels above that. In simple words, it was taking them less than a month

to close on junior level roles and between one to two months for mid- and upper-management roles. They were witnessing a hiring ratio of 1:4, that is, one out of the four candidates who made it to the functional interview round was given an offer. The acceptance rate (describing the fraction of people who accepted the final offers) was a whopping 92–95 per cent. In March 2020, Unacademy had 580 employees in total. By December 2021, the number had shot up to 2,100 full-time employees and 1,400 people in the Sales team. But with progress came more responsibility.

Tina stared at the email in front of her. It was an anonymous email sent by someone claiming to be an Unacademy employee. The email was a desperate plea for intervention. Tina read it again and again. She immediately set up a meeting with Gaurav. 'Somebody is trying to tell us that a manager is abusing his power and creating a hostile environment in his team. He is using his influence and the women in that team are no longer feeling safe.'

Indian start-ups have not kept themselves bereft of sexual harassment allegations. If anything, their lack of personnel and resources focusing on such borderline issues make them a bigger breeding ground for the power imbalance that often leads to harassment. The alleged manager was a high-performer and a valued resource. Gaurav and the leadership team unanimously asked HR to resolve the issue with an iron fist. HR investigated the accusations and when it came to light that many women in the said manager's team were indeed feeling threatened, the manager was shown the way out. 'There was no discussion required. We have always believed that we owe the safest of workplaces to our employees and if anyone tries to jeopardize it, we don't have a place for them,' says Tina.

For the time being, Unacademy had dodged a bullet.

However, it could see issues that still needed its attention. Another manager was complaining that one of his resources was being poached by a competitor and that he needs to retain him at any cost. He wanted to give a salary hike and bonus to this person. In another case, the happiness and culture survey results were out. Employees were not happy with different salaries at the same level. Two engineers who hailed from the same college and had been hired in the same month had found out that their salaries were different. Their manager was now pushing for an unfair hike so that he could bring them to the same level.

Tina had seen such requests before. In her experience, the people who wanted to leave extorted such hikes and then left after six months anyway. She had to think of a way to let these managers understand the issue from the company's perspective. The company had outgrown the stage where Tina alone could handle employee woes. After a discussion with Gaurav, Tina pulled out another page from David Ulrich's famous HR model and decided to build a Centre of Excellence (CoE) team. In HR parlance, the Ulrich model describes a basic structure for organizing a company's HR function into three components: HRBPs, CoE and Shared Services.

Tina had already tasted success with HRBPs and believed a CoE team would help navigate the essential rite of passage for Unacademy to transition from a start-up to a mature organization. As any organization grows from one orbit to another, it needs new practices. CoEs are relatively small teams of experts with specialist HR knowledge who work together to develop such best practices and implement them organization-wide with the help of HRBPs. These often include learning and development, compensation and benefits, employee relations, organization development, change

management and recruitment.

Her search for a leader of CoE led her to Diksha Fouzdar. Diksha's 12 years of HR experience after an MBA from Symbiosis Centre for Management and Human Resource Development, Pune, had seen her traversing the intricate hallways of the pharmaceutical sector at Ranbaxy and Strides Pharma. In between, she had acted as a HR consultant to manage the people policies at five of Diageo's manufacturing plants in Karnataka. Steve Correa, who was the chief human resource officer of Diageo India at the time, impressed with her work, had asked her to join full-time as the HRBP for all corporate functions at Diageo India. When Unacademy offered her a position, she reflected on her past experience. While she had ably handled the workforce at these established companies, start-ups were a 'different beast.'

Her mind went to what her husband had experienced at Flipkart. 'The first five to seven years of any high-growth start-up is a period of turmoil. My husband was there at Flipkart in its initial years. They had seen a chief HR officer (CHRO) moving out, a product guy who came from Google joining in and moving out within a year and so on,' she told me. She didn't expect things to be any different at Unacademy. Besides, Tina had apprised her of the challenges. Although Unacademy was at a more stable footing now, there were a couple of products in its portfolio that were running like mini start-ups under Unacademy's umbrella. Graphy was one such product run by Commonfloor founder Sumit Jain. Graphy had undergone three pivots in three months. 'When the businesses pivot, the roles change, deliverables change, some people may no longer even be relevant but you can't just let them go. So, you try to fit them elsewhere in the company. These are very complex things to manage.' But, at this stage of her career, Diksha felt ready for a new challenge.

She joined Unacademy as a senior director in HR in April 2021 and started a new team called the CoE team. As she passed the hallways of the Unacademy office, she noticed multiple framed typographic posters that depicted the company's leadership principles in minimalistic visualizations:

We are a sportsteam, not a family

Be impatient for action, not results

Pay attention to the details

Show, don't tell

Insist on the highest of standards

Learn and unlearn

Think unconventionally

Be overtly transparent

She was curious to find out how these principles were translating to employee behaviour. Are they relevant in a six-year-old Unacademy? Can the leadership precisely define them without leaving any ambiguity in interpretation? She made a mental note to take these questions up with the leadership later. For now, she had a lot to help Tina with.

GETTING SHIT DONE

The first mammoth task that lay ahead for Diksha was to bring the company on an annual appraisal cycle. So far, HR was doing two appraisals, one in April and another one in October, for expedited performance-rewarding. With the headcount crossing 3,500 non-sales employees, Diksha set the wheels in motion for Unacademy's first unified Performance Management System (PMS) targeted to finish by the end of July 2021.

With one stone, she was targeting two big birds. First and foremost, making the appraisal process robust; second, addressing compensation parity concerns and ensuring that

employees at the same level are compensated fairly with respect to each other. Let us first understand how parity was addressed.

Diksha had discussed the outcome of the X to 10X culture survey that Tina's team had closed last month. Employees had called out the discrepancies in the salaries compared to their peers. They both thought that the annual performance management event is an effective way of addressing these. CoE published the salary ranges for people at each level within Unacademy (Tech organization had its own ranges). Specifically, she introduced a framework which was a combination of 'compa-ratio, level and rating' to address parity for deserving talent. Compa-ratio (comparison ratio) is a compensation metric that is calculated as the employee's current salary divided by the median of the current market rate range for his position as defined by the company's competitive pay policy. CoE advised the managers to decide the increments based on their reportee's level as well as compa-ratio and rating. Diksha explains with an example, 'So, a person who has been given a four rating but is at a lower compa-ratio will see a higher increment compared to a person who is at four rating but at a higher compa-ratio.' They went on to automatically populate the increments that an employee was entitled to based on their formula in the PMs. It was now up to the manager to use it as a reference and decide the increments.

Second, CoE attacked the systemic flaws in how appraisals were being conducted so far in the company. While employees knew their metrics and goals informally, these goals were not recorded in any system. 'How can you evaluate someone if there are no goals to check? It is unfair for the employees.' To address this, CoE came up with a process of self-review. The idea was simple but powerful. HR asked the employees

to write their own elaborate reviews capturing their biggest achievements as well as what they could not accomplish. Secondly, they were asked to talk about their strengths and areas for further development. This was a new exercise for employees and managers alike. So, Diksha worked with the HRBPs to create a training module that educated employees to prepare them for writing effective annual reviews and helped managers understand the new PMS process and how to share feedback with their reportees. Diksha was pleasantly surprised with the results. 'More than 90 per cent of employees filled their reviews on Lattice and some were done very well. We were greatly appreciated for this intervention.' Going forward, Diksha decided to continue the self-review and make the goal-setting process more robust.

The humongous task of bringing 3,500 plus full-time employees to the same annual cycle had taken four months but finally, Diksha and Tina were able to bring the PMS to a successful completion. Ninety-five per cent of the employees reported that their managers engaged with them during the PMS process. Seventy-six per cent of employees also felt that the feedback given to them was actionable and productive. At the organizational level, CoE efforts were showing results. Gaurav advocated in favour of all employees doing proper goal setting exercises. To set an example, he started doing goal-setting with business unit leaders once every month. The results are trickling down effectively—while only 3.4 per cent employees had set their goals in the June-end quarter, the number was up to 15 per cent for the quarter ending in September 2021.

When Leigh Buchanan wrote in *Inc.*, 'Between start-up and maturity, companies navigate a period of adolescence that— like its biological counterpart—is awkward and uncertain,'

she couldn't have been more precise.[25] Unacademy is going through such an adolescent phase and what is at stake is not something as binary as survival but something more complex. The company has to make complicated decisions and hard choices amidst a surge of self-doubt—is it focusing on the right things? Are the goals appropriate? Would it keep growing? Diksha has been brought in to help navigate some of these challenges at the employee management level but change, at its very core, is uncomfortable.

Many millennial managers, unexposed to strict HR structures and practices before, initially resisted complying with these changes in the appraisal process. Diksha noticed that unlike at the previous MNCs that she had worked at, there was no full stop to the discussions even after the performance management process had been completed. Managers demanded unreasonable salary increases for their employees, fearing they would otherwise leave. Their concerns needed to be dealt with delicately. Diksha asked the managers why they thought the employees would leave their teams. Most of them carried the impression that talent can only be retained through compensation. 'Then instead of trying to stop the ones who leave for money, why not do succession planning?' was Diksha's antidote to the unsolvable problem. An important part of the talent management process, succession planning is the act of grooming internal people with an intention of letting them fill key positions when the time comes. It entails identifying critical resources and preparing replacements to remove dependency on

---

[25] Buchanan, Leigh. 'How to Manage Your Company's Awkward Adolescence', Inc., September 2015, https://www.inc.com/magazine/201509/leigh-buchanan/your-awkward-phase-and-why-you-should-love-it.html. Accessed on 16 December 2021.

those resources. Diksha is introducing Unacademy's young workforce to long-established HR practices. She is showing them how performance management and talent planning is not about bringing everyone up to the same salary but about differentially rewarding and developing the top talent. The company would do well to identify and nurture its top talent, while not becoming dependent on it with the succession planning process.

However, handling the managers' objections is only part of the job. Every HR personnel knows that compensation dissatisfaction is not the only reason why employees quit, although, it remains the oft-quoted one. Start-ups like Unacademy see an average attrition rate of 40 per cent in Sales and 20 per cent or more in Technology teams. One feedback that was captured in the previous surveys was that there was no closure on the issues people had raised in the past. Employees felt their concerns were identified but not registered. Work-life balance is one such issue of contention. There is always noise about it but '*sab kuch fizzle ho jaata hai* (everything fizzles out)', in their words.

Work-life balance is a topic that stumps all high-growth start-ups. Roman remembers working from the office till 26 November 2019 and catching a last-minute flight to Jaipur to be there for his own wedding on the 30th. Even in Jaipur, there wasn't a single day when Roman and Gaurav were not meeting to discuss Unacademy's rapid expansion. Since the time she had started seeing Roman to 2 December 2019, when she landed in Bengaluru as his newly-wed wife, Spriha Choubey knew what she was getting into but still, the first sight of their new apartment left her flabbergasted. 'I had just taken possession of the new apartment the day I left for Jaipur. So, when we both came back after our wedding, the flat was still a mess,' Roman told me. While for the founders, the

sacrifices become a part of their routine life, other employees have different expectations.

One specific employee did not have an issue with working hard or long hours but he faced another challenge. 'I am a morning person whereas my whole team is full of night owls. It stresses me out because I get messages when I am going to bed,' he shared. 'I had to make it clear at some point that I will start my day early and finish early. Eventually, they started respecting my preferences.' Sometimes, there are solutions, other times there are not. HRBPs are trying to address such challenges in their business units, coming up with policies like 'unplug hours', but it is one of those topics that baffles all high-growth start-ups. Tina and Gaurav are more realistic about it. 'We are in an experimentation and rapid expansion stage. It comes at a certain cost. We don't claim otherwise in our interviews.'

When Gaurav announced a four-day company-wide holiday in September 2021 for people to take a well-deserved break, it was a signal that the company has started to think of the greater good of the people who make it what it is.

STEPPING UP WHEN IT MATTERS

Running a start-up has its own hazards—overlooking health is one of them. No stranger to the perils of start-up life, Gaurav had hired Arooshi Singh to teach yoga and meditation to him and Roman in October 2017. Seeing her passion for health and wellness, Gaurav invited her to teach the whole team. 'I had done a lot of weekend workshops for corporate clients but it was really cool that Gaurav was inviting me to do it full-time for his employees. I remember the team was just 50 people at the time but the energy was amazing. They were fun, dynamic and curious people. I gave them surya namaskar

(sun salutation) and push up challenges,' Arooshi told me. Apart from yoga, she started conducting meditation sessions after which the employees would ask her a lot of questions—'I am 24, why should I meditate?' 'My work is high energy, will meditating slow me down?' Arooshi found herself discussing metaphysics, spirituality and every topic under the sun. She was loving the vibe of the team and became Unacademy's in-house wellness consultant.

In April 2020, she was asked to lead the Employee Experience and Welfare team where she took care of various touchpoints in the employee journey, right from designing a personalized welcome kit, to buddy programme, to sending curated hampers to all the employees on crossing special milestones and so on. She feels that Gaurav's obsession for quality and concern for the company has only sharpened over time. 'He is one of those CEOs who still thinks about creating a better employee experience every day. That keeps me motivated.'

Unacademy's focus on wellness revealed itself in its full proportion when the second wave of the COVID-19 pandemic wreaked devastation all across India. A report prepared by the Centre for Global Development called it 'India's worst tragedy since Partition in 1947.'[26] Indian companies would remember it as the biggest test of their resilience. As soon as it became clear that the hospitals were running out of something as basic as beds and oxygen, Unacademy sprang to action. In April 2021, Gaurav and Vivek called a meeting with Arooshi to brainstorm ideas for providing additional support to their

---

[26]Mordani, Sneha. '2nd Covid Wave Was India's Worst Tragedy Since Partition, Saw up to 49 Lakh Excess Deaths: Report', India Today, 21 July 2021, https://www.indiatoday.in/coronavirus-outbreak/story/2nd-covid-wave-was-india-worst-tragedy-since-partition-saw-up-to-49-lakh-excess-deaths-1830894-2021-07-21. Accessed on 16 December 2021.

people beyond standard health insurance. This is when they took a major step to extend COVID-19 benefits not only to employees but also to their educators. Steps like these were deeply appreciated by the educators who otherwise would have no employment benefits in contractual positions.

Arooshi spearheaded a UCARE (Unacademy Covid Assessment and Relief Essentials) programme that included COVID-specific benefits. Beyond the regular extra leave and flexible work hours, Unacademy offered exclusive oxygen concentrators, practo membership, grief counselling support, Swiggy/Zomato vouchers, etc. The company wanted to extend healthcare benefits but insurance companies were inundated and unable to help. Gaurav used his personal connections to get an additional insurance coverage of ₹1.5 lakh which could be used by employees' or educators' families alike and opened his email for any queries. He would keep a close eye on how the UCARE programme was rolling out. Tina calls it Gaurav's knack for leadership. 'He is minutely involved whenever a new initiative is being launched. He would ask probing questions to determine how we are thinking about implementing something. He would give a lot of input in those days. Once he sees that the team has a clear road map and is looking capable to handle it, he steps back.' This way, Gaurav is gifted at the ability to see the big picture while paying attention to the finer details.

Nothing brings people together like a tragedy. Unacademy lost five educators and two employees to the pandemic. This was the time when Indians leaned on one another to help find basic resources such as oxygen concentrators, hospital beds and Covid medicines. Gaurav had created a slack channel #covid-help to enable anyone to ask for help internally. When the requests flooded beyond their expectations, Vivek started an Internal Covid Response Team (ICRT) for enabling

systematic support. War room associates were appointed who collected requests from COVID-19-affected employees and passed it on to the zonal leaders who would:

1. Contact the admin team to help find hospital beds, ICUs, RT-PCR test locations, oxygen masks, etc., in their respective regions.
2. Reach out to a 100-member volunteer team to source verified details.
3. Amplify the requests on social media channels for broader reach.

'It was devastating to hear a fellow employee begging for plasma for his parents. We had never seen anything like this before and when things started becoming really bad, everyone stepped up without a second thought. People started volunteering to provide home-cooked food or find medicines,' Arooshi recalls. The UCARE programme saw 18 people availing salary advances, 6,300 practo enrollments, 30 people availing mid-term insurance inclusions and so on. At a time when many start-ups had no clue how to help their employees and were being called out for jeopardizing their employees' safety by asking them to come to work, Unacademy had stepped up when it mattered. The leadership also learned first-hand that it is possible to be high-performing as well as employee-friendly. Arooshi was promoted to associate director as a part of the People, Experience and Culture team in July 2021.

WE ARE A SPORTSTEAM, NOT A FAMILY

Elad Gil wrote in his book *High Growth Handbook*:

You do not need a VP engineering who has run a 10,000-person organization when you only have

20 engineers. Instead, hire someone who has led a 50 to 100 person team and can scale up your org to the right level over the next 12–18 months. Either that person will grow with the team or you will need to hire someone new in the future.[27]

Elad believes that it is unrealistic to hire for posterity. When a start-up is growing exponentially, the founders, at best, can hope to hire for the next few years. Unacademy would also learn that there is no permanent fit and when the time comes to choose between stability, seniority and growth; growth always wins.

Growth is great. Growth is what start-ups live for. But, growth is also unsettling. As founders try to bring in more capable executives and stabilize the company from the top, older employees feel at the centre of the hurricane. Every few months, they might be reporting to new managers and be given new goals to work on. The same people who loved building the company in the initial days may be thrown off by new structures and processes. Their roles and scope of work starts narrowing down and it can get very uncomfortable for those who are used to the fluidity of the earlier days. The employees who are able to adapt to these new constraints have a great chance at growing with the company. These faithful old-timers who evolved as Unacademy scaled became precious resources. However, those who could not deal with it found themselves out of step with the company's new rhythm and soon got churned out.

Almost every year, Unacademy has not shied away from overhauling the management to keep up with the growth of the company. Whenever leadership questions arose, Gaurav

---

[27]Gil, Elad. *High Growth Handbook*, Stripe Press, 2018.

turned to one of the first cultural principles he had designed for the company—We are a sports team, not a family. He made it a point to reward performance, not people. The same employee might be given a shout out for achieving a big milestone and also called out for slipping on another aspect of his or her work—all on the same day. A senior leader recalls, 'The month in which I had exceeded my revenue expectation and my learner NPS was more than 95 per cent, in the same month, I have been criticized because there was a negative comment from a user. To a newcomer, the first critical feedback looks ruthless but when he sees that everybody is being treated the same way, it becomes liberating. People who are driven to do the greatest work of their lives fit in but anyone who comes in taking it as just another job may not survive.' Ultimately, managers embrace these values in their own leadership style. One of Vivek's reportees, Balaji Ramachandran, told me, 'Vivek was upset when I did not deliver what I had committed. I told him that I would submit it the next day but he pointed out that it was supposed to have happened the same day. It did not matter that my previous project had been super successful. I respect that and would do the same with my team.' The founders and top leaders had worked hard and long to set the tone for Unacademy's growth DNA through these cultural values.

Tina feels that there are employees who are great in a certain phase of the company and not in another phase. It is an important realization for both the company as well as employees to make sure they grow together or grow apart.

Managers are mindful to deal with this gracefully. Disha Agarwal had led the Business teams effectively till 2019 despite her lack of leadership experience before Unacademy. However, the business was now exploding. Gaurav sat her down and told her that he would need to bring a more experienced leader for the business. 'I really appreciated that he talked to me and

involved me in this process. And I was fully aligned because I thought I could also grow more under a capable mentor. So, I told him that I would be happy to support in any way possible. He then made sure that I got to meet anyone he was shortlisting. This is how I met Ankita Tandon when she was being considered for the role. Gaurav asked for my feedback and I told him that I would be very happy to work with her,' Disha told me. She is now an associate vice president in the Business team.

In a sports team, it is all about meritocracy but as a mindful organization, Unacademy leaders try to communicate transparently and make a place for people to keep growing within the company. When it doesn't work out internally, they make the tough call of replacing the leadership. Tina takes her own example. 'I have had good success in growing the company to 5,000 people but if the systems need to be tweaked now to be more systematic, then I should be open to working with people who can do that. The leader has to do what is good for the company.'

There is no section in this book that defines Unacademy's culture. If you were looking for that, sorry to disappoint you! Does that mean that Unacademy has no culture? Far from it. Patrick Collison (founder of Stripe) says that there is a fine line between being explicit about your culture and being overly wedded to it—'One of the most difficult exercises in judgment that has to be applied by the leaders of a start-up is continually balancing this tension.'[28]

As the ouroboros depicted, Unacademy continues to grow and eat itself in the sixth year of its existence. So far, it has prioritized winning over anything else. But Gaurav has been building a strong leadership team around himself to make sure they keep learning and unlearning. The Unacademy that will

---

[28]Ibid.

exist when this book reaches its readers will be undeniably different than the one I am writing about now. If not, it would be a shame, because, that would mean it has lost its DNA of growth.

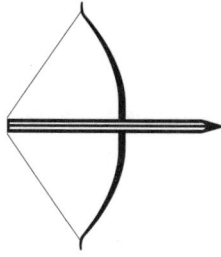

SEVEN

SUPERPOWER 6: BRAND AS THE NORTH STAR

How Unacademy Is Developing an Unbeatable Brand

Culture guides employees in the absence of their leaders. Brand is what stays in the mind of users long after the founders are gone.

Apple released its hallmark 'Think Different' ad campaign with the 'To the Crazy Ones' commercial after Steve Jobs returned to the company for a second innings at the company he had founded and was thereafter forced to leave. Jobs was instrumental in every aspect of the campaign right from choosing the slogan, to creative depiction, to expediting its execution. Two versions of the narration in the television ad were created in the development process: one narrated by Jobs and one by Richard Dreyfuss. While most of the employees at Apple voted in favour of Job's version, Jobs himself decided to air Dreyfuss's version at the last moment, saying it was about Apple and not about him. Jobs, who loved every bit of the limelight, would never have let go of such an opportunity in

his younger days. But, in his second innings, Jobs was creating something bigger than a name for himself—he was creating a brand that would outlast anyone associated with Apple. That is what great founders do.

Unacademy is in its infancy compared to the big brands we see out there. Nonetheless, the team is focusing on building a brand that lasts in the long term.

'Marketing, if treated as a product in itself, drives better growth,' said Gaurav in a tweet. He went on to give examples of Michelin star restaurants and Apple events and Nike films that are treated not as a means to an end but as products in themselves. He professes that every company today is a media and content company. Traditional marketing does not work anymore. This product-first approach has been followed rigorously by Unacademy's Marketing team since day one. Their budgets may have increased and more channels now may be available at their disposal but it is the core product mindset that has made its branding efforts stand apart.

DEFINING THE BRAND

'In my very first week, I proposed something and Gaurav thought it was a shitty idea. I had never heard someone be so direct with their feedback. It said a lot about Unacademy's expectations from its employees,' says Shweta Sivasankaran. 'It truly made an impact on how I ended up working. And I was okay with someone expecting a lot from me and telling me if I do something badly rather than not giving me a chance to do anything worthwhile.'

Shweta came to Unacademy as a marketing manager in 2018, fresh from her ISB MBA and with bare minimum prior marketing experience. In her first year, she would get an unparallaled opportunity to shape Unacademy's brand

narrative. A few weeks into her job, she told Gaurav that Unacademy should have a brand book.

'Okay, do you know how to make one?' Gaurav replied.

'No. But I can learn.'

'Okay, you have three months to do it.'

As Shweta started working on the brand book, she started conversations around brand perception that could set the tone for the company's marketing activities from the early days on. These would also reveal Gaurav's thought process on marketing.

'From the beginning, Gaurav was so passionate about building the right brand. He is a person who doesn't miss the forest for the trees. Because of working with him so closely, we also learned that we can never compromise on the brand image for any short-term gains. This is why we never thought about gimmicky things like advertising discounts or prices. It was always about the big picture; that we are here to transform the lives of people. For many of us, it may be another exam but for so many people, it is the means to their livelihood. And that gives us a certain responsibility.'

Shweta completed Unacademy's first brand book which spelled out the brand's tagline, vision, purpose, values and personality in more concrete terms. While the tagline 'India's largest learning platform' has stayed on, the messaging has evolved with the company's growth. It also laid the guidelines on how the brand is to be portrayed in 360-degree marketing campaigns. For example, the team decided that the brand's tonality has to be eloquent, encouraging and engaging. It was decided that complicated messaging and jargon was not the way forward for the company. While sounding obvious, such detailed guidelines acted as an easy-to-use checklist when designing any new initiative. Since then, the company has taken it to heart that their campaigns must stand out and never be boring or uninteresting.

INTEGRATED BRAND PLACEMENT

April 2019

The protagonist Vaibhav Pandey is about to cry. Despite his best efforts, he is struggling to solve the question paper given by his IIT-JEE coaching teacher. Just as his shoulders are sagging and head about to slump, his friend Uday pats him on his back enthusiastically. He hands over his phone to Vaibhav and says, '*Uday Gupta kabhi apne punters ko nahi bhoolta. Ye le...* (Uday Gupta never forgets his friends. Take this...)' Vaibhav looks at the phone. Vineet Loomba's lecture on 'Revision Course on Differential Calculus' is showing on the screen. Uday adds, '*Maine Unacademy ka annual subscription le liya hai... Sirf tere liye. Ja attend kar jitne live lectures attend kar sakta hai* (I have bought Unacademy's annual subscription only for you. You can now attend as many live lectures as you want).' Vaibhav goes on to revisit the concepts he has found difficult to grasp so far and looks relaxed and hopeful by the time the episode ends.

The scene barely takes a minute in one of the 30 minute-long episode of *Kota Factory*—a web series created by TVF that chronicles life at Kota, the hub for IIT-JEE coaching. But anyone who has binge-watched the series cannot miss Unacademy's name placed strategically throughout the story. *Kota Factory* went viral like many of the other TVF series and anyone who harboured IIT dreams and thought of going to Kota saw it. Moreover, if there was anything that stuck on to the viewer's memory as much as the famed Jeetu Sir, it was the fact that the Unacademy app has live lectures from some of the most popular IIT-JEE educators in the country.

Gaurav believes that today's audience is too clever to tolerate old-school sales(y) campaigns. He likes to practise

the art of integrated brand placement. He explains the concept via the example of the sitcom *F.R.I.E.N.D.S.* 'Do you remember the episode where Rachel breaks Joey's recliner and replaces it with an advanced model of the La-Z-Boy? The whole episode is focused on that chair. Did it ever feel like you were watching an advertisement?' The example can be extended further because the sitcom had a lot of clever brand mentions and placements. Who can forget the recurring name of Bloomingdales or Ralph Lauren or a whole episode dedicated to Pottery Barn?

When cleverly placed as a part of the main story itself, brand names have a much-higher chance of staying in our memories (a concept known as brand recall). Gaurav had successfully experimented with integrated campaigns back in his Commonfloor days when he had convinced TVF to create a series *Permanent Roommates* based on the lives of flatmates. The success story continued with *Kota Factory* (rated 9.2 on IMDB), *Aspirants* (rated 9.7 on IMDB) and *Operation MBBS* (rated 8.9 on IMDB). All of these were a path-breaking attempt at painting the viewpoint of an average student who finds himself dealing with the intense academic pressure of preparing for Indian competitive exams, a character who is otherwise considered too mundane and boring to talk about in everyday conversations. This is what made them utterly relatable to the crores of teenagers appearing for these exams—the very segment that Unacademy wants to attract.

However, integrated brand campaigns may be deceptive in their apparent simplicity. Is getting 'viral' as simple as paying a renowned creative agency such as TVF? If so, why aren't more brands doing it? The answer lies in whether you have enough clarity about your brand or not. For the campaign to have the desired affect, you need a clear vision and a lot of behind the scenes prep. TVF can lend its creative chops to make any idea

come alive but only a few people know the crucial role played by Unacademy in finding the right narrative.

Shweta remembers the day in August 2018 when Gaurav told her to accompany him for a marketing meeting. She still had no clue who they were meeting when they reached the Oberoi. That is when she saw the familiar faces walking in. The only difference was that she had seen them only on-screen so far. Gaurav had invited TVF team because he wanted them to create a web series for Unacademy. The next few meetings proved to her how detail-oriented Gaurav is. 'Gaurav would discuss the content he wanted, in minute detail, with TVF's creative team. He even had a clear vision when it came to building the characters and said he wanted a character that really cares about their students. That led to Jeetu Bhaiya being written.' Apart from the storyline, Unacademy also made it clear that they want a 100 per cent family-friendly, clean show. The dialogues and humour were tailored accordingly. It spoke to the company's far-sightedness when the series positioned Unacademy not as a competitor to the established coaching industry but as an on-demand supplement to learning.

And, was it a coincidence that the protagonist was a student with two sidekicks and a wise teacher? Perhaps TVF team had just finished a helpful reading of *Harry Potter*.

BUILDING THE TEAM

Until the summer of 2019, Unacademy had barely opened its wallet for traditional marketing unlike its biggest competitor BYJU'S, who had spent ₹450 crore on advertising alone in the previous financial year. Its campaigns featuring Shah Rukh Khan and the official sponsorship of the Indian cricket team had put its name front and centre in Indian households. It is only after finding its product-market fit with Unacademy Plus

that Unacademy could afford to start thinking of traditional PR or advertising. Gaurav, now for the first time, started looking for a head of Marketing.

This is when Karan Shroff, the head of Brand Marketing at Xiaomi India, came onto his radar. From the time he had joined Xiaomi in June 2015, the brand had grown by leaps and bounds. Karan himself had spearheaded iconic campaigns including 'Naya Note' and 'Kiska Baja'. One of the questions Gaurav asked him was the name of the brands that he looks up to. When he mentioned Apple, Nike and Coca Cola, Gaurav's ears perked up. It was not easy for Karan to switch from a company like Xiaomi, which was making a lot of noise, to a relatively lesser-known start-up like Unacademy. Gaurav kept pursuing nonetheless. Karan also appreciated Gaurav's own forte at marketing and storytelling. Looking at Gaurav's vision for Unacademy's brand convinced Karan that this could be his unfettered chance to experiment and do something groundbreaking.

'*Zyada se zyada* (what's the worst that can happen), it wouldn't work. I am 30. If I don't take a chance now, when will I take it?' With this thought, Karan joined Unacademy in August 2019 and went on to build a 50-plus-people-strong Marketing organization. The first 12 months was a tough period to start with. At that time, there were only six to seven people in the Marketing team who were handling everything and the expectation was to put out Unacademy's first mammoth campaign. Karan noticed a very different side of the media industry when he started to approach them on behalf of Unacademy. 'The same people who were chasing me at Xiaomi would go cold on my requests. They would say "*Ye toh abhi chhota company hai, ye hum nahi kar sakte*" (Your company is very small, we cannot do this for you). It made me realize who my true connections were and who were not. There

were people like Puneet Kapoor (Lowe Lintas, ex-McCann Worldgroup) and Bhairav Shanth (ITW Consulting) who stuck with me and I will never forget that. My objective has always been to build the biggest, "baddest" brand out there and that's what we set out to do, it didn't matter how small our company was. We partnered with those who were willing to take that journey. Once we were on TV, IPL [Indian Premier League], etc., it changed the way we were perceived. During the lockdown, we closed on Virat Kohli for our legends series, all while working from home. That's how far we have come.'

Karan was born in Mumbai but has spent half of his life and most of his career in Bengaluru. Coming from a lower-income household, Karan had to finance his own college education. Very early on, he had imbibed that if he wanted something, he would work hard for it. 'If you have ever gone to a mall and someone has made you fill out an application form for a credit card etc., you have met someone like me,' he told me. 'I used to volunteer for those small jobs to make money while in college. Everyday I would finish my classes and then head out for these jobs. Some people might have thought *ki ye kya* (what are these) menial jobs *hain* because you get like ₹150 or ₹200 rupees per day, right? But I looked at them as something to prove myself with. Can I be the best among these guys? People would run as soon as their eight hours were done but I would stay back and help out. I wanted my work to be so good that the clients and those people should say that "hey I want that volunteer again", you know?'

His dedication caught the attention of people from IBM GPJ (George P. Johnson—selected partner for IBM's exhibition management services worldwide) who offered him a consulting project while he was still in college. An opportunity to work with such global brands got him not only the exposure to big-budget events but also mentorship

by experts. He learned his early grooming lessons in those jobs—'how to talk, how to carry myself' and so on.

A role like chief marketing officer (CMO) does not come easily. Shannon Stubo Brayton (ex-CMO at LinkedIn) mentions in the *High Growth Handbook* by Elad Gil that, 'To be a successful marketing leader, you have to have a little bit of knowledge of a hundred different skills. Everything from copywriting to creativity to research to NPS.' When reflecting on his own strengths, Karan believes the same. 'There are people far more educated and talented than me when it comes to individual functions. But, one thing where I excel would be the hunger to get things done. Throughout my life, I have seen struggles and that has made me hungry. So, I would probably say that my strength is that I am the hungriest of them all.'

Karan also attributes much of his success to people who helped him along the way. This is why when it comes to leading his own team, he is more of a 'team player' than an authority figure. The unique camaraderie reflects in his relationship with his people. He cares not only about performance but also that his team is 'nice and friendly' with each other. When conducting hiring interviews, he likes to check if a candidate has strong team spirit or not. When he had to let go of one employee from his team, he considered it his own failure as a leader. There was an instance where two employees were not getting along with each other and it was impacting the team performance. He called both of them to his cabin and told them, 'I am giving you 15 minutes. You have to resolve your conflict now and get back to work. I don't care who is right or wrong. If you cannot work with each other, I will fire both of you. So, figure out if both of you want to stay or both of you want to leave.' Then he left the room and closed the door behind him. The employees stayed and made sure their personal conflicts did not spill out after that.

His mantra is, 'It doesn't matter how you do it, just do it.' He is a leader who has high expectations but also leads by initiative. 'I am always available to my team. I wouldn't ask anyone in my team to do something which I wouldn't be comfortable doing myself.' There was a time when his team was negotiating with a TV channel for sponsorship. The channel was quoting ₹16 crore and Karan asked his team to do it at half the ask. The team tried but ultimately told Karan it looks impossible. '*Chalo, kar ke dekhte hain* (Let's try and do it),' Karan told them with a twinkle in his eyes. He got on calls with his team and they were able to close the deal finally at ₹7 crore.

'To be honest, I wasn't doing it to show off. Sometimes, I don't even know if what I say will work or not but I want them to think that if Karan can do it, so can we,' he told me. 'This has happened so many times now that the team knows if I said "*Mai karke dikhaun* (Shall I do it and show it to you)?", I believe it is doable. I know they can do it too and now they have started doing it. *Ab toh team wale bolne lag gaye hain ki "Karan mai kar ke dikhaati hun"* (Now my team has started saying that Karan, "I will do it and show it to you"). That is what I wanted. And frankly, we would not be here if it was not for the team. We aim high and set impossible targets. We are able to achieve them only because every single person here is driven and works hard for it.'

STICK TO THE BRAND

When it comes to putting the name of Unacademy out there, Gaurav is a stickler for the tone of their messaging. He is clear that everything they say has to be about learners and the spirit of studying.

In August 2019, Virat Kohli was in top form in the Indian

tour of West Indies. He had hit two back-to-back centuries and his name was trending on every social media platform in India. Unacademy's Marketing team tweeted a congratulatory message and a quiz question—'What was the last biggest performance by Virat Kohli?' As soon as Gaurav saw that, he messaged Karan, 'Why are we tweeting about Virat Kohli in a way that has nothing to do with education?' While Karan defended the tweet calling it in-moment marketing, Gaurav reprimanded the team for deviating from the brand. 'What we should have tweeted was something like "while your idol is hitting centuries on the ground, how many of you are sticking to your study schedule?"' Karan and Gaurav agreed to disagree on this particular episode.

Gaurav does not shy away from speaking his mind and a leader working under him soon realizes that he expected the same from him. This wouldn't be the last time the two of them disagreed but Gaurav would give Karan full freedom to experiment creatively and blow his mind away. And Karan would do exactly that with the upcoming campaigns.

LET'S CRACK IT

There was no breathing time for Karan as he joined the company in its coming-of-age moment. It was time for Unacademy to become a mainstream brand and Karan undertook the behemoth task of creating Unacademy's first ATL campaign. 'ATL' stands for 'Above the Line'—meaning an ad campaign that is going to be deployed to a wider target audience such as on television, radio and/or billboards. He shortlisted three agencies to pitch to him and Gaurav. After going through the ideas, they were sold on the slogan that was proposed by McCann. 'It was so simple, yet so big—"Let's Crack It!" We felt it made perfect sense for our brand because

of the word "let's". It reinforces our value as a brand. We have never been about tall claims, we have always laid emphasis on understanding our learners and this simple phrase did justice to that. The phrase was laden with hope and encouragement,' says Karan.

Typically, it takes four to five months for a campaign pitch to make it to the big-screen commercial but in the spirit of its hallmark penchant for speed, Unacademy asked McCann to deliver it in less than two months. They did it in 45 days. Again, the speed reflects the clarity that Unacademy had for the brand. Shweta recalls one of their meetings with McCann. 'We were telling them that few of our educators have written defining books on their subjects and many students come to our app after hearing that they can directly learn from the experts whose books they have been reading.' This description translated verbatim into one of the three campaigns. Shot in the smoggy streets of Delhi, the campaign showed a student spending a day looking for 'Chauhan Sir's book', which was out of stock. In the evening, he is sitting with a friend whose phone pops up the message—K.C. Chauhan is now live on Unacademy.[29]

Second was shot in the *Tumhari Sulu* fame house in Mumbai where a student in a middle-class family is sacrificing watching a cricket match and instead studying to make his dream come true. Karan's eyes light up when he talks about the third one though. 'We believed that the story of determination would come out best through the rocky yet vivid terrains of Ladakh, and we decided at the last minute to shoot it in Leh.'

[29]'Unacademy Launches "Let's Crack It" Campaign', *ET Brand Equity*, 22 November 2019, https://brandequity.economictimes.indiatimes.com/ news/advertising/unacademy-launches-lets-crack-it-campaign/72183670. Accessed on 17 December 2021.

So what if it's the nippy month of November? So what if they say you need a minimum of 48 hours to acclimatize? The team reached Leh when the temperatures were crashing to minus eight degrees. Many of them fell sick on the first day but the shooting had begun as planned at the twentieth hour itself. When Karan saw the final version, he knew all that pain had been worthwhile.

The film features a girl supporting her family at their own eatery in a remote area of Leh. She has been washing cups and cooking for the customers till the tail end of the evening. All of a sudden, she sees the notification that Biology class is going live on the Unacademy app. She grabs her scarf and car keys, informs her mom that it's her class time and rushes out. As soon as she gets in the car, the viewer wonders why she needs the car for an online class. Well, she just rolls up the car windows and sets her phone on the steering wheel to finally watch the live class and study in peace. The window glass reflects the snowy peaks of the Himalayas. Even in the thinnest of civilizations, the Unacademy app lets her study from the best teachers.[30] 'We wanted this film to convey the message that no journey is too rocky, if you want to embark on it. It's your determination that counts. She maintains a balance between her personal responsibilities and her studies with the help of Unacademy,' Karan adds.

The team gathered together nervously when the campaign was finally ready to go on air on 22 November 2019. Turns out, the celebrations had just started as they garnered 33 million views in the first 24 hours. Unacademy was no longer an Internet phenomenon—it was about to become a household name. Karan was named as the CMO in September 2020.

---

[30]Ibid.

THE IPL SIXERS

'I don't like it,' Gaurav told Karan.

'I think it will work. Trust me,' Karan replied. '*Nahi kaam kare toh fire kar dena* (if it doesn't work, fire me),' Karan broke the silence after a few seconds.

'That's not required. Okay, let's do it if you believe in it,' Gaurav gave him the go-ahead.

'Gaurav and I rarely agree on ideas. We always have different views but it's more of a debate rather than a fight. We both add a lot of value to the end results. See, we both believe in taking risks and experimenting and we both want the company to be successful. So, it is a partnership of mutual trust and respect. There were teething issues in the start. Knowing how much of a perfectionist Gaurav can be, he would keep himself very involved in what we were doing. Eventually, he saw my obsession and passion for my work. We wouldn't see eye-to-eye on certain campaigns but Gaurav always trusted me and let the team experiment. That is what makes our partnership so successful.'

Having tasted success with their first ATL campaigns, the Marketing team was now geared to experiment on an even bigger stage. The opportunity came when Unacademy became an official sponsor of the IPL tournament in 2020. The IPL finale of 2020 was scheduled to take place on 10 November. The team wanted to end the tournament with a big bang, something that would stay in the minds of the audience long after the tournament had ended. Unacademy decided to premier a new ad film on 8 November.

Associate director of Marketing, Arpita Bhattacharya, recounts the making of the iconic 'Cracking the Game' or more popularly known as the '*Kya-Seekha* (what did you learn)' ad film. 'We wanted to do something different from

run-of-the-mill ads. For us, Unacademy is all about learning. So how do we integrate learning with cricket was the question, all the while keeping it fun and fast-paced as our target audience is students. As a part of the sponsorship, we had access to all the match footage for promotional purposes. We thought why not use that and stitch a story around learning. We drew a correlation between different scientific concepts and the game.'

The first step was to write the script. Once that was written, Unacademy had to scout for appropriate footage. So, every day, the Marketing team would sit and watch the footage to pick such moments. 'We would keep doing this every single day for weeks. We would then share that footage with our agency and they would help create a film. Of course, new footage was coming in every day. So, till the last day, our agency was updating the video. The footage had to align perfectly with the script. For example, we had Dhoni's footage and his hand motions aligned with making a right-angled triangle. So, we used that for the Pythagoras theorem!'

The end result was a high-speed montage of a few of IPL's most memorable moments to a catchy tune. The ad starts with a voiceover saying, '*Oh student log, is IPL se kya seekha* (Hey students, what did you learn from the IPL)?' It went on to map everything from mathematical formulae to physics' laws.[31] It was a first-of-its-kind film in India. Most of the brands use such prime-time rights to talk about their product offering and make a sales pitch. It was an audacious bet by the company

[31]'Unacademy's Viral Ad Draws a Correlation Between Students' Desire to Learn and On-Field Cricket Action', *Business Insider*, 10 November 2021, https://www.businessinsider.in/advertising/brands/news/unacademys-viral-ad-draws-a-correlation-between-students-desire-to-learn-and-on-field-cricket-action/articleshow/79148201.cms. Accessed on 17 December 2021.

and till the last minute, Karan had no clue if it would pay off. Even within the company, opinions were divided. Some loved it, some didn't.

The 75-seconds ad film premiered on 8 November and within 24 hours, all doubts were put to rest when it clocked 2.8 million views on Twitter, with close to 8,000 retweets and 45,000 favourites. The film, loved by students, media and experts alike, was lauded especially for its product-first approach. Many compared it to Nike ads in storytelling and editing—a towering compliment for an Indian company.

Unacademy would go on to become an official sponsor of the IPL in 2021 as well. This time, they would break all the ceilings for brand integration and set new precedents for marketing in India. Combining Gaurav's flair for integration with Karan's eye for storytelling, Unacademy came up with advertisements which take place inside the commentator box. There's a short match clip, cut to Harsha Bhogle and Sunil Gavaskar (or other brand ambassadors) chatting in the box where they are discussing the match but also subtly referring to Unacademy's benefits, cut to the Unacademy banner on the ground.[32] The crisp editing made the whole ad look like a part of the live match itself and this led to interesting reactions from the audience. The brilliance of the campaign lies in its seamless continuity—the commercials would appear usually at the end of ad breaks and start with footage from the match. Many viewers who would disperse off in the ad breaks would come back running as soon as the ad started only to realize the match is yet to resume.

Many viewers loved it, some were frustrated by it but

---

[32]'Unacademy Hijacks the Commentary Box in the New Campaign for IPL 2021', *Media Samosa*, 14 April 2021, https://mediasamosa.com/2021/04/14/unacademy-ipl-2021-campaign/. Accessed on 17 December 2021.

nobody could ignore it. Karan says, 'The whole point of brand campaigns is to start conversations and have people talk about it. And, on that yardstick, the ads were a massive success.'

WORKING WITH GOVERNMENTS

'In a sector like education, you cannot ignore the government's role,' Karan says. With brand campaigns doing well and their Marketing team gaining confidence, Karan decided to figure out ways to work with the government. He had been thinking about working with the government for some time but knew it was a different ball game altogether. He was used to closing deals with private companies, partners, vendors and media channels but government officials work very differently. He floated around an opening for director of Government Relations and ended up interviewing Sumanta Dey who was working at Flipkart in those days. Since it is a new kind of role where start-ups do not have clear expectations, Karan asked him to prepare a presentation on his interpretation of this function.

Sumanta knew what government collaboration could look like in e-commerce but education was new for him as well. So, he did a deep dive into Unacademy's offerings, government's initiatives in education and how they can mutually benefit each other. Instead of making the presentation for the function of government relations alone, he made the presentation for a function of Corporate Affairs, which also included public policy, PR, Corporate Social Responsibility (CSR), sustainability, etc. 'I added milestones that we can achieve in nine months, 18 months and 36 months, and showed a long-term path. I think Karan really liked that.'

For the uninitiated, the Corporate Affairs team is responsible for all internal and external relations management

with central and local governments and quasi-government bodies. An increasing scrutiny of online businesses, 24x7 news coverage and social media activism has made this role more critical than ever before. In 2018, Facebook appointed Nick Clegg as the company's new VP, Global Affairs and Communications. Clegg had served as a British MP and deputy prime minister of the UK. High-growth start-ups have been known to pay attention to this function mostly as a reactionary measure when governments pass any regulation that is detrimental to business. Or, as in Facebook's case, the function became critical when the company was drawing flak because security concerns and its lack of moderation.

Unacademy, however, is in a sector that is looked at favourably by the State. Building a team proactively to work with the government, therefore, made sense. At Flipkart, Sumanta had been assisting the senior vice president (SVP) and chief corporate affairs officer (CCAO) find ways to collaborate with the government and deal with e-commerce regulations. At Unacademy, he joined as the director, Corporate Affairs in July 2020. There was no one to guide him. This gave him a wide canvas to experiment with. Soon, he was immersed in his new role with full sincerity. He started conversations with the government of Karnataka to help out students in government colleges crack exams such as railways, banking and SSC which can help them land jobs directly.

'In education, like many other sectors in India, you cannot grasp the extent of any problem you're trying to solve unless you go to its grassroots level. For an edtech company, you cannot make a true impact until you speak to the government.' As the conversations went on, he started understanding the non-obvious aspects of the issues around education. 'I'm speaking to a government official in a large state who has hundreds of schools under his management. He told me

that oftentimes the issue of a digital divide between the well-to-do and the needy drives decision-making which leads to procurement of thousands of devices at huge cost to the exchequer. But buying devices is only a fraction of the solution because unless you have landing applications, educational content that is periodically refreshed, etc., the devices have little use. Purchasing devices is a one-time exercise, while content and learning outcomes partnership requires much deeper operational collaboration. At the same time, I see an innate appreciation of the need for technology in education. I have not yet met a single official who has been dismissive of the work being done by reputed edtech platforms. What matters is finding the right solution.'

Sumanta realized that giving away subscriptions would also be akin to taking a shortcut. He, instead, started working with government officials to come up with a plan that is actionable and will directly benefit the students. In his first victory, Unacademy signed an MoU with the Department of Collegiate and Technical Education, government of Karnataka, to conduct a series of aptitude and scholarship tests in the state. The most meritorious and purposeful students in these tests would then receive scholarships to study for a competitive government exam on Unacademy. It is a win-win for both parties. Apart from the goodwill with the government, Unacademy has an opportunity to access and impact a much larger section of the student population. Previously, their scholarship tests were taken by 50,000 students but now they can reach many lakhs of students studying in government schools. For Unacademy, it is an altogether new traction channel. 'The benefit is threefold— reputation, social and business,' says Sumanta.

In October 2021, Unacademy signed an MoU with the government of Tripura leading to a unique partnership in which Unacademy would help prepare 250 girl students

from Tripura for the NDA exam. It is worth nothing that the Government of India, in a historic decision, has decided to allow women into the NDA from 2022 onwards[33], which has been a male bastion till now. 'The power of Unacademy's platform and our vision to democratize education comes alive through such partnerships,' Sumanta says. 'With this partnership, we can reach out to and prepare girl students, not just from Agartala—which, because of its capital-city status, already has some coaching institutes—but even those who live in far-flung, hard-to-reach areas of the state. I believe even if one of these 250 aspirants crack the NDA, the whole exercise was worth it.'

Sumanta is talking to other state governments including that of Jammu and Kashmir, Odisha and Jharkhand, to strike up similar initiatives or find newer areas of collaboration. 'If the good work continues, our voices are more likely to be heard when India's education policies are being shaped. What can be more satisfying?' Unacademy's goal of building a brand that truly democratizes education goes through the bureaucratic hallways and Sumanta is making sure the journey remains frictionless.

---

[33]'Women Can Join NDA, Centre Informs Supreme Court', *Hindustan Times*, 8 September 2021, https://www.hindustantimes.com/india-news/women-cadets-will-be-allowed-to-join-nda-centre-informs-supreme-court-101631087888411.html. Accessed on 17 December 2021.

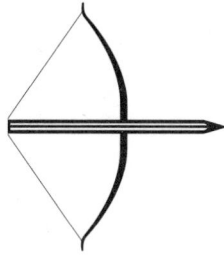

EIGHT

SUPERPOWER 7:
VELOCITY AS A MOAT

How Unacademy Consistently Stays Ahead of Its Competition

The Indian edtech sector was scaling new heights. On 13 January 2021, Amazon announced the launch of Amazon Academy to help students prepare for competitive entrance exams like the IIT-JEE by providing curated learning content, live lectures and assessment material.[34] The COVID-19 lockdowns increased funding in edtech start-ups by four times, as compared to the previous year. A significant piece of the funding resulted in consolidation efforts such as the behemoth BYJU'S acquisition of other funded players like Toppr and veterans like Akash Education.[35]

---

[34]'"Amazon Academy" Launched to Help Students Prepare for Competitive Entrance Exams', Amazon, 13 January 2021, https://www.aboutamazon.in/news/innovation/amazon-academy-launched-to-help-students-prepare-for-competitive-entrance-exams. Accessed on 17 December 2021.
[35]Bhalla, Tarush. 'BYJU'S Continues Acquisition Spree, Acquires Toppr and Great Learning', 26 *Mint,* July 2021, https://www.livemint.com/education/news/byjus-continues-acquisition-spree-acquires-toppr-and-great-learning-11627218110917.html. Accessed on 17 December 2021;

Amazon's entry was a loud and clear foghorn that it won't let go of any big, price-sensitive market even if it is something as unexpected as test preparation. Unacademy knew it had to compete against well-funded players and to be fair, it had been doing exactly that for some time.

With his first-principles and original thinking, Gaurav made bold bets such as the path-breaking subscription model that catapulted Unacademy ahead, leaving its competitors playing the catch-up game. Paul Graham said in an old essay dating all the way back to 2001, 'Software is a very competitive business, prone to natural monopolies. A company that gets software written faster and better will, all other things being equal, put its competitors out of business.'[36] In a sector like edtech that doesn't leave much scope for differentiation in the offering, speed is an unbeatable advantage. All things being equal, a company that executes faster is the company that stays ahead.

However, imagine the scenario that one moves fast—very fast—but, in the wrong direction. A visual of a fast-moving Aston Martin from a James Bond movie entering a highway on the wrong side of the road should do the trick. Although the nice explosion on the screen is likely to boost box-office collections, wrong direction in real life is hardly going to be forgiving, forget rewarding! Relying on speed alone may, therefore, prove to be an impulsive and premature decision. The students of physics will identify speed as a scalar quantity defined by the rate at which an object covers distance. There

Sneha Shah and Alnoor Peermohamed. 'BYJU'S Acquires Aakash Educational Services in Nearly $1-Billion Deal', *The Economic Times*, 6 April 2021, https://economictimes.indiatimes.com/tech/startups/byjus-to-acquire-aakash-educational-services-in-700-million-deal/articleshow/81910598.cms?from=mdr. Accessed on 17 December 2021.

[36]Graham, Paul. *Hackers and Painters: Big Ideas from the Computer Age*, O'Reilly Media, 2004.

is a better term that we can use for our intent here—velocity. Simply put, velocity is speed with a direction.

Speed in the right direction is the moat that can lead to spectacular outcomes for start-ups. Unacademy orients itself with data and then achieves unparalleled results by speed of execution.

DIRECTION COMES FROM THE RIGHT DATA

Vivek's eyes were glued to the big TV screen in his office when I walked in. The big white screen had a column of numbers for various examination categories. Vivek was studying today's revenue numbers for each category and the percentage increase over the previous day. 'Yeah, we are a numbers-driven organization,' he acknowledged while switching it off and turning his attention to me. Unacademy heavily uses Slack for internal communications. Slack has different channels for important metrics tracked by different teams. The numbers are updated transparently every 15 minutes so that everybody knows where they stand. Being the one responsible for all profit-and-loss activities, Vivek avidly tracks the revenue numbers, number of subscribers and so on. Apart from the team-specific metrics, everybody can see customer satisfaction ratings such as learner NPS and negative reviews on common channels.

Unacademy is not unique in its pursuit of the metrics. Every tech start-up today is obsessed with data. However, being obsessed with data and knowing what data to look at are two different things. At Startup School (a free online programme run by YCombinator for founders actively pursuing their own start-up), start-ups are asked to decide one single primary metric (sometimes referred to as North Star metric) and then update it weekly. Focusing on one single primary metric helps the

founders not get lost in the data. This primary metric for most of the early stage start-ups ends up being revenue or active users. Once supplemented with three to four secondary metrics, they can get a good 360-degree view of the health of any company. For example, focusing on the primary metric of active users alone can be misleading if you don't track the retention rate.

The cost of badly chosen metrics can devolve a company's growth pursuit into a futile chase. If not checked, the worst-case scenario can lead to what is known as the cobra effect. In 2016, Wells Fargo, a respected bank in the US, introduced and impressed overly-ambitious sales goals to be met by its sales force. On the face of losing their careers upon not meeting such quotas, few employees ended up opening millions of fraudulent savings and checking accounts on behalf of Wells Fargo clients without their consent. The bank faced a penalty of $185 million as a result of the illegal activity and billions in lawsuits thereafter.

The cobra effect describes an extreme case of perverse incentives whereby an adopted strategy or solution to a problem makes the problem worse due to unseen consequences. The origins of the name of this concept are very interesting. Once upon a time, the officials of the British government were terrified by a large number of venomous cobra snakes in Delhi. To solve the problem, the government offered bounties for dead cobras. Bring a dead cobra and get your reward. Little did they know that enterprising people eventually started breeding cobras so that they could kill more of those and collect more rewards. The scheme that was originally intended to reduce the number of cobras ended up incentivizing people to grow more of them.

Many companies in the edtech sector are frowned upon for practising aggressive sales-driven growth. Unacademy, as the founders profess, is trying to stay away from such tactics.

One way to achieve this is to focus on the right metrics. As has been described, Gaurav made learner satisfaction the core metric for everyone in the company. Whereas a metric like revenue could incentivize employees to take shortcuts that could hurt the company in the long run (akin to the Wells Fargo example), a metric like learner satisfaction is harder to manipulate.

We looked at how Balaji manages a team called Learner NPS, which is responsible for tracking and improving learner satisfaction. His North Star metric is 'Plus subscription satisfaction ratings'. In simpler words, it equates to how satisfied a subscriber is with the Unacademy experience. He explains, 'We ask the learners to rate their experience on a scale of zero to five. This is collected every 28 days on the app and it's a moving cohort. We track it for each category and then we calculate the rating for overall TestPrep business. Our target is to maintain a minimum of 4.3 stars out of five for every category. What this means is that 80 per cent or more of my categories should have a subscriber satisfaction rating between four and five. So for instance, our IIT-JEE rating is at 4.31 right now, our UPSC rating is close to 4.29 and our GATE rating is at 4.35. So we know, broadly, things are going fine.'

While numbers are the driving force, it is important not to get bogged down in them. 'If a category is at 4.29 today, then we don't say that this category is doing badly. We instead look at it and ask, "Do we know what's wrong with this category and are we taking actions to fix it?"' The next step after tracking is to move the needle forward. 'I ask myself how can I get our average to 4.4 instead of 4.3 or how do I move this category from 4.5 to 4.6.'

This might boil down to noticing the comments that the learners leave or asking for feature suggestions. Balaji cites an example in the IIT-JEE category, 'We found a clear gap. Our

classes and tests are fantastic but we don't have notes, and notes are critical for IIT-JEE because you cannot go through a large textbook; you need very crisp notes that you can read on your phone or you can download and view. We identified the gap and there is no quick solution but we have started working on it. I think we are now at a stage where 33 per cent of our IIT-JEE notes are live and soon, it will be 100 per cent.' Balaji is hopeful that that would boost the category rating even higher.

DATA MEANS QUICKER COURSE CORRECTION

Unacademy uses monthly (weekly in some cases) goal setting and key performance indicators (KPIs) for tracking the performance of its employees. One of the KPIs that Punith Reddy (director, Business) was assigned to was to grow the paid subscribers on the Unacademy app. One month, he noticed that his monthly target looked unreachable according to Slack projections. He still had one week to go. 'We came up with a surprise scholarship test wherein students could compete for scholarships and other prizes. These scholarship tests have been a great way to attract new users to check out our app. Once they sign up on the platform, they can see our vast selection of courses, watch a few free classes and then eventually become subscribers.'

Given the past performance of their scholarship test events, Punith can say with enough confidence that such a test would deliver the results he is looking for. But that's not all. When you are on top of your metrics day in and day out, you start connecting the dots in a nuanced way. Punith takes the use case further to explain.

Let's say even after the scholarship announcement, the number of subscribers are falling slightly short. Punith used the 'hook' of scholarship tests but the hook has not

reached the audience as wide as he had hoped. How can he leverage existing resources at his disposal to increase the reach of scholarship announcements? Another metric he has been tracking is the number of views per video for different educators on their YouTube channel.

'We can basically ask one of our top educators who has a big following on YouTube to just go live and announce that we have a big test coming. He can also add a more personal touch, such as "we have created some challenging questions and you should take this test!" He might even offer to personally felicitate the top scorers virtually, etc. Once he says that, there's a very good chance that we will get a boost in users. So, there are immediate interventions you can do if you know your data.' Punith watches his data every day, so he knows who his top educators are and who commands the kind of viewership that would lead to immediate enrollments.

This is a simplistic example inspired from real events. But, there is something deeper going on here and brings us to another exciting concept—'input metrics.'

HOW UNACADEMY USES INPUT METRICS

One of the companies that is infamous for its non-revenue metrics is Amazon. In his letter to his shareholders for the year 2009, Amazon's CEO Jeff Bezos wrote that 'In the 452 goals [mentioned above in the statement], the terms net income, gross profit or margin and operating profit are not used even once.'[37] The problem with revenue or profit as the sole metric is that one cannot really control them directly. Even if revenue is higher this week and the team doesn't know why, tracking it is hardly going to deliver any useful insight.

[37]Bogos, Jeff. '2009 Letter to shareholders', Amazon, https:cutt.ly/DAiScbO. Accessed on 2 March 2022.

In their book *Working Backwards*, long-time Amazon employees Colin Bryar and Bill Carr talk about five mechanisms that played a pivotal role in driving the success of the trillion dollar behemoth that Amazon has become. One of them is 'metrics: manage your inputs, not your outputs'.[38] Amazon relies heavily on identifying correct, controllable input metrics even if it means following a lengthier and costlier process of trial and error. The examples of such controllable input metrics that they cite include reducing the 'internal costs' so that Amazon can affordably lower product prices, adding 'new items for sale' on the website or reducing the 'standard delivery time'. All these metrics, when optimized, will deliver the desired output metrics such as the monthly revenue. The authors reinforce that output metrics show results whereas input metrics provide guidance. So, instead of focusing on output metrics, it is better to track controllable input metrics.

Gaurav quotes a simpler example to explain the same. 'I know people who are looking for jobs in my network. I tell them that instead of focusing on getting X number of job offers, why don't you focus on giving 10 times more interviews in the next 60 days? If you give so many interviews, the offers will follow.' The idea is to focus on what you can control. In this regard, controllable input metric is the Silicon Valley equivalent of ancient wisdom from the Hindu scripture, The Gita—'कर्मण्येवाधिकारस्ते मा फलेषु कदाचन' which translates to 'on your duty only, you have a right. Not on the fruits of it, ever.' Like Amazon, Unacademy is shifting its focus from output metrics to input metrics.

Let's go back to Punith's example from the last section.

---

[38]Colin Bryar and Bill Carr. *Working Backwards: Insights, Stories and Secrets from Inside Amazon*, St. Martin's Press, 2021.

As we saw, he is responsible for growing the 'number of paid subscribers' on the Unacademy app. As a director in the Business team in those days, he had a team of 30 people under him. Punith tracks the funnel of paid subscribers. At some point, almost every paid subscriber has been a free user who watched a few free courses and then decided to upgrade to a subscription plan. 'It tells me that if more users sign up on the app, more of them are likely to upgrade at some point.' Going further up this funnel, a major portion of sign-ups come from people who browse through Unacademy YouTube channels. 'So, I know that if I increase YouTube views, I can generate more free sign-ups and then, more paid subscriptions. What I can do is divide my basic KPI into smaller input KPIs and assign them to different people in my team. This also helped me decide the KPIs for my team.'

The application of KPIs trickles down neatly. Continuing with the above case, let's say a deputy of Punith is given the KPI to do 40 million YouTube views for a particular category next month. One can either post more videos to get these views or increase the views per video to meet the target. The deputy might pay more educators to create more videos and increase the eyeballs this month. However, there may be a budget constraint next month which means that the deputy cannot pay more educators to drive more videos. Instead, he would look for qualitative ways to improve the SEO and click through rate (CTR) to make sure the videos attract more views and clicks.

The deputy can make it more granular and look at the views generated by different kinds of videos being posted on the YouTube channel. It was observed that non-academic videos including fun or motivational content garner higher views per video. To meet his aggressive number of views this month, the deputy might decide to amp up the non-academic content on the channel. Or he might end up taking the 'announce a

scholarship test' route as we discussed in the previous section.

The number of videos, conducting scholarship tests and the SEO (views/video) become the input metrics or levers for the YouTube channel views which becomes the growth lever for the number of new sign-ups which, in turn, is a growth lever for the number of subscribers. Identifying such input levers across the board helps Unacademy stay on course towards its goals without getting lost.

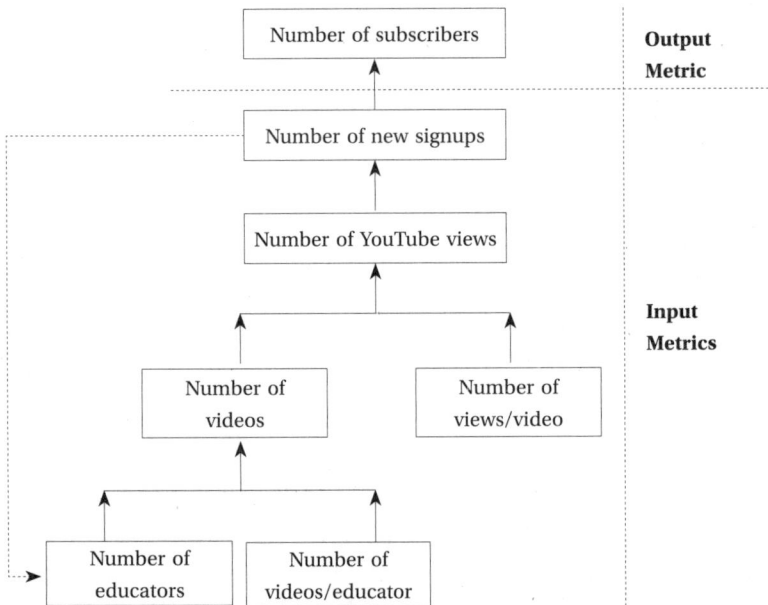

Fig. 1. Example use case of input and output metrics.

What we are doing here is going down the funnel to identify the input metrics or levers for the bigger output metric—'number of subscribers' (see Fig. 1). In fact, the 'number of videos' can be improved further by onboarding more educators on the channel. Interestingly, as the number of sign-ups increases, it again attracts more educators to join the platform, thereby

completing a nice cycle. Punith does not have direct control over the 'number of subscribers', but he can control how many educators are onboarded, how many videos are produced and so on. Each team identifies such input metrics with regards to its primary output metric and creates KPIs around those input metrics.

Similarly, Balaji can pander to his learner satisfaction metric by controlling the levers of 'number of calls made to the users who left a bad rating', 'response times on the customer support chats', etc. On the other end, the Marketing team tracks the number of views on their brand campaigns. Apart from tracking, the leaders make sure that the KPIs are aggressive and that the teams are never settling in their comfort zones.

Using data as a compass keeps Unacademy on its course towards its iconic goals and prepares it to execute at a speed seen in very few start-ups.

BUILDING A MINDSET FOR SPEED

When the world was crippled by the deadly spread of the novel coronavirus in 2020, the very existence of life came into question. The world's best minds committed to work out a solution in the collective spirit of humanity. It was Pfizer/BioNTech which produced the first vaccine to receive emergency-use listing from the World Health Organization (WHO) in December 2020.

Normally, vaccine development takes eight to 10 years. Previously, the fastest vaccine ever developed was the mumps vaccine (Merck licensed Mumpsvax) which took four years to come to market. Let that sink in. The first-known case of COVID-19 was traced to 17 November 2019. Pfizer launched a vaccine for this deadly virus in approximately one small year. This is mind-bending speed for something as complicated

as a vaccine. Their efforts were rewarded when the vaccine generated $3.5 billion in revenue for Pfizer in the first three months of 2021 alone.

In a self-authored *Harvard Business Review* article, Pfizer CEO Albert Bourla sheds light on how his team achieved the impossible. He writes:

> We decided to work on several vaccine candidates in parallel instead of testing the most promising ones in sequence, as was usual. This was financially risky but, again, would generate results more quickly. We also declined government funding, to liberate our scientists from bureaucracy and protect them from unnecessary slowdowns.[39]

But these are tactical choices. He talks about changing the mindset itself:

> When you set a huge goal, you must encourage the out-of-the-box thinking required to achieve it. What worked in the past won't build you a new reality. In the spring of 2020 various teams presented senior leaders and me with multiple ideas for solving particular problems: 'One, two, three. This is what has been done before.' We kept asking them for a fourth, fifth, and sixth choice, and creatively, they complied. After a few months it became a habit. People brainstormed new options on their own.[40]

In the early days, a start-up's agility is the function of the agility of its founders (in particular, the leading founder). In later days,

---

[39]Bourla, Albert. 'The CEO of Pfizer on Developing a Vaccine in Record Time', *Harvard Business Review,* May–June 2021, https://hbr.org/2021/05/the-ceo-of-pfizer-on-developing-a-vaccine-in-record-time. Accessed on 17 December 2021.
[40]Ibid.

however, a company's agility is the function of its culture and collective mindset. Gaurav has always been a human dynamo and a quick decision maker. With his assertive personality, he has been able to ingrain the same alacrity in his leadership—part through inspiration, part through enforcement.

Ankita Tandon, previous director of Business, told me, 'Having worked at multiple tech organizations, I can say hand to heart that you won't see this speed of execution anywhere else. I never even imagined that such a speed was possible. I learnt this at Unacademy.'

However, embracing speed is awkward if you are not used to it. Archit Nanda had almost quit his internship at Unacademy when the going got a bit too fast. A Mechanical Engineering student at IIT Bombay, Archit was interviewing for a strategy internship with Unacademy in April 2020. Since Archit came through a referral, Gaurav ended up personally interviewing him. After a few brief questions about his activities and projects, Gaurav gave him a market research assignment. 'He wanted me to make a competitive benchmarking presentation for a Chinese edtech firm. And he wanted it done in the next 24 hours. It was really hard to find any information because Chinese websites do not get translated well. So, I had to look into their SEC filings and dig out all the data. Anyway, I worked really hard that night and sent him the PPT file on time,' Archit told me.

Gaurav looked at Archit's submission and told him that he liked it but he would rate it at five out of 10. Next, he offered him the internship and asked for Archit's expectations on the stipend. When Archit mentioned that he is okay with the company's standard offer, Gaurav told him not to be diplomatic and quote a number. When Archit finally quoted a number, Gaurav counter-offered with a slightly higher number.

Archit was excited at the prospect of working with Gaurav but before he could breathe a sigh of relief, Gaurav had assigned him tasks for the next 15–20 days. On top of this, he also wanted him to redo the presentation within the next three days and make it a nine out of 10 this time. 'This was all happening on WhatsApp, and he types really fast. In five minutes, he had assigned me all of this work.' Archit started with gusto but soon found himself meandering an uphill road of Gaurav's expectations. 'He gave me a task to research some of the bigger Chinese edtech apps. He wanted me to buy their subscriptions, understand their offerings and present a report to him. And I was like, how am I going to download a Chinese app and understand it? I really had no clue how to even start. So, I reached out to Gaurav and told him that these are the challenges and I don't think I can do it.'

Archit was taken aback at Gaurav's response. 'If you want to work with me, I don't want to hear no for an answer. You have all the resources at your disposal. You can spend money, you can hire people, figure out how to do it,' Gaurav had messaged him. The next day, Archit's thoughts were racing. 'I knew that working with Gaurav was very rewarding but I was also thinking that I am just an intern. How do I hire Chinese-speaking interns, you know? I felt really overwhelmed and did not think I could fulfil his expectations.' After much thought, Archit sent Gaurav a message expressing his apprehension about being able to perform in his role and offered to give Garurav recommendation of his batchmates who could do the job.

If Gaurav had been harsh in his expectations till now, he was equally unfiltered in responding to Archit's concerns. He told him that he had liked his work and he hoped Archit would continue, but if not, he wished him the best. This was the first time Archit realized that Gaurav actually likes his

work. 'That five out of 10 comment had really thrown me. But then, I learned that his expectations are different from other people. You can never really be 10 on 10 for him. And then he added, "Usually people don't say no to working with me, but it's cool." And I was taken aback again. Here was a CEO, spending so much time on an intern, and if he thinks I can do this, then I should try harder. That was the only thought in my head. So, I shared my concerns and we discussed how we could make it work.'

Archit took back his resignation that day and continued working with Unacademy long after his internship was over. He became a part of the CEO's office team which works closely with Gaurav. Once Archit espoused Unacademy's way of working, he found the work extremely fulfilling as well as rewarding. Many young employees are hungry to get their hands dirty and do real projects. On that front, Archit would find his learnings unparalleled.

IMPATIENCE FOR ACTION, NOT RESULTS

Hemesh vividly remembers the crazy month of January 2019. 'Until the last second, we were fixing bugs but we went live on our target date. It was 29 January, I think... yes, 29 January.'

In December 2018, Unacademy's 'paid live classes' product had generated a monthly revenue of ₹3 crore. In the last week of December, however, Gaurav had announced that they were shutting down that product and launching a new subscription model. He and Hemesh had even set a launch date for it— 29 January. Switching business models required non-trivial intervention on the tech as well as business front. The older product had to be shut down and Gaurav needed some time to negotiate the existing contracts with the educators. 'Most of the people were out for New Year's celebration. So, we could

actually only start working on 2 January,' Hemesh told me. A month was the bare minimum they would have required. A month is what they gave themselves—not a day more.

Hemesh informed his team (which was less than 25 engineers at the time) that they were up for a new challenge together. Steve Jobs, in his time, was infamous for setting audacious goals in front of Apple and NeXT engineers. But, instead of rebelling, his engineers were known to deliver within deadlines that other companies deemed impossible. Brent Schlender aptly described the phenomenon in his bestselling biography *Becoming Steve Jobs*—'Steve understood that engineers, at heart, are problem solvers. They thrive on digging their way out of sinkholes, especially the gnarly kind with no clear path forward.'[41]

Hemesh personally prefers to think of new projects as challenges to conquer rather than tasks with tedious deadlines. He realized that his engineers were the same. Instead of telling his team that they have to extend their working hours, he told them how the new product would solve their biggest headaches, how it was their biggest test of innovation yet and he asked them, 'Can we do it?' The response was a unanimous 'Yes.'

Hemesh brainstormed the features required for the new product with his team and analysed how they could reuse parts from the older one. 'Earlier it was like a marketplace. A user could browse through the courses, look at the educator's profile and buy any course individually. Each course had its own number of seats, starting date and price. We could reuse some of it but we needed a lot of new modules to make the subscriptions work—subscription management, access management to determine who can access what courses,

---

[41]Brent Schlender and Rick Tetzeli. *Becoming Steve Jobs: The Evolution of a Reckless Upstart into a Visionary Leader,* Crown Business, 2016.

checkout management to introduce multiple payment options, etc. But more importantly, the design itself needed to be revamped.' Needless to say, both the front end and back end needed significant tinkering. Hemesh's Tech and Product team got to work.

That one month flew by and before they knew, the deadline was hovering over their shoulders. On the evening of 29 January, the whole team gathered in the office and put up a countdown timer on the big screen for the launch at midnight. 'People were hanging out, having fun and working, too. The energy was electric. There was a point when the countdown timer was going down and we were still fixing bugs,' Hemesh adds with a chuckle. 'When the entire team goes through a strong challenge together, it makes the bond stronger. People wanted to contribute and not get left behind. They didn't want to sit on the sidelines. It was one of those times that brought us closer as a team.'

Ankita Tandon remembers her own share of impossible deadlines. 'COVID-19 cases were steadily rising and we were planning to start remote working around 16 March 2020. People were not going to the office anymore and just figuring out how to work effectively from their homes. On 17th morning, Gaurav called me and told me, "Fuck it, let's launch the K–12 category." We had been toying with it for some time. He said this is a watershed moment for us. "We don't know how long this lockdown will last." Let's not overthink it, let's just launch and see where it goes. In the evening, we did a quick huddle to discuss the details. I put together the team, a basic structure of what was to be done and Gaurav gave us 1 April 2020 as a deadline. And we made it, you know. The beta version of the K–12 category was launched on 1 April.' Ankita takes a pause before adding, 'I think that was when Gaurav's "I will not listen to no" attitude just percolated through the

team.' There was no looking back.

Everybody who has worked with Gaurav and Hemesh has their own stories of imbibing their taste for speed. Arushi Mudgal (HRBP of Technology) recounts the tale from one of her early days when she was about to set the organizational structure for the Technology and Product team. 'Hemesh and I sat on a Monday to think about it. There were no designation metrics or competencies defined for promotions at that time. I thought we would get it done gradually that week. Hemesh started brainstorming and three hours later, we had come up with the designation metrics for the entire Product and Tech organization! I still cannot believe that such an exercise had been done in three hours.' Mayank Garg reflects on his time working under Gaurav, 'He is clear about what he wants and he clarifies his vision to the minutest details, which is great. It allows the team to work very swiftly.' Hemesh agrees, 'We spend a lot of time thinking and developing clarity first. Once we have that, we are able to move extremely fast.'

One might mistake speed for impatience. As Naval Ravikant once tweeted, 'Impatience for actions, patience for results'[42], the distinction lies in the driving force behind the impatience. If a manager checks in every day to ask an employee why a sales objective has not been reached, his impatience for results can be seen as harassment. But, if the manager enables his employee to understand the right input levers and checks in on whether necessary actions are being taken to move those levers, his impatience can be productive. Controllable input metrics in combination with impatience for acting on those metrics has been yielding excellent results for Unacademy.

---

[42]@naval, Twitter, 18 June 2018, https://twitter.com/naval/status/10085332 13919133697?lang=en. Accessed on 17 December 2021.

SPEED COMES FROM PODS AND 'PROCESSIFICATION'

Apart from inculcating a mindset for aggressive deadlines and quick action, Unacademy made several choices in the way teams are structured and work together to expedite the execution. Speed in innovation or new initiatives is derived from smaller teams (or pods) whereas the speed in repetitive tasks is enabled via 'processification' such as creating playbooks and automations.

Let's look at the speed in hiring itself. When the newly-appointed head of HR, Tina Balachandran, had to quickly expand the Sales team, she knew it was not possible to do it manually. There was no time for expanding the in-house recruiting team either. So, Tina, Ankita and Karthik (head of Sales) came up with a process to expedite the hiring process by using technology. 'Earlier, we were manually screening, which was time-consuming. We switched to a video profiling process wherein the candidate had to submit a video essay to introduce themselves on a tool called Loom. We started using that to screen people and also maintain it as a profiler record for ourselves so that later on, if any manager wanted to check out a candidate, he could just look at their video. We could check for attitude and personality without individually talking to every candidate. It was a game changer. We still use it in our sales hiring process,' Tina told me.

Further, they created practices to ensure hiring decisions were made faster. Every interview was conducted by a panel consisting of four to five different interviewers. Each member was asked to individually rate the candidate and then the scores were revealed all at once within an agreed-upon time frame. If anyone rated the interviewee below eight, he would not end up being hired. Such processes helped HR to rapidly

hire in the earlier days when the goal was not to do things perfectly but to keep moving. Later on, experienced leaders like Umesh Bude helped formalize the hiring process more effectively so as to help hire 150 plus engineers in a short period of time. The idea is to set processes and perfect them over a period of time rather than getting stuck in analysis paralysis.

Unacademy relies heavily on playbooks for any high-stake task which involves team coordination and is time-sensitive. The Unacademy app offers courses for 70 plus examination categories, some of which were launched within highly-compressed deadlines (such as K–12 beta launched by Ankita). Over the years, Unacademy has perfected the launch of any new category down to a T using launch playbooks. These playbooks define which categories to start, where to find educators, how to find them, what are the metrics to look at, what does the growth path look like, how to go about scaling the category, what checkpoints to keep in mind while scaling the categories, the kind of positioning of the content we want, all of these things. Teams might change, people in-charge might change, but the work doesn't stop when you have such playbooks in place.

Lastly, Unacademy is minimizing the number of touchpoints within and between the teams to enable swift decision-making. Taking his cue from Amazon's famous 'two-pizza rule', Hemesh decided to strip down the size of the Tech teams to the level where the entire team can be fed by not more than two pizzas. Such a small team size, as Jeff Bezos realized, has multiple benefits. In an interesting experiment conducted by researchers Bradley Staats, Katherine Milkman and Craig Fox, it was discovered that when tasked to build the same Lego figure, two-person teams took 36 minutes while four-person teams took 52 minutes to finish—over 44 per cent longer. The researchers went on to publish a paper called

'The Team Scaling Fallacy: Underestimating the Declining Efficiency of Larger Teams' which shows that as team size increases, people increasingly underestimate the number of labour hours required to complete projects.[43] Combine this with the ease of communication, coordination and intimacy possible in smaller teams and one comes to a conclusion that the ideal team size is six to 10 members. Moving to 'two-pizza'-sized teams and small pods has allowed rapid experiments and innovation to thrive in the Technology and Product teams.

On the other hand, the Business organization noticed that their content always has to be up to date if they want to win the trust of their learners. Punith explains, 'Let's say the education minister has announced that NEET-UG exam will only happen once this year, not twice like IIT-JEE and we are postponing the date from 3 May to 1 August. When you have such an important notification or update, you immediately have to come up with a video to explain the impact of this news.' This requires their educators to be uber-responsive in making their content. Earlier, the category teams had a few relationship managers handling a bulk of the educators. This made it difficult for the relationship manager to catch hold of a particular educator and coordinate the content creation as fast as they wanted to. So, the category teams ended up assigning dedicated relationship managers for each educator. Punith adds, 'These relationship managers talk to their assigned educator daily to plan the content. So, if a news update video needs to be created, the relevant manager passes it along to

[43]Staats, B.R., et al. 'The Team Scaling Fallacy: Underestimating the Declining Efficiency of Larger Teams', *Organizational Behavior and Human Decision Processes*, Vol. 118, No. 2, Elsevier 2012, pp. 132–142, https://doi.org/10.1016/j.obhdp.2012.03.002. Accessed on 17 December 2021.

the educator who comes up with the video. All this can happen only if we work together on a daily basis which is only possible when we have enough relationship managers.'

Apart from the core teams, Gaurav has appointed a brigade of go-getters and generalists as a part of his CEO's office team. The team oversees anything that Gaurav deems important enough but doesn't have time to deal with himself. These may include issues that need escalation, user-facing features that need more research or simply experiments. Archit Nanda, a member of this team who report directly to Gaurav, shared that he has created and sent 530 plus documents to him over the past one and a half years. He recalls, 'For any particular feature we might just end up calling 500 to 1000 learners to understand the issues they're facing. Now, once you've called 1,000 learners for one feature or one product, I think you exhaust the number of insights that you can get. Then we compile the results and Gaurav picks up the points he likes best and forwards them to the relevant teams so that they can use them.' The team has become an expert on data crunching, drawing insights and enabling cross-teams ideation. Archit has learned that the whole purpose of his job is to enable Gaurav to execute faster. He makes sure to keep his reports or discussion documents leaner on text and heavier on visuals and lists so that Gaurav can quickly skim through them.

In one instance, the Marketing team needed something from the Business team and there were delays. The CEO's team stepped in and helped close the loop. With this team, Gaurav can now wield his wisdom on a diverse set of projects running throughout the company without spending as much time.

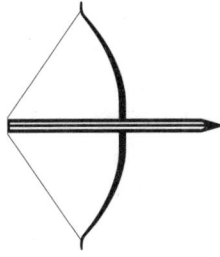

NINE

SUPERPOWER 8:
ATTRACTING THE MENTORS

How Unacademy Built an Enviable Team of Investors and Mentors

It was 2007. Gaurav looked at his watch again in annoyance. As soon as he saw Roman coming out of the tuition class, he blurted, 'I am going to be late again.' They hopped into the car, Gaurav praying that he reaches the school in time. This would be the typical daily routine for both of them in their teenage years as they would share rides to tuition classes and thereon to school. 'You are asking so many questions to the teachers, we always get late,' Gaurav would mutter with no response from Roman.

Roman was one of those typical frontbenchers who answered all the questions correctly and topped the exams. Gaurav initially saw him as an anti-social, uber-intelligent guy who acted beyond his years. Once or twice Gaurav had asked Roman's advice on a few of his academic queries and the way Roman had explained the concept to him had left a deep impression on Gaurav. Before he knew it, he was calling Roman whenever he faced a difficult situation—not just academics but also in his personal life. It was a particularly low and depressive

phase in his life when Gaurav started appreciating this unique camaraderie they shared. Roman would always pick up his calls, even late at night, to try to help him think straight. At times, it would mean just doling out words of wisdom—'you should eat healthy, don't ever smoke, don't ever drink, read every day' and so on. Gaurav recalls a particular tip, 'He had told me that at the end of every day, we should rate how well our day went. If the rating is low for consecutive days, that means we are doing something wrong.' These sermons are now popularly known as 'Roman's rituals' in the Unacademy community. Gaurav was perhaps the first recipient of it.

Most of the other kids were intimidated by Roman's academic prowess but Gaurav had never been shy. He saw a wise guy and had decided that he could learn from Roman. Roman might have shared his insights with other people as well but Gaurav was not a passive listener who would simply nod and go back to the same old way of doing things. He started appreciating and applying those pieces of advice.

People who have interacted closely with Gaurav, even those who are much senior to him, comment on being astounded by his capacity to learn and grow. What he did with Roman was only the beginning. Then, he repeated the same with the next successful person he would meet in his life; then with one more and again with more. This is how the eternal student in him transformed into one of the most successful entrepreneurs in India. Moreover, Unacademy has benefitted from the presence of strong mentors time and time again.

DEEPINDER GOYAL: *'KYUN MILNA HAI YAAR?'*

We hear stories about how Mark Zuckerberg was mentored by Steve Jobs or how Bill Gates benefitted from Warren Buffet's mentorship. The reality is more sobering. Once you are

already famous, you can get popular and successful people to agree to talk to you. Or, if you hail from a famed institute, it is easier for you to connect to other people who are also emotionally attached to the same institute. This is why IITians and BITSians benefit from the heavyweight names of their alma mater. But for an average person with no enviable pedigree, finding mentors is a grind. The story is no different for Gaurav Munjal. If you look at the list of angel investors or board members associated with Unacademy, you might mistakenly think Gaurav hails from a secret club where he met all these incredible people. Rest assured, he was rejected more times than one can imagine. And, if there indeed is a club that he is a member of, its name is 'hustle.'

Networking, like making money, is one of those activities Indians are conditioned to loathe. Everybody wants to do it but talking publicly about it is considered rude. While Westerners ask each other out for coffee chats or informational interviews all the time, these kinds of 'professional getting to know you' rituals simply do not work with Indians. On the one hand, remote relatives do not shy away from asking how much someone's kid is making. On the other, no one likes to meet, help out or advise a stranger. We are a strange society in that way. And this bizarre social dynamic stops a lot of people from finding help. One has to be thick-skinned to not take lack of responses or rejections personally. Gaurav Munjal, fortunately, never had that problem.

The young entrepreneur in Gaurav admired Deepinder Goyal and the way he was building Zomato. He wanted to meet him to get advice on building Unacademy. 'This is a guy who has built one of the largest consumer companies in India, so why not ask him directly? That is how I think,' Gaurav told me. But Deepinder was always too busy to meet. Gaurav kept emailing him and it was after the fourth email

that Deepinder replied in one line, '*Arre kyun milna hai yaar?
Apna kaam kar lo* (Why do you want to meet? Just focus on
your work).' Gaurav persisted. In January 2016, Gaurav was
attending a start-up event in Gurgaon and someone called
out his name. It was Deepinder. Although Unacademy had
got the nod from the angels for an investment of $500,000
by this time, it had not officially announced the round yet.
Gaurav started pitching to Deepinder with a hope if bringing
him in as an investor. It was a short meeting and Deepinder
asked him to email him. Gaurav went back to Bengaluru and
emailed him again. Finally Deepinder agreed to meet for 15
minutes. Gaurav took another flight to Delhi for that fifteen-
minute meeting.

'I valued his time, so I prepared five questions that I was
going to ask him. The advice that he gave me has really stayed
with me all this while. He said, "traction is as important as the
product. Fifty per cent of your time should be spent on the
product and 50 per cent on traction." Advice number two was to
grow 1 per cent every day. This was translated into a mandate
for our Content team that we need to grow 25–30 per cent
month on month.' Gaurav attributes the consistent growth that
they have achieved to that 15-minute meeting. Deepinder did
not invest in Unacademy in 2016 but the relationship gates
had opened. Deepinder would eventually join as an investor
in Unacademy's Series H funding round in August 2021.

Be it picking up a phone or sending messages or walking
up to strangers, Gaurav believes in making things happen.
Once he was vacationing at Sun-n-Sand in Mumbai when
he spotted Akshay Kumar. 'So, we just went to him and told
him what we were doing. Many people overthink that.' This
promptness to make the move combined with his ability to
tell a story around his ideas makes him persuasive as well
as memorable. And when opportunities are not presenting

themselves, he creates them. The way he assembled a star-studded team of angel investors for his seed round goes to show how he does not leave things up to chance.

SUMIT JAIN: 'HAVE PRIDE BUT DON'T OPERATE FROM A PLACE OF PRIDE'

Sumit Jain was one of the first founders to have spotted the winning traits in Gaurav and that is why he had acquired Flat.to simply so that Gaurav could work with him.

When Gaurav and Hemesh quit Commonfloor in 2015 to start working full-time on Unacademy, they felt the need to associate themselves with successful entrepreneurs and bring in mentors and angel investors who would be their go-to people for advice. Gaurav had always understood the power of long-term relationships. He knew that reaching out to people when you need something is the worst way to build any relationship. Sumit Jain, Aakrit Vaish and Bhavin Turakhia were his closest and most-trusted aides at that point. He reached out to them to raise investment as well as find contacts. Although Aakrit and Bhavin did not participate, Sumit not only invested but also introduced him to Sujeet Kumar (co-founder, Udaan) and others who agreed to meet him.

Sumit had even become the reference for early-stage investors who were contemplating making an investment in Unacademy. They were worried because they had heard that Gaurav is tough to work with. Sumit would candidly highlight his unique entrepreneurial traits. 'I remember some of them would ask if Gaurav can work well with others because until then Gaurav had not scaled a company or created big teams. I would tell them that Gaurav has no tolerance for working with bad talent but it is a great sign because he would make sure he

hires a good team. I told them, the fact that he does not like processes means that he will build a superior, product-based organization where processes are not the most important criteria of success,' Sumit told me.

Whenever an employee asked for Sumit's opinion on whether or not to work at Unacademy, he only had good things to say. 'I used to tell them that you will either love working with Gaurav or you hate it, but you will not regret working with him. It will be an unforgettable learning experience and that is why you should not leave such an opportunity.' After all, Sumit had seen, up close, both Gaurav's brilliance and restlessness. At one point, Sumit was exhausted with Gaurav's flurry of messages. 'He replies fast on WhatsApp and expects the same of others. I remember deliberately delaying replying to his messages because otherwise he would start chatting right there on WhatsApp.'

There came a time when Sumit was contemplating his next innings in the start-up world after Commonfloor. Unacademy had grown quite big by this time but Gaurav would discuss ideas with Sumit. One of the ideas that excited them both was that of Graphy—to create interactive content that mixes various media formats. Gaurav told him that Unacademy would be a strategic investor. 'On 1 April 2020, we decided that I would start Graphy. The earlier decision had been that Unacademy would just be an investor, but later we decided on Graphy being a part of Unacademy and I am happy with that decision. On 3 April, we officially started Graphy,' Sumit remembers.

When asked what he most enjoys about working with Gaurav, Sumit paused before answering. 'There are many things to admire in Gaurav. But he has perfected the combination of being high on ambition but low on ego and this makes him a great leader. Every entrepreneur has ego—when you're building a company from the ground up,

everything is personal. But Gaurav doesn't operate from a place of ego when it comes to maintaining relationships. If Gaurav offends anyone, he will be the first to apologize. And he doesn't mind saying it publicly either. He does not take things personally and is looking to grow and learn from the experience. He will ask people how to do something openly. He will not say that I am bigger than Sumit now and why should I chase him for a meeting? If he wants to meet me, he will go to any length to make the meeting happen. He will not let any ego come in between.'

Destiny had turned back the clock. Now, once again, Sumit Jain and Gaurav Munjal are working together and looking forward to creating a great product.

SUJEET KUMAR: 'GAURAV IS THE DHONI OF THE START-UP WORLD'

Gaurav and Roman reached Novotel on Outer Ring Road, Bengaluru. They were about to pitch to Sujeet Kumar. Having made money from his stake in Flipkart, Sujeet used to invest actively in start-ups. He patiently heard their stories. 'If a guy has an AIIMS and IAS background and leaves it all for a star-up, he's worth listening to, right?' Sujeet told me with a smile. 'In my experience, start-ups anyway have to iterate. What matters to me is the founder—how hungry, clear, straight-thinking, problem-solving and creative they are. I saw all those things in them. While the product or problem statement was not clear, the medium was very clear. They had good traction on YouTube. I like to work with good people and learn something from them. Being an investor is all about helping, learning and making it happen.'

It did not take long for Sujeet to make up his mind to invest. Roman's commitment and Gaurav's dedication convinced him

that this could grow big. When Gaurav asked him to put ₹10 lakh, Sujeet replied in his straight-shooting panache, '*10 lakh me kya hoga?* (₹10 lakh would not be enough). Take at least $100,000.' Gaurav could not have asked for anything better and Unacademy secured its first angel. Sujeet invested in every subsequent round till the company crossed $500 million in valuation.

'If the meeting went well, I would always ask to get introduced to two or three more people. Amod Malviya from Udaan chose not to invest but, ultimately, we pitched to everyone,' Gaurav told me. Sujeet also helped them connect to his friends from Flipkart—Kalyan Krishnamurthy and the Bansals.

Having secured such leads, Gaurav made a full 15-day plan to carpet-bomb every angel he could. He and Roman would attend start-up events and parties and look around to spot investors. This is how they found Rajan Anandan. Gaurav also remembered Karthik Reddy from Blume Ventures from back in the Flatchat days. He had expressed an interest in investing whenever Gaurav embarked on a new venture. He reached out to Karthik, who readily agreed to participate in the seed round as well. Once they had secured a few popular investors, it built credibility and it became easier to approach others. Their adolescent confidence was burgeoning. This is when Gaurav took a chance that he otherwise wouldn't have.

Sachin Bansal and Vijay Shekhar Sharma had expressed an interest to invest but had not confirmed yet. Gaurav wanted to close the seed round but didn't want to do it without them. He emailed Vijay that Sachin is in and waited. Vijay replied back to him that he is in too. Gaurav now emailed Sachin that Vijay is also in. Sachin said he will invest. By the time Unacademy closed its seed round, it had few of the most imposing names in its cap table.

Sujeet calls him the Dhoni of start-ups. 'In start-ups, you see most success stories coming from people with strong pedigree—IIT, BITS Pilani, IIMs. When they build something, it is other people from their institutes who support them. But not with Gaurav. In the cricket world, we have M.S. Dhoni. A lot of cricketers come from Bangalore, Mumbai and Delhi because the institutes in these cities have developed machinery that nurtures talent and produces successful cricketers. But Dhoni ruled the game for 20 years and you don't see anyone else like him coming from Ranchi. It is sheer talent,' Sujeet told me. 'Gaurav is the same. He arrived on his own and how he did it has not been replicated. Full credit goes to him.'

AAKRIT VAISH: *'GHAR KI MURGI'* SYNDROME

In May 2015, Gaurav informed Aakrit, his partner at Flat.to that he was going to work on Unacademy full-time. 'He and Roman both used to come to Mumbai frequently for fundraising. They stayed at my house on every visit. I am sure Gaurav has spent about 25–30 nights at my place. We would talk about Unacademy, but funnily enough, I did not invest in the first round. Everyone invested and I didn't,' Aakrit chuckles. 'Maybe it was a case of the *"ghar ki murgi"* syndrome (an idiom that means "not realizing the value of your closed ones") because I knew him so closely. I guess I was also in a tough spot professionally and personally, and I just couldn't think of anything else.'

While Aakrit did miss that early entry into Unacademy, Gaurav kept checking with him every subsequent funding round if he was ready to invest. 'I could have invested at the valuation of $3 million but I invested in the Series D round when they had already reached the valuation of $250 million.'

Gaurav called Aakrit up just before the Series D fundraising

round was concluding. He knew that Aakrit had by then sold his company Haptik to Reliance and had liquidity to invest in Unacademy.

'Look, I want you to invest now,' Gaurav told him.

'Yeah but it's still a lot of money, you know. Let me think about it.'

Gaurav followed up after a few days of silence. 'If you don't invest now, you'll regret it later.'

The message was not lost on Aakrit this time. Gaurav did not need his $100–200,000 investment but he wanted to make sure that Aakrit got to participate before the valuation got too big for individual checks.

'Kudos to him for almost forcing me into it. What I realized, and this is something I had probably missed out on in the Flat.to days, is how much Gaurav values his relationships and that he would go the length to protect the people that he values. I guess good founders are like that. If you think about it, there are only a few people like that in our lives that we can be candid with, right? Our relationship went back such a long way that we had seen the good and bad in each other. So I can see why Gaurav was always so frank with me.

SAMEER GUGLANI: 'NON-TRANSACTIONAL RELATIONSHIPS'

This capacity to not only attract or chase advisors but also keep them involved, even when you don't need them, reveals itself in many of Gaurav's other relationships too. Sameer Guglani had stopped investing in start-ups actively after 2014 but Gaurav always considered him to be his advisor. When Roman had been pondering over the question of whether to quit the IAS or not, Gaurav had taken him to meet Sameer and have a chat about it. Sameer had warmed up to Gaurav

because, unlike many adrenaline-filled young entrepreneurs who ask for advice but don't really put it to practice, Gaurav was 'different'. 'People always come back with more problems, having ignored our previous conversations. So it was interesting that Gaurav always explained how the previously discussed steps had worked out for him, before moving on to the new challenge he was facing and needed advice on. So, for me, it was a nurturing relationship. He keeps in touch, keeps you updated,' Sameer told me.

Sameer had watched him in that larval stage when he was a kid from Jaipur, striving to make a name for himself. 'There are hang-ups and issues that can deter a person's progress at that age, but Gaurav has always shown great maturity. In the earlier days, the comparatives were who got into IIT and who didn't, after that it became who is a unicorn founder and who isn't, now the comparatives are Netflix, you know. It has been a journey where the competitive force has faded into the background and the desire to do something great has taken over. He is still young, but far more mature. Many entrepreneurs secure funding, but not all grow along with the company.'

Around 2017, when Gaurav was raising money from Nexus Venture Partners, Gaurav had called Sameer up and said that he wanted him to be a formal advisor for Unacademy. 'I told him that I am not practising commercial interests in life anymore, and wasn't sure if I'd add value to a commercial venture. He said he wanted that kind of energy to be a part of the comapny. So, I said okay,' Sameer recalls. He offered advisor equity to Sameer even though Sameer had told him that he would help him irrespective of it. 'He did some calculations and told me that he is allocating so and so equity to me. Over the next year, although I had spoken to Roman and Gaurav personally many times, I had not contributed to any formal meetings. I did not feel like I was contributing anything.'

When they met the next time, Sameer brought the topic up. 'I told him that Unacademy should take back the shares because I don't think I have contributed much. Gaurav said they still wanted me to retain the shares because I have contributed to their growth in the past. Maybe it was a token of appreciation or a gesture of gratitude or whatever. This is a rare sight in the start-up world. And I have seen it many times in Morpheus too. Over the years, I have been involved with many founders and sometimes, there were people *jinki start-up nahi chali but future me kuch aur chal gaya* (whose start-ups did not take off but they found success in some other venture later). It's not common for people to come back and appreciate you for something that happened in the past. I know that Gaurav has done this with other people too, not just me. He doesn't treat his relationships as transactions. It builds goodwill and respect.'

BHAVIN TURAKHIA: 'DON'T LOOK AT YOUR FEET'

'When you are learning how to snowboard, one of the biggest mistakes you can make is looking down at your feet. Since your feet are strapped in, you keep looking down to make sure you can still move your feet. Now, good coaches will constantly remind you to not look at your feet. They, instead, ask you to focus on the direction you want to go in, and many are surprised by how the body adapts to move in that direction. Your body will get you there. So if you're constantly thinking big, your mind will constantly spot the opportunities that will take you there,' Bhavin Turakhia told me.

If there is one entrepreneur who has influenced Gaurav the most, it is Bhavin. From the moment Gaurav stepped into the Directi office to secure a sponsorship for his college fest, his ambitions took off. He decided to intern at Directi

and take guidance from the people who had created 'such an awesome place'.

Born and raised in Mumbai, Bhavin devours books, a habit he inculcated from watching his father. Between grades six to 10, he read a ton of biographies including ones written on the founders of Apple, Microsoft, IBM, Xerox, etc.—companies that were shaping the new digital era. This, in turn, made him curious about computer programming. So, he would spend every minute of his spare time writing code in his school's computer labs. He then started consuming books on programming and practising each lesson mentioned in those books. His father's reinforcement of the idea that he can achieve whatever he sets his mind to and the fact that all these technological advancements that he was reading about had been spearheaded by humans like him led to his precocious appreciation and talent for entrepreneurship.

He started writing software and assembling computers for pocket money. 'I would buy parts from Lamington and Grant Road and then assemble them. After that, I would go to Khar and Bandra and knock door to door, asking people if they wanted to buy computers,' Bhavin told me about his first sales experience. Just as Bhavin was getting his first taste of entrepreneurship, the Internet arrived. 'I remember being so enamoured by the Internet. That you could transfer any information from and to anywhere in the world in real time was fascinating. It made me wonder about the possibilities.' In order to harness this new power, Bhavin created a website for finding and matching jobs. But of course, there were not enough people on the Internet back then. 'There were hardly 40,000 people using the Internet then. After a year and a half of doing that and finding no success, my brother Divyank and I started our first company called Directi, in 1998. The whole idea here was that more people wanted to build their

presence on the Internet and they would need web access, email accounts, etc. So, we thought that we could build something which would enable that. Also, it would be a large enough market unlike my previous idea.'

Bhavin's father loaned him ₹25,000 to buy their first server and they started selling web-hosting services to various companies. 'We got our big break at NASSCOM's conference in Pragati Maidan, Delhi. We didn't even have the money to set up our booth. So, what we did was that, instead of selling to the attendees, we went booth to booth and sold our services to all the exhibitors. We made more sales in three days than we had in the last three months. That gave us the confidence and money to grow.'

Having survived the dot-com bust, Directi expanded its portfolio to a lot of different web-based products and services catering to a growing customer base across the globe. Further, being techies at heart, Bhavin and Divyank set a high bar for their hiring processes. 'In 2006–2007, we started aggressive campus recruitment. For this, we had designed a rigorous interview process. It was almost impossible to pass. I spent a lot of time working with my engineering team to create these really hard algorithmic challenges. Then, we went to various different campuses and selected the best of the best. I remember, initially, we had received 6,000 applications and we ended up hiring, maybe, 50 of them.' Directi had even created CodeChef, a website which posted a bunch of programming contests to help programmers practise their coding skills and knowledge. With such initiatives, Directi had become the hub for the best programmers across the country and this geek buzz was not lost on Gaurav. He worked hard to crack the internship and found his way in to the office that he so badly wanted to join.

The way Bhavin had built Directi, designed the office spaces and created a nerdy culture—all of it left a mark on Gaurav's

adolescent mind. In particular, he admired the CodeChef platform they had built. Once an intern, he strived to capture Bhavin's attention and get his mentorship. Bhavin remembers his first impression of Gaurav. 'He kept coming to my cabin and discussing or pitching different ideas and apps that he was building with his friends. He even pitched to me different videos he wanted to create for CodeChef on YouTube. I did not take any notice in the beginning, but he was so persistent that I relented.' This is how Gaurav forged his first mentorship, and although Bhavin would not give any significant time to him until much later, he had created a first-degree connection with him. And when Unacademy would become big enough to start expanding into programming lessons in 2020, he would acquire the same CodeChef platform.

Bhavin and Divyank were becoming influential figures in the tech circles in India especially after their net worth shot up as a result of successful sales of a few Directi business units. A lot of the highly-skilled programmers within the company looked up to their entrepreneurial journey and would go on to found their own start-ups. 'I counted with my HR that roughly 64 people had left Directi to start their own venture and I think that is a great outcome for us,' Bhavin told me. 'This is why, when Gaurav came to tell me that he was resigning to start Flat.to, I was not surprised.'

Once Gaurav had started Unacademy, he kept asking Bhavin to invest and even join Unacademy's board. But Bhavin did not want to commit a lot of time and kept declining. It was later in 2016, when Bhavin was spending a lot of time in Dubai that Gaurav was finally able to pull him in. 'One day, he randomly called me to say that he and his family are going to be in Dubai for a vacation and that he would like to meet. So I invited him to my house. In that meeting, he finally convinced me to join the board,' says Bhavin. 'Do you

want know the funny part? I found out later that he had no vacation plans in Dubai. He had dragged his family out there just so that he could get a 30-minute meeting with me.'

One can see parallels between Bhavin and Gaurav's ravenous appetite for knowledge that they fulfil via reading. One area where Gaurav credits Bhavin is his ability to point him to the right books whenever he approaches him for a problem. In turn, Bhavin gets amazed by how quickly Gaurav imbibes the lessons and executes them. Bhavin has seen him metamorphose from an enthusiastic college student to a visionary leader.

'The thing that excites me about Unacademy is the difference between a tech-first company and a tech-enabled company or the difference between being digital and being digitized. Most of the companies in edtech are actually just digitizing education in some form. But Unacademy is building a tech platform. This is like Amazon versus Barnes and Noble or Netflix versus Blockbuster. Unacademy is a very product-driven company. For example, I remember this board meeting where they were giving a demo of a cool new product feature which makes them detect if an educator is wearing Unacademy T-shirts or not. That's what I mean when I say they aren't just tech-enabled, they have tech at their core. It has been an amazing ride watching the company grow. I am glad Gaurav convinced me to join the board,' Bhavin says.

SAMEER BRIJ VERMA: 'UNADULTERATED INTENSITY'

It was June 2016. In the very first meeting, Gaurav left an indelible impression on Sameer Brij Verma. 'He was so much in control of the conversation, of what he wanted to do, how he wanted to do it. It was unusual to see that in a guy in his 20s.'

As a managing director at Nexus Venture Partners, Sameer has been an early stage investor in over 60 ventures, including the likes of Postman, Infra.Market, Hasura.io, Zolo and Ultrahuman. A colleague had introduced him to Gaurav Munjal. In his words, 'The name Unacademy itself stayed on in our minds'. Two things had stood out for Sameer—Gaurav's passion for education and his understanding of new-age social media channels like YouTube and Quora. The meeting was short but Sameer had asked Gaurav to meet him again the next day, for dinner. During this dinner conversation, they discussed why UPSC is the right exam to go after, how the app would position their content and so on. Gaurav kept alluding to building a fast-growing company but also seemed to have enough grasp on how to go about it. Sameer found the discussion so riveting that he offered to drop Gaurav home. On the way, Gaurav took out the book he was reading from his bag and gave it to Sameer. It was called *Exponential Organizations* (written by Michael S. Malone, Salim Ismail and Yuri van Geest). Sameer recalls what Gaurav had said to him, 'He told me that he had been reading that book and that it had made him think of what he had learnt from building Flatchat, how he could build Unacademy differently and how a platform company in India should be built. And he gave me the book, you know. I just felt there was something crazy, edgy and brilliant about this guy.'

Within a week, Sameer had invited Gaurav to his office in Mumbai to talk to his Product team. 'Usually, all our meetings are presentation based where people presented decks, etc., but I had told Gaurav that I don't need any deck. We just chatted over the whiteboard. Everybody in the team really liked him.' Gaurav then flew back to Bengaluru and Sameer followed over the weekend. When Sameer went to Unacademy's office in Indiranagar, he had a clear mission. He

got straight to the point. 'I have really enjoyed our discussion and Nexus would like to invest. What do you say?'

Gaurav looked at him strangely and asked, 'Are you sure? You don't need more time?'

'No, I don't need more time.'

'But I do,' Gaurav hesitated.

'Okay, but I am not leaving till I have an answer.'

Gaurav realized Sameer meant business. 'Okay, why don't you meet my Product team first?'

Once they had met and looked around the office, they came back to Gaurav's cabin. Sameer asked him to connect his laptop to the printer and printed out the term sheet he had brought with him.

'I did not leave for four and a half hours until I had that signed term sheet in my hand,' Sameer chuckles. 'I believed Gaurav to be this "crazy" founder with his own version of reality and if anybody could make it come true, it is him. We wanted to be a part of that ride. It all happened within a week. There was no presentation, no long negotiation. He kept thanking me for having faith and that was it. In fact, I was so happy I decided to take a stroll to Toit and have a drink all by myself to celebrate.' Investor deals rarely happen so swiftly but it is all about who is chasing whom. Entrepreneurs spend years going from one VC meeting to another, not knowing why it isn't working out. When investors want to invest, they don't waste any time.

Gaurav often advises founders to be finicky about bringing the right advisors and board members on, instead of anybody who is willing to throw money. Nexus Venture Partners remains the biggest shareholder on Unacademy's cap table. Even after investing in early 2017, Sameer did not push for monetization. Instead, he let the founders take their time to figure out the right business model. 'When we were writing

that check, BYJU'S was already valued at $600 million. This was the kind of gap that existed in edtech, But then there is Gaurav, who came from the shadows trying to build the second-largest edtech company in the world, and possessing a very different approach in life,' Sameer recalls.

Time and time again, his patience and trust has been rewarded and faith reinforced in the company. He particularly refers to the period when Unacademy decided to pivot to the subscription-based Plus model in January 2019. 'That was a pivotal moment for them. It took six weeks of unadulterated intensity to make that thing work. I don't think the team did anything else or even go home to sleep. Even today, Gaurav comes home at 1 a.m., every night. I know this because he is my neighbour. They are working day and night.'

Talking about Gaurav, the biggest thing Sameer admires is his ability to compartmentalize the strengths of different advisors. 'One notable thing is that he's put together a board of very strong people who have empowered him and have a deep amount of trust and faith in him. Nobody is second-guessing him. Then, he's aware of how Shailendra or Sujeet or I can help him. He knows our individual strengths. So he can get holistic advice about different areas from the company he keeps. That's actually an exceptionally smart thing to do.'

SHAILENDRA SINGH: 'DUALITY'

Right from the first meeting, Gaurav had hit it off with Shailendra Singh. It became this quintessential investor–founder relationship that Gaurav believed would brace Unacademy to scale greater heights. Taking Shailendra's inputs about live classes or trying out a successful subscription model pivot had proved Gaurav's trust had been well founded. While Gaurav benefitted from Shailendra's wider perspective,

given Sequoia's global presence, Shailendra felt more invested in Unacademy's success because of Gaurav's ability to blitzscale and his readiness to apply himself. A mutual respect and admiration burgeoned.

Shailendra noticed some eccentric traits that made Gaurav stand apart, for example, his obsession with having a four-year runway. When Unacademy was raising Series D round of $50 million, it still had its last round's capital in the bank. When Shailendra asked Gaurav why he wants to raise money if he is yet to spend his last round, Gaurav told him about his fixation.

'That is the amount I feel comfortable with, else I start losing sleep,' Gaurav explains to me later. 'I start fundraising when I have 24 months of runway and I get anxious if I have only 18 months left. I called Shailendra at 2 a.m. once to ask him to put more money in that round. And then, he said, "Please message me before you call at 2 a.m." The point is, when we are sick, our bodies cannot function. Similarly, if an organization does not have enough cash in the bank, it cannot function well. You cannot innovate, you cannot make bold bets. It's a no-brainer for me—why wouldn't you keep enough cash?'

Over time, Shailendra started appreciating Gaurav's cautious approach. He explains, 'Many founders underestimate costs and overestimate revenues. You think you have 24 months of runway when you really have only 14. When they are eight months in, they realize that they have only six months left. And then, they panic. Now, when you are under pressure, you make tactical choices, not long-term decisions. So, it makes sense that Gaurav is being risk averse when it comes to having a big margin of safety. It also shows how badly he wants to win because he does not care as much about dilution. This is a unique trait actually. Ambitious founders like Gaurav are often risk-seeking but when it comes to funding, Gaurav is restrained and risk-averse.

This coming together of opposing traits in founders can lead to very powerful outcomes, in my opinion.' Shailendra calls it the duality principle whereby a person or an entity can demonstrate the best of opposing philosophies—risk-seeking in goals and risk-averseness in fundraising, in case of Gaurav.

It helped that Shailendra had worked with other creative founders before. He was able to temper Gaurav's impulsiveness and channel it into well-thought-out decisions. 'Sometimes Gaurav calls me to share ideas and I tell him I'll talk to him in three days and see if he still wants to do it. And then normally, by the third day, he tells me he doesn't want to do it anymore. I just tell him that I know what's happening to him. That I've seen it before and that we'll talk in three days. I promise him that we'll have a full chat if he still likes the idea in three days.' At other times, he puts forth a sobering perspective to keep Gaurav grounded. 'There is a simple misconception that many founders harbour. They feel they need to grow double or triple every year. I often tell Gaurav that you can grow 29 times more in 10 years by simply improving by 40 per cent year on year. You don't need to worry about three times the growth every year because that is not sustainable in the long run.'

The relationship has grown in trust, transcending the limitations of a founder-investor connection. Gaurav doesn't hesitate in taking Shailendra's opinion on matters of any importance, especially, after noting that his advice is not self-serving. 'He has not only helped me build a better business, but also be a better person,' admits Gaurav.

KUNAL SHAH: 'CLOSE THE LOOP'

Kunal is not a typical mentor.

'Why are you being rude?' Gaurav messaged Kunal Shah.

'I am not rude; I am just efficient in the way I speak. If you

feel offended by it, then it's on you. I have never said anything bad to you or about you. I am just speaking what I think is the truth, in a straightforward manner,' Kunal responded.

'Hmm.'

'Maybe you need more people who can be blunt with you. My job is not to be nice but to be honest and truthful. I have no incentive to be nice. There are many people who can be nice to you.'

Most people inadvertently surround themselves with yes-men and others who can stroke their egos. Gaurav's early interactions with Kunal would rattle his basic need for validation and his insecurities. There was a time when Gaurav would react to every crisis with the same amount of intensity. So, Kunal once told him, 'If everything shakes you equally, then you are not built of substance yet. You have to decide what level of issues can shake you. There should be a team under you to worry about some of these things.'

'I don't think he really liked me in those days, but to his credit, he took those conversations well,' Kunal told me. The fact that Gaurav appreciated Kunal's straight talk and took his feedback seriously shows his authenticity in his quest for self-improvement. In Kunal, Gaurav found an honest sounding board, someone who could give him the bitter pill or unembellished truth when required.

Their first interaction dates back to the time when Gaurav was studying at NMIMS and Kunal (who also hails from NMIMS) had come to judge a start-up competition. Gaurav was one of the participants and the most enthusiastic student in the lot. Kunal judged his pitch to be the second-best in the competition and when Gaurav asked him why, he told him that he could have thought out the idea in more detail. Gaurav then added that the pitch that had won the first prize was also his idea. Once the ice was broken, Gaurav kept in touch with

Kunal—sending him updates now and then. 'He always had an edge. Even in the early days, he was very good with the content game. He had that joy of understanding content which comes naturally to him and this is something beyond education. I can recollect his immense hustle and ability to push everyone around him to work on his ideas. Ultimately, that's what happened when he was able to convince people like Roman to join him and that is powerful,' Kunal remembers.

It was sometime after he had sold his company Flat.to to Commonfloor that he had the most revealing conversation with Kunal. Since both of them used to live in Mumbai at that time but would travel to Bengaluru a lot for work, they would bump into each other on flights between Mumbai and Bengaluru. 'I remember him walking up to me on that Indigo flight as I sat in the exit row. He started discussing his current real estate start-up but he talked so much more passionately about Unacademy, which was just a YouTube channel back then. That is when I told him that it was clear that he was passionate about Unacademy and asked him why he was wasting his time with real estate,' Kunal says.

They went on to discuss the number of views that their videos were garnering, etc. Kunal pointed out to him that the videos pertaining to exam preparation were garnering more views. 'Why don't you just build on top of this?' Kunal asked. If Gaurav had been on the fence about devoting his full attention to Unacademy until then, this conversation spurred him to think about it more seriously.

Kunal is not a big believer in mentorships and never had mentors of his own. 'We are all stuck in our urgent and important tasks but there are people we can trust who can give us the zoomed-out perspective and show us what we cannot see for ourselves. Maybe I was doing that with Gaurav. I don't know if you can call it mentorship. We have not met

in a long time, but if we need anything, we ping each other and that's how it should be.'

Once Gaurav had quit Commonfloor, Kunal invested in Unacademy's seed round. 'To me, it did not matter what he was building. I believed that given this particular category of government exams, it was a case of founder-market fit by design. He and Roman were the right people to build something like this.'

Long story short, Kunal put his faith in Unacademy and Gaurav. This is why when he was spending some time as an advisor at Sequoia Capital, he was able to nudge Shailendra Singh to make an investment too. Kunal had already invested in Unacademy as an angel and was familiar with Gaurav's modus operandi. He took Shailendra to Unacademy's office for the first time and the rest is history.

Kunal believes that technology can serve an existing motivation well but it cannot create new motivation. 'For example, Amazon can deliver you the shampoo you desire but it cannot make you desire the shampoo. The desire for Unacademy's category was already high among the people.' Still, it was hard for Sequoia to lead a round into a start-up that did not have a monetization model. The app was pre-revenue. He adds, 'Government exams are one of the top Google searches in India. If people want it so desperately, how hard would it be to monetize this? See, if we cannot monetize people's need for getting education, then we can't monetize anything in India. My push was largely with the intent that it doesn't matter if they haven't monetized yet but they can when they try. I guess Shailendra agreed.'

Kunal Shah and Shailendra Singh visiting Unacademy's office in 2017 (from left to right: Roman Saini, Kunal Shah, Shailendra Singh, Gaurav Munjal)

After that, it was a matter of execution, which Unacademy had been learning to do faster and faster. 'One of Gaurav's biggest strengths is to move very quickly and then look at data to build conviction. That is rare in founders. Many people take months to align, but he quickly adopts a new idea as he did with live classes and then subscription models. He built a high-quality product in a very short time. That is why Sequoia felt like doubling down and they have invested in every round thereafter. Speed has nothing to do with the size of the company. You can be a very large company and still be fast. The competition is always between those who can move fast and those who cannot.'

So, what made the 'too blunt to be pleasant' connection between Kunal and Gaurav turn into a strong kinship? Kunal

believes it is Gaurav's ability to 'close the loop'. 'If you see that the person took your feedback and changed because of it or that he implemented things, it motivates you to help him more. Many founders don't do a good job of closing the loop. I approach you when I want to learn from you but I never tell you what I did with your advice or if I made any changes. I remember Gaurav doing a decent job at that, you could see the changes he would make based on what you told him. That is what makes people want to help him because not all of them are financially invested in his success. I think that's the main reason why he has been able to have good relationships with so many people.'

Kunal shares examples of where Gaurav heeded his suggestions. Be it introducing EMI payments or figuring out a way for motivating educators via prestige rather than money, Gaurav was quick in implementing ideas. 'I told him to hire and retain certain kinds of people and he has done that really well—how to pick some investor over another or how to negotiate when he has the option. I am not saying this to take credit because I am sure he talks to many people and he takes inputs from everyone. But it feels good to see that our discussions are not futile. I remember when we were discussing how YouTube gives awards to people who cross half a million or a million views, etc., and then he adopted the same. Next time, he showed me the trophy that Unacademy had designed to award the educators.'

WHAT MAKES A MENTOR TICK?

It is hard to imagine that Gaurav knew how successful he would be one day or that he was building relationships as a premeditated business strategy. One can still forge initial connections but nurturing them over long periods of time

is an area where most people stumble. Gaurav has mastered the art of relationships and one could argue that most of it came to him naturally.

However, the good news is that this 'art of attracting mentors' appears to be learnable. A deeper look reveals the traits that have attracted his mentors and well-wishers to stay invested in his progress. Anyone can take a cue from his playbook because whatever he is doing seems to be working well for Unacademy.

1. Ability to listen and close the loop

There's none so deaf as those who will not hear. Assertive and ambitious founders often succumb to obstinate deafness. Any mentor would give up fast on a person who is not open to advice. Sameer Brij Verma comments how many people mistake Gaurav for being bad at taking feedback. 'In my experience, he listens very carefully. He may not immediately agree but he will listen and be open to changing his stance after giving it due thought. Initially, it appeared that he was not paying attention but he would always come back to me after two hours and say that he had thought about it and that he agreed. He is open to listening to a different point of view. Of course, if he thinks he is right, he works very hard to convince you to see his side as well. I think that is remarkable.'

Aakrit remembers the time when Gaurav had messaged him in 2020 that he is building Graphy as a new product with Sumit Jain and raising capital for it. Unacademy had already stabilized by then and Gaurav had a list of people ready to invest.

'The round is coming together. Are you in? Reply by end of day,' Gaurav messaged Aakrit.

'Yes, I am in.'

However, Aakrit had a new thought the next day which he

shared with Gaurav. 'I messaged him, "Hey, food for thought—all large conglomerates never raise early-stage capital for new products. They end up owning them for a long time and spin them out into separately valued entities much later only if it makes sense to do so." And, he said, "Okay let me think about it". And that was that. Next day, he dropped a message to everybody saying that they are no longer raising separate capital for Graphy and would be continuing it as a product under Unacademy itself. I think it was a good decision in the long run.'

As Kunal Shah pointed out, Gaurav not only acts on the advice shared by mentors, he also updates them as he does so, thereby generating in them a feeling of having contributed to something significant. This acts as a powerful non-financial motivation for people to see him succeed.

2. Being generous with time and energy

Sameer Guglani commented on Gaurav's talent at keeping the relationships non-transactional and empowering people around him. 'Many entrepreneurs are like this tree which grows so big, it doesn't allow any other trees to flourish in its shadow. Gaurav has not had that issue till now. He doesn't feel threatened. In fact, he invites smart people to work with him.' Be it investing in Sumit's intitiative with Graphy or supporting many engineers who left Unacademy to start their own companies, Gaurav tries to retain and support talented people in any way he can.

Despite the ever-increasing responsibilities on his shoulders, Gaurav makes time for his relationships with the same diligence as before.

Sumit remembers, 'I was in the US and messaged him at 6 p.m. EST. I was going to be free for four to six hours and asked him if he knew any people I could meet there.

It must have been 2 or 3 a.m. in the Indian time zone but he gave me five contacts and I met those people in the next four to five hours. Two of them were very close friends of Gaurav. Very busy people tend not to have time for friends but Gaurav responds within minutes. He has somehow managed to keep his friendships alive. He has people ready to receive him in almost every city he goes to. So, while he has so many connections, he is not your typical networking guy who goes to conferences and collects contacts. He invests time and energy in them.'

People remember not what you say but how you make them feel. Almost everyone who has interacted with Gaurav for a substantial length of time calls him a reliable friend.

3. Talk their language

'*Yaar ye tum books vooks mujhe mat batao* (please don't discuss books with me)'—that is what Sujeet Kumar would tell Gaurav whenever he started talking about what he had learned from reading some book. Soon, Gaurav realized that Sujeet is not a book person and he would keep those discussions reserved for people like Bhavin who are avid readers. The crux is that Gaurav deciphers the strengths and interests of people around him and ensures that discussions remain relevant for them as well.

4. Keep it interesting

There is a WhatsApp group that all Unacademy's board members are a part of. Shailendra Singh calls their group's updates a 'drip feed of the drug of growth.'

He adds how Gaurav's daily updates, reviews, testimonials and milestones on the group keeps his investors rooting for him. 'It is a real-time stream of data that he shares, which helps the investors develop an intuitive sense of how the business is performing. It also makes board meetings somewhat of

a formality because we are already up-to-date on what's happening. There are no sudden shocks. Every update, especially a good one, acts like a booster shot. It makes your investors your champions.'

Bhavin Turakhia was amazed at the volume of information in the group as well. 'It is the chattiest group ever. I can tell you nobody in the world sends so much information and data about their business and I'm not saying by a factor of one or two. It's like 10, 20, 30 times higher than any other company that I've invested in or I'm on the board of or I've seen reporting. So, Unacademy is really numbers-driven.'

Bhavin had his own share of 'fun' when Unacademy asked him to test out and demo the new 'live classes' product they were creating in 2017. 'I remember they were trying to demonstrate Unacademy's new features for teaching. Gaurav asked me to pretend to be a teacher and conduct a mock session in a board meeting to showcase the features. So, I created a small course on an entrepreneurial topic using Unacademy's platform for the rest of the board members. It was almost like a show. It was quite interesting.'

Gaurav regularly invites Roman, Hemesh and other executives to present their updates and get a chance for the board to know the whole team. One time, he also sent a seating plan before a board meeting to experiment how the arrangement impacts the speed of approvals. By keeping the meetings interesting and sharing the progress or roadblocks transparently on the group, he keeps everyone engaged and emotionally invested in the company. It has also earned Unacademy a deep trust from its investors and advisors.

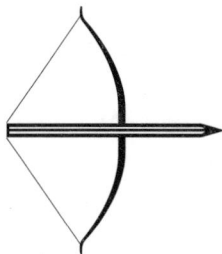

EPILOGUE

Long before they had started Unacademy, Gaurav had told Roman and Hemesh that he would be running a unicorn company before he turned 30. The prophecy came to life when Unacademy crossed $1 billion in valuation in September 2020—days before Gaurav turned 30.

In August 2021, Unacademy's valuation jumped to $3.44 billion.

Gaurav's pursuit for mastery continues inside and outside the company. In November 2020, he finally caught up with Reed Hastings (CEO, Netflix) over a video call.

In September 2021, Unacademy created a 'partner' programme to recognize any leader who has been as instrumental in the company's growth as a co-founder. It was decided to give the title 'partner' to such leaders in an effort to publicly acknowledge their contributions. Karan Shroff became the first leader to be elevated to the position of a partner. With this initiative, Unacademy is solidifying its human capital and empowering its most valuable leaders.

Unacademy has so far focused on the TestPrep business which is the major contributor to its revenues. The book has examined, in depth, the strategies that helped it grow its business and impact from a nondescript YouTube channel to India's second-largest edtech company. One of the things that Unacademy has done well so far is not following the competition and innovating on its own. With a leadership

team more or less in place and comfortable access to funds, Unacademy is eyeing more territories beyond TestPrep.

Unacademy is looking to create two to three other product lines which can grow as big as its current TestPrep business ($200 million in ARR). The most promising category is its K–12 segment which has grown to $18 million in ARR. Further, the company is increasing its bets on other products such as Relevel which is a hiring platform that empowers candidates to showcase their skills through tests and get coveted jobs. With fresh infusion of $20 million, Relevel aims to become the go-to product for millions of job seekers in the country.

The management is bullish that there are white spaces in the industry locally and globally where Unacademy can make a significant headway. At the same time, they are also cognizant of challenges that lie in growth and expectations management. 'The battle is ours to lose. If we cannot create a $50 billion company from where we are today, it means we messed up somewhere,' says a senior leader.

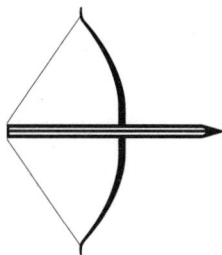

THE CHARACTERS

You would find the following names appearing inside the book. In case you feel like checking who's who, you can come back and look them up here. I have sorted the employees in the order of their date of joining Unacademy.

Founders and Employees:

- Gaurav Munjal—co-founder and chief executive officer
- Roman Saini—co-founder and vice president (Content Sales)
- Hemesh Singh—co-founder and chief technology officer
- Sachin Gupta—co-founder, left Unacademy to pursue other interests in 2017
- Alok Maurya—ex-director (Tech), joined in March 2016 and left in 2021
- Disha Agarwal—assistant vice president (Business), joined in May 2017
- Abhishek Srivastava—director (Business), joined in October 2017
- Arooshi Singh—associate director (HR), joined in October 2017
- Mayank Garg—ex-category leader (Business) and ex-senior product manager (Tech), joined in October 2017 and left Unacademy to pursue other interests in 2021

- Shweta Sivasankaran—director (Marketing), joined in May 2018
- Dinesh Godara—founder of WifiStudy, joined Unacademy after they acquired WifiStudy in November 2018 and left to pursue a new start-up idea in 2020
- Shubham Kumar Boundia—senior product manager (Tech), joined in March 2019
- Ankita Tandon—ex-vice president (Business), joined in October 2019 and left Unacademy to pursue other interests in 2021
- Karan Shroff—chief marketing officer and partner, joined in September 2019
- Karthik Kailash—vice president (Sales), joined in October 2019
- Arushi Mudgal—senior manager (HR), joined in November 2019
- Tina Balachandran—vice president (HR), joined in December 2019
- Jerin Kesavan—head of Talent Acquisition (HR), joined in March 2020
- Archit Nanda—director (CEO's office), joined in April 2020
- Aditi Arora—senior category manager (Business), joined in June 2020
- Umesh Bude—senior vice president (Tech), joined in July 2020
- Arpita Bhattacharya—director (Marketing), joined in July 2020
- Sumanta Dey—assistant vice president (Corporate Affairs), joined in July 2020
- Balaji Ramachandran—associate Director (Business), joined in July 2020

- Vivek Sinha—chief operating officer, joined in September 2020
- Jitender Kumar—director (Tech), joined in May 2021
- Diksha Fouzdar—senior director (HR), joined in April 2021

Educators:

- Mansoorali Kappungal—top educator for Kerala PSC, teaching since June 2018
- Sudarshan Gurjar—top educator for UPSC, teaching since June 2018
- Prateek Jain—top educator for IIT-JEE and NEET, teaching since July 2019

Mentors and Friends:

- Kunal Shah—founder (Freecharge and CRED)
- Bhavin Turakhia—co-founder (Directi, Radix, Flock, Zeta)
- Aakrit Vaish—co-founder (Flat.to and Haptik)
- Sameer Guglani—co-founder (Madhouse, Morpheus Accelerator)
- Sumit Jain—co-founder (CommonFloor, Graphy)
- Sujeet Kumar—co-founder (Udaan)
- Sameer Brij Verma—managing director (Nexus Venture Partners)
- Shailendra Singh—managing director (Sequoia Capital)

GRATITUDE

सरस्वति महाभागे विद्ये कमललोचने।
विद्यारूपे विशालाक्षि विद्यां देहि नमोस्तुते॥

Above all, I am beholden to Devi Saraswati for giving us the power of thought and ability to capture its essence in language. She is the container of all answers, I bow to her for making this book flow into existence.

Among the mortal beings, I have many to thank as well. First and foremost, the depth of this book is a result of the cooperation of Team Unacademy who let me go down my own rabbit holes and connect the dots. They opened their doors and shared some of the internal data which otherwise would be hard to procure. If we are to have better business literature in India, we would benefit from the open-mindedness of our businesses in sharing their wisdom. To that end, I could not have expected more generosity from Team Unacademy.

This book would not have been possible without the people in and around Unacademy who candidly talked to me and let me peek into their sacred work lives. Most of the quotes that appear in the narrative are picked from the interviews I conducted personally. In a few cases, I relied on other news sources to fill the gaps. Some people shared stories but wished to stay anonymous. I have respected their wishes and covered only the parts I could corroborate with other parties involved in the conversation. Since I had already interviewed the founders for my last book, I had an open connection with them and familiarity with their working styles. Nonetheless, it was again a pleasure to pick their brains and get them to open their chest of insights and stories more widely than they normally do.

During the writing of this book, my father had to undergo open-heart surgery. As I sat the night before his surgery, I stared at the screen, unable to write any longer. It was my father,

my silent co-author, with whom I used to share the progress of this book. His excitement matched mine, he was the one person who got what it was like to 'be writing'—not only the thrill of seeing your name on something that will outlast you but also the torturous dark moments of self-doubt. His power of wielding words far exceeds mine but he never embraced writing as a full-time vocation, he chose to provide for us, his family. I do not know if he would have been a better writer or a better father, not because I have any doubt on his pen but because he did set the bar of fatherhood extremely high.

As he slept that night in the hospital, my well of inspiration dried but I also realized that getting to write was my privilege. It was the biggest blessing we both shared—the ability to find joy in penning words down. The surgery finished before time and the surgeon assured our family that it could not have gone any smoother. As my father recovered, I wrote with force, reckoning, urgency and this book came to life. Thank you, father, for kindling the writer in me and being my eternal co-author.

I am grateful to Eaishvarya, my partner in every sense. Only you could assuage my fears, my doubts and my vulnerabilities in the writing process. Thank you for being my rock.

There are friends who hang out with you and there are friends who elevate you. I am forever indebted to Sameer Guglani, Umesh Rangasamy and Alok Kejriwal without whose advice and encouragement, the book would not be in your hands. Special thanks to my author friends, Ravi Nawal and Kavita Devgan for their expert inputs on publishing matters.

The wonderful Dibakar Ghosh and his whole team at Rupa are responsible for the timely and expert execution of this book. Thanks to them for making the book enjoyable.

Lastly, I remember my unborn child, one who did not see the light of the day. You changed me forever and made me experience emotions I had never known to exist. This one is for you.

Praise for the book

'Very few founders have the gumption to convert a passion project on YouTube into a formidable business. Nistha has been able to bring out the essence of what makes Unacademy an excellent case study for new-age Internet startups. Must-read.'

—Kunal Shah
Founder of CRED

'I have had the opportunity to observe the Unacademy founders closely for many years. They exemplify how to consistently evolve, think big, question the norm and work to raise the bar personally and professionally. I recommend this book to everyone who does not conform to societal frameworks and boundaries, and wants to create a unique journey and in the process create a once-in-a-lifetime story.'

—Shradha Sharma
Founder, CEO and chief editor of YourStory

'At a time when our country's education sector is struggling to resurge from the shambles of the pandemic, innovative edtech start-ups like Unacademy are reimagining and diversifying the way learning is perceived by millions. Unacademy exemplifies how harnessing the power of digital tools and tech innovation can transform an entire sector, culminating into larger societal education and economic progress. Having seen how the founders have built the company with grit and determination, I can say this book is a much-needed read for any budding entrepreneur.'

—Harshil Mathur
CEO and co-founder of Razorpay

'Gaurav, Hemesh and Roman's journey with Unacademy has been nothing short of spectacular. Over the many years that I've worked with them, their obsession to serve audiences at scale, shines through the most. *Unstartup* is an exciting read for anyone aspiring to build a fundamentally strong brand that can change the lives of millions.'

—Aditi Shrivastava
Co-founder and CEO, Pocket Aces

unsto.......

Nistha Tripathi is on a mission to make business books interesting to read. A bestselling start-up author, her last book *No Shortcuts* featured stories of 15 successful Indian entrepreneurs because she was tired of turning to Silicon Valley books for advice on building start-ups in India.

After completing a degree in Engineering from University of Illinois, she joined New York University to pursue an MBA but dropped out. Thereafter, she worked on Wall Street and with a few fast-growing start-ups in Manhattan, where she developed a keen understanding of business strategy. She organized NYU Stern's first Entrepreneurship Summit that featured the likes of Seth Godin and Chris Dixon. After returning to India, Nistha founded India's leading career consulting community—Scholar Strategy. It has helped hundreds of applicants get into top MS and MBA programmes in the US including MIT, Harvard and Stanford. She is an active career coach (certified with NeuroLeadership Institute, USA), acclaimed author and a prolific speaker. She has given talks at leading start-up events and college start-up fests.

With 100,000 plus followers and more than 12 million views on her content across Quora, LinkedIn and Instagram, Nistha actively writes on entrepreneurship, career advice and pursuing one's passion. Her articles have appeared on *Entrepreneur, Time, DailyO, DNA, The Tribune* and other leading media outlets.

Follow her on:
Instagram: @nistha00
Twitter: @nisthatripathi
LinkedIn: https://www.linkedin.com/in/nisthatripathi/